ENTREPRENEURIAL ROLE OF DEVELOPMENT BANKS IN BACKWARD AREAS

About the Author

KALPANA VAISH (*b.* 1959) has brilliant academic record to her credit. She passed M. Com. in 1981 from Shri Ram College of Commerce securing first position in University of Delhi. She obtained Ph.D. from Meerut University in 1990. Since 1981, she is working as a Lecturer in the Department of Commerce, Daulat Ram College, University of Delhi.

Entrepreneurial Role of Development Banks in Backward Areas

Kalpana Vaish
Daulat Ram College
University of Delhi
Delhi

CONCEPT PUBLISHING COMPANY, NEW DELHI 110059

ISBN 81-7022-470-5

First Published 1993

Kalpana Vaish (*b.* 1959)

Published and Printed by
Ashok Kumar Mittal
Concept Publishing Company
A/15-16, Commercial Block, Mohan Garden
NEW DELHI 110059 (India)

Lasertypeset by
Microtech Advance Printing Systems (Pvt.) Ltd.
H-13, Bali Nagar,
NEW DELHI 110015

Dedicated to
my father-in-law
Late Shri Jai Narayan Vaish
Principal, Shri Ram College of Commerce, Delhi

Preface

The emergence of a network of Development Banks in India during post-independence era could perhaps be termed as the most significant financial innovation. At the advent of political independence in 1947, the country's industrial scene was marked by a narrow industrial base reflected in the problems of acute shortage of capital and absence of developed capital market to mobilise resources for productive avenues. The nation was faced with a financial and socio-economic structure that was by and large inhibitive of rapid economic progress. There was a wide gap between the rising aspirations of the people for a fast rate of economic development and social advance and the scanty nature of basic ingredients of development to translate them into reality. The establishment of Development Banks was one of the steps to supply the missing links of the growth process.

Development Banks have been set up with the objective of providing medium and long term industrial finance to assist the growth and development of industry in India as an integral part of the planned economic development of the country. Besides finance, however, some equally important desiderata of industrialisation are entrepreneurial ability, careful selection and formulation of projects and technical and managerial competence to plan and operate industrial enterprises. These factors are more crucial for developing nations where the experiences in and exposures to industrial development have been inadequate. Therefore, the role of development banks in a developing country like India is much broader than that of mere financing agencies; and increasing emphasis has been placed not only on the 'banking' aspect of their operations but also on the 'development' aspect so that both financial and non-financial inputs flow under planned direction to expedite the pace of industrial development in consonance with national objectives and priorities. Industrial Finance Corporation of India (IFCI) has been the pioneer development bank in India set up in 1948. The fact that IFCI's existence is almost as old as country's independence inevitably expects a greater commitment on the part of IFCI to fulfil its role as a 'development bank of a developing nation'.

This study attempts to analyse the developmental or promotional role of IFCI and its contribution to the development of backward areas in the country. The objective is to critically highlight and evaluate IFCI's role in channelisation of its direct financial assistance to the projects set up in backward areas and the various promotional activities undertaken as supportive measures — like participation in industrial potential surveys, development of institutional infrastructure for technical consultancy services, risk capital assistance, management and entrepreneurship development, support for rural development, promotional schemes for tiny, village and small industries sector and promotion of research studies etc. — to accelerate the process of industrialisation in the country.

The efficacy and success, or otherwise, of these developmental measures have been judged on the basis of utilisation of allocated resources in achieving their stated objectives and the extent to which the benefits to be derived from such activities have proliferated for the development of industrially backward areas. The study reveals that in spite of policy declarations and financial and promotional measures undertaken to reduce regional industrial imbalances and step up efforts for backward area development, the results achieved have not come up to expectations. Analysing the difficulties encountered, the shortcomings, lags and lacunae in the administered policies and programmes, the study attempts to suggest, in a modest way, measures to enhance the efficiency of the existing efforts and new dimensions to the arena of developmental activities to respond to the challenging task of accelerating development of less-developed areas.

The source material employed in this study has been collected from various Government Reports, Reports of the Planning Commission, Committees and Working Groups, Annual

Reports and Operational Statistics of IFCI, IDBI and ICICI, Annual Reports of Technical Consultancy Organisations, Risk Capital Foundation, Proceedings of the Seminars organised by IDBI and MDI and several other research studies and references related to the subject which have been enlisted in the Bibliography at the end.

It has been my privilege to carry out this work under the guidance of Prof. K.N. Nagar, Principal, D.N. College and Dean of Commerce Faculty, Meerut University, Meerut, and Dr. C.B. Gupta, Director, Birla Institute of Management Technology, New Delhi. In pursuit of this study, I have received valuable assistance from many quarters. I gratefully acknowledge the help and co-operation rendered to me by the entire staff of IFCI, IDBI and ICICI, the staff of Risk Capital and Technology Finance Corporation (RCTC) and various Technical Consultancy Organisations in the country in procurement and collection of the relevant data. In particular, I express my sincere thanks to Shri Din Dayal, Manager, Promotional Activities Division of IFCI, Shri Mohan Singh, Secretary, RCTC, Shri P.C. Hada, Secretary, RAJCON, Jaipur, and Dr. J.C. Verma of IFCI with whom I discussed many issues relating to the study. I express my gratitude to Prof. L.C. Gupta, Dean (Research), Management Development Institute, who enriched my understanding of the subject. I sincerely acknowledge the help received from Shri Kulwant Rai Mittal, D.K. Agencies Pvt. Ltd., Mohan Garden, New Delhi, in connection with procuring various Reports of the Committees, Working Groups, Planning Commission and NCDBA. My thanks are due to all my teachers and colleagues for their encouragement and help in this work.

The blessings of my father-in law Late Shri Jai Narayan Vaish, an eminent educationist and philanthropist, have always been a source of inspiration to me. My parents Shri Vidya Ratna, Reader Shri Ram College of Commerce and Smt. Kusum Vidyaratna, Reader, Lady Shri Ram College, University of Delhi, have consistently encouraged me in my endeavours and taken pride in my success.

Words are insufficient to appreciate the affectionate cooperation of my husband Dr. P.K. Vaish, Eye Surgeon, and the interest and attention which he has keenly lavished upon all my academic work. My sons Anurag and Anshuman deserve a special mention who sacrificed their right on my leisure to see my work accomplished.

All credit goes to the Concept Publishing Company, New Delhi, for their meticulous job in publishing this work.

Delhi
November 14, 1992

KALPANA VAISH

Department of Commerce,
Daulat Ram College,
University of Delhi.

CONTENTS

LIST OF ANNEXURES

APPENDICES

LIST OF TABLES

1

Introduction

Development Banks: Objectives & Functions:

Development Banks, a post-war financial innovation, are a familiar feature of the financial system of practically every country, though more pronounced in the developing economies. In the years after the World War II, a number of countries gained political independence and wanted to bring about rapid economic development and social progress. Unlike the western countries, where the availability of capital and other basic ingredients of development was not difficult, the developing nations were faced with the problem of non- availability or inadequacy of the fundamental factors of development. Besides acute shortage of capital,[1] these countries had low levels of income and savings, and a major proportion of the meagre savings that existed could not be effectively channelised into productive investment in the absence of a developed capital market.[2] There was also a shortage of people with necessary technical and managerial competence who could profitably make use of the available investment opportunities.

With such economic background, these countries were in search of an agency which could supply both financial and non-financial missing links in the growth process, and this constituted the rationale for the evolution of the development banks in almost all the countries of the developing world.

These banks differ widely in respect of their ownership, sources of finance, objectives, methods and scope of operations depending upon the peculiar social, economic and political framework within which they have to function. However, they have all been devised to provide atleast a few, if not all, the fundamental ingredients of economic development, the lack or inadequacy of which would inhibit the pace of industrial

---

1 Boskey Shirley, *Problems & Practices of Development Banks*, Chap. 1, p.3.
2 *Ibid.*, p.4.

progress.[3] A development bank is intended to provide the necessary capital, enterprise, managerial and technical know-how and also assist in building up the financial and socio-economic infrastructure favourable to quick economic development.

The provision of finance is the hard-core of a development bank's activity.[4] The most important function of the development bank is to provide term-capital for financing the long-term need of industrial enterprises. Apart from this, to stimulate capital market they extend financial assistance in several others forms, such as grant of loans with or without security in national or foreign currency, subscription to and underwriting of shares, bonds and debentures of corporate firms, guaranteeing domestic or foreign loans and guaranteeing deferred payment in respect of imports of plant and machinery.

But the task of development banks goes far beyond the conventional function of providing finance to qualifed entrepreneurs. In developing countries like India, the non-financial or promotional activities of development banks are equally important. Non-financial bottlenecks sometimes become more critical to a fast rate of industrialization than the financial difficulties. The development banks are therefore expected to perform a host of promotional activities designed to accelerate the pace of industrial development, so that not only capital but all other ingredients of economic development flow under planned direction to irrigate and fertilise the arid regions and transform them into economically developed fruitful areas.[5]

One of the important aspects of the promotional role of development banks is to reduce regional imbalances and foster the development of backward regions. To achieve this objective, they grant financial assitance at concessional rates to attract projects in backward areas. They also conduct techno-economic surveys in these regions to assess the industrial potential and

---

3 Basu S.K., *Theory & Practice of Development Banking,* Chap. 1., p.1.

4 Diamond William, Second IFCI Silver Jubilee Memorial Lecture, 1974. Extracted from *Search Light on Development Banking - Compendium of IFCI Silver Jubilee Memorial Lectures,* p.56

5 Basu S.K., *op. cit.,* Chap. 8, p. 89.

problems of these areas and to bring to light new project ideas and investment proposals that should be undertaken on a priority basis.

With a view to help the development of backward areas and fill up gaps in the institutional infrastructure at the regional levels, the development banks set up technical consultancy centres which conduct potential surveys at the district levels, screen the identified project ideas and undertake detailed feasibility studies to help the prospective entrepreneurs. They also promote new enterprises and encourage new and technician entrepreneurs to take up identified projects. The Technical Training & Management Development Institutes set up by the development banks organise entrepreneurship and management development programmes to impart and upgrade technical and managerial skills of entrepreneurs and executives.

Fostering the growth of rural, tiny, small and medium scale sectors is yet another dimension of the promotional role of development banks. They operate several schemes of subsidies and concessional assistance and provide guidance in identification, formulation, implementation and operation of industrial projects in these sectors.

The development banks, in their financial operations, have to pay a due regard to the promotional aspect of their functions. This implies that while selecting projects for assistance, they have to be guided not only by considerations of commercial profitability, but also those of broad socio-economic commitments of the country. In doing so, they may sometimes even have to compromise their commercial interests, for example, by providing assistance at concessional rates or promoting a project in less developed area which may be more expensive than the same in some developed region. In short, the development banks have to work as an instrument of economic development in conformity with the national objectives, plans and priorities.

Development Banking in India:

The idea of establishing special institutions for the provision of finance for the industry was put forth as far back as 1931 by the Central Banking Enquiry Committee. The Committee recommended the creation of Provincial Industrial Credit Corporations and an all-India Institution for the purpose of meeting the financial requirements of industries of regional and national importance respectively.[6] However, nothing concrete was done till the beginning of 1945.

After the World War II, the problems of modernisation, expansion, and reorganization of existing industries and establishment of new industrial units could no longer be ignored. The need to establish special financial institutions to provide adequate finance to industry became inevitable. The matter was examined by the Finance Department of the Central Government and a detailed study was made by the Reserve Bank of India in May, 1945.

The study proceeded on the premise that specialised financial institutions should be set up at the all-India and the regional levels and also indicated the respective fields of their operations.[7] Accordingly, a number of development banks were established in quick succession soon after independence to expedite the pace of industrial development of the country. Some of the development banks established in the country such as Industrial Finance Corporation of India (IFCI), National Industrial Development Corporation (NIDC), Industrial Credit & Investment Corporation of India (ICICI), National Small Industries Corporation (NSIC), and Refinance Corporation for Industry Ltd. (RCI) operated at the all-India level; while State Financial Corporations (SFCs) and State Industrial Development/Investment Corporations (SIDCs/SIICs) operated at the state level.

IFCI was the first to be set up in 1948 and mark the beginning of the era of development banking in India. The basic objective was to make long term credit available to public limited companies and industrial cooperatives. The establishment of SFCs at the state level was considered almost simultaneously to supplement the work of IFCI by making finance available to small and medium industrial units and the first SFC set up in 1949 was Tamil Nadu Industrial Investment Corporation (TIIC). In 1951,

6 Report of Central Banking Enquiry Committee, 1931, p.5.
7 Simha S.L.N., *Development Banking in India*, IFMR, Madras, 1976, p.34.

State Financial Corporation Act was passed by the Parliament enabling legislation under which more SFCs could be established in different states as the counterpart institutions of IFCI at the national level. At present there are 19 such SFCs working in different states.

To view the problem of industrial financing with a more dynamic approach and add 'developmental' dimension to the mere financial working of the development banks, National Industrial Development Corporation (NIDC) and Industrial Credit & Investment Corporation of India (ICICI) were set up in 1954 and 1955 respectively. The purpose of NIDC was to provide both finance and entreprenurship to industry. It was expected to formulate projects, prepare feasibility studies and establish and run industrial enterprises. Although ambitious in design, it ultimately degenerated into a financing agency for rehabilitation and modernization of cotton and jute textile industries. At present it has ceased to be a financing institution for private industry and acts merely as a consultancy organisation.

The Industrial Credit & Investment Corporation of India was established in 1955 as a public company with support from Government of India, the World Bank, the Commonwealth Development Finance Company and other foreign institutions. The activities of ICICI were more diversified in so far as it engaged in direct investment in shares of industrial units, underwriting of issues of capital, guarantee of loans and channelisation of foreign currency loans from the World Bank to private industry in India.

In the same year, National Small Industries Corporation was set up by the Government of India specially to assist small scale units through promotional, marketing, financing and other activities. In June 1958, Refinance Corporation for Industry Ltd. was established to provide refinance to Commercial Banks and subsequently from 1962 to SFCs also, for the medium term-loans extended by them to medium sized borrowers in the private sector. RCI was later merged with the IDBI w.e.f. September 1, 1964.

At the State-level, State Industrial Development/Investment Corporations were set up from 1960 onwards for the promotion, management and financing of industrial concerns. They paid special attention to problems of industrial development in the relatively backward areas and extended help to entrepreneurs with regard to the supply of infrastructure facilities. At present there are 26 such SIDCs/SIICs operating in the country.

These development banks concentrated mainly on providing financial assistance of various kinds to different sectors. The proliferation of financial agencies that had taken place over the years, however, was not matched by any effective mechanism to coordinate and integrate their activities, with the result that there was little synchronization and often overlapping in their financial operations. Therefore there was an utmost need for a coordinating machinery to bring about inter-institutional cooperation and establish working relationships in the efforts of these institutions.

It was in response to this need that Industrial Development Bank of India (IDBI) was set up in 1964 as the apex development bank of the country. IDBI was assigned the responsibility to function not only as a financing and developmental agency to plan, promote and develop industries and bridge financial and non-financial gaps in the process of industrial development, but also to coordinate the activities of other financial institutions in the country. IDBI performed the much needed coordinative function by setting up Inter-Institutional Groups (IIGs) comprising the representatives of IDBI, IFCI, ICICI, SFCs, SIDCs and leading commercial banks. 23 such IIGs have since been established in different states of the country. The Heads of the institutions hold monthly inter-institutional meetings and the senior executives meet fortnightly to secure coordination in the financial and promotional activities of development banks and discuss matters relating to project financing on consortium basis. In 1975-76, the three all-India institutions, viz. IDBI, IFCI and ICICI jointly constituted inter-institutional Committee consisting of their senior executives and evolved a system of common loan application form and common appraisal of projects. Under this system of consortium financing and single-window dispensation of credit, the applicants now have to approach anyone of these institutions for assistance, which serves as the "Lead Institution" to undertake detailed project appraisal for the applicant and the decisions of the Lead Institution are accepted by others thereby avoiding duplication of efforts.

The latest in the series of all-India institutions is Industrial Reconstruction Corporation of India (IRCI) set up in 1971 with the main objective of rehabilitating sick units. From March 20, 1985, this institution has been renamed as Industrial Reconstruction Bank of India (IRBI) to provide assistance for reconstruction and rehabilitation of sick industrial units and also perform a wide range of developmental activities such as providing infrastructure facilities, consultancy and managerial services and machinery or other equipment on lease or hire-purchase basis to industrial concerns.

In addition to these institutions, Unit Trust of India (UTI) set up in 1964 and Life Insurance and General Insurance Corporations of India (LIC & GIC) established in 1956 and 1973 respectively, also to a certain extent, meet the financial requirements of the industrial sector as they work in close association with all-India Financial Institutions to provide finance on a consortium basis.

The discussion in the foregoing paragraphs is mainly intended to give an introduction to the concept and functions of development banks in general and growth of development banking in India.

2

IFCI and its Operations

Industrial Finance Corporation of India (IFCI) was the first development bank established in the country in 1948 under an Act of Parliament. Introducing the Bill in the Constituent Assembly on 20th November, 1947, the then and the first Finance Minister of Independent India, Hon'ble Mr. Shanmukham Chetty had stated:

> *"With the inauguration of independent India and our anxiety to go ahead full speed with the industrial development of the country, the setting up of an Industrial Finance Corporation has acquired a new significance..... I must frankly say that the object of this Bill is to set up a Finance Corporation for the purpose of financing the large scale industries in this country...... It is my intention, after this Bill has been placed on the Statute Book, to persuade the Provincial Governments to set up similar Industrial Finance Corporations in each province......mainly to finance small scale industries."* [1]

The Bill was passed and became an Act on 27th March, 1948, and on 1st July, 1948, IFCI opened its doors for business. The entire share capital of IFCI was subscribed by the Central Government, the RBI, Scheduled Banks and other financial institutions. The Government and the RBI share-holdings were transferred to the Industrial Development Bank of India in 1964 on the establishment of the latter. At present, IFCI is a subsidiary of IDBI and functions under its guidance and control. Epitomised in IFCI are now four decades of service to the growth and development of Indian industry.

IFCI was established with the main objective of making "medium and long term credits more readily available to industrial concerns in India, particularly in circumstances where normal banking accomodation is inappropriate or recourse to

---

1 Extracted from *IFCI, A saga of 35 years of service to industry,* (pages not numbered)

capital issue methods is impracticable"[2] This functional arena of IFCI has been enlarged from time to time through several amendments made by the Parliament to the IFC Act, 1948, which aim to provide IFCI the requisite dynamism and adaptability to the changing socio-economic environment, increase flexibility in its operations, improve its organisational efficiency and effectiveness, and above all, its usefulness to industry and national economy. IFCI's role now extends to the entire industrial spectrum in the country, in particular, encompassing:

— Project Financing Operations,

— Promotional Activities.

Project Financing Operations:

Under its project financing operations, IFCI provides financial assistance to eligible industrial concerns in corporate and/or cooperative sector, for setting up new industrial projects as also for the expansion, diversification and modernisation of the existing ones, in the form of Rupee and Foreign Currency Loans, underwriting and/or direct subscription to shares/debentures as also guarantees for deferred payments and foreign loans.

The following paragraphs give an account of the project financing operations of IFCI, classified as Plan-wise, Facility-wise, Sector-wise, Industry-wise and Purpose-wise assistance sanctioned, which reflect the growth and diversification of IFCI's operations over the past four decades of planned development in the country.

I. Plan-wise Assistance Sanctioned:

Table 2.1 indicates that starting with a modest business of Rs. 3.25 crores in 1948-49, the first year of its operations, IFCI's quantum of assistance has grown over the years and amounted to Rs. 853.02 crores in 1986-87. The total cumulative assistance sanctioned by IFCI upto June, 1987 stood at Rs. 4042.58 crores to 2541 projects. A look at the disbursements as a percentage of sanctions indicates that the total cumulative disbursements upto June, 1987 were Rs. 2886.54 crores which were 71.4% of the cumulative sanctions.

---

2 Preamble to IFC Act, 1948, as amended up to date, 1987, p. 5.

Table 2.1

Plan-wise Assistance sanctioned and disbursed by IFCI

Crores Rs.

Year ending 30th June		Net financial assistance sanctioned	Net Financial sanction disbursed
	1949-51	8.13	5.79
I Plan	1952-56	27.03	10.94
II Plan	1957-61	73.00	57.04
III Plan	1962-66	179.65	145.02
Annual Plans	1967	20.29	45.99
	1968	17.50	33.01
	1969	28.68	19.11
IV Plan	1970-74	173.56	141.80
V Plan	1975-78	284.65	216.71
Annual Plans	1979	149.56	73.96
	1980	155.58	96.56
VI Plan	1981	198.45	133.68
	1982	256.56	188.25
	1983	263.60	223.27
	1984	343.12	256.69
	1985	448.78	317.95
VII Plan	1986	561.42	413.92
	1987	853.02	506.85
		4042.58	2886.54

Source: IFCI, Operational Statistics, 1986-87, p-42.

II. Facility-wise Assistance Sanctioned:

IFCI provides direct financial assistance to industrial projects in one or more of the following forms:

1. Rupee Loans.
2. Sub-loans in foreign currencies out of the foreign exchange lines of credit made available to it.
3. Underwriting of and/or direct subscription to the shares and debentures of public limited companies.
4. Guaranteeing of:
   a) deferred payments for machinery imported from abroad or purchased within the country,
   b) foreign currency loans raised by industrial concerns from foreign institutions and
   c) rupee loans raised by industrial concerns from scheduled banks, cooperative banks or the public market.

Table 2.2 indicates the facility-wise classification of assistance sanctioned by IFCI in the past six years and cumulatively upto June, 1987.

About 90% of IFCI's assistance is in the form of loans. An emerging trend in the facility-wise assistance granted by IFCI is the rising share of foreign currency loans in its assistance portfolio. The sanctions of foreign currency loans which commenced from 1960-61 now account for about 18.5% of the total quantum of assistance sanctioned as indicated by the figures as on June 30, 1987. The assistance sanctioned in the form of rupee-loans is 71.4% of the total assistance.

The underwriting and direct subscription operations of IFCI are generally catalytic in nature. Initially, IFCI was prohibited from subscribing to the share capital of companies presumably because equity investment was considered risky, though it was empowered to underwrite shares, and hold the same for a limited period. This evoked criticism and IFCI Act was suitably amended in 1960 to authorise the Corporation to subscribe to the share capital also. It is interesting to quote here the words of William Diamond, *"Indeed, equity rather than loans is often the appropriate*

TABLE - 2.2

Facility-wise Assistance Sanctioned by IFCI

Facility	1981-82		1982-83		1983-84		1984-85		1985-86		1986-87		Upto June 1987	
	Amt.	%	Amt.	%	Amt.	%	Amt.	%	Amt.	%	Amt.	%	Amt.	%
Rupee Loans	209.54	81.7	221.50	84.0	236.11	68.8	288.00	64.2	368.78	65.7	600.64	70.5	2886.06	71.4
Foreign Currency Loans	22.93	8.9	17.92	6.8	63.85	18.6	104.40	23.2	138.64	24.7	194.49	22.8	748.41	18.5
Underwriting/ Direct Subscription	19.51	7.6	18.47	7.0	35.90	10.5	33.06	7.4	38.02	6.8	56.64	6.6	296.87	7.3
Guarantees	4.58	1.8	5.71	2.2	7.26	2.1	23.32	5.2	15.98	2.8	1.25	.1	111.24	2.8
	256.56		263.60		343.12		448.78		561.42		853.02		4042.58	

Source: Prepared from IFCI, Operational Statistics, 1987 p. 13 and IFCI Annual Report, 1987 p. 41.

way of providing the required capital. This may especially be the case with a new enterprise or a rapidly expanding one, on which fixed debt beyond a certain level might place an intolerable burden....... and a development bank ought to be prepared to take equity participation in lieu of or in addition to making loans." [3] S.K. Basu has also expressed that *"Admittedly development banks have to take risks; indeed it is in their very nature, and their policies must be free from the inhibiting conservatism of ordinary banks."* [4] Therefore, after 1960, with a view to provide a measure of relief to small and medium-sized industrial units, IFCI started direct subscription to their share capital on selective basis where the amount for subscription including promoters' contribution does not exceed Rs. 25 lakhs. This facility is not available to rights issue made by existing companies.

The idea is to help small entrepreneurs and save their expenditure on advertisement, printing etc. besides underwriting commission and brokerage involved in making the public issue through prospectus. However, as is evident from Table 2.2, underwriting and direct subscription operations of IFCI account for only 7.3% and assistance in the form of guarantees amount to 2.8% of the total assistance sanctioned by IFCI as on 30th June, 1987, on cumulative basis.

A more helping hand in the field of direct subscription and underwriting activities is welcome on the part of IFCI to stimulate capital market activity and enable the small entrepreneurs raise finance in the initial stages of their business when they find it hard to do so due to their doubtful credit-worthiness.

III. Sector-wise Assistance Sanctioned:

IFCI provides financial assistance to industrial projects both in the corporate sector; whether public, private or joint; and the cooperative sector. **Table 2.3** indicates a sector-wise classification of the assistance sanctioned by IFCI in 1986-87 and cumulatively upto June, 1987.

In 1986-87, 530 projects (95.3% of the total projects assisted)

---

3 Diamond William, *op. cit., p.52.*

4 Basu S.K., *op. cit., p.31.*

Table 2.3

Sector-wise Assistance Sanctioned by IFCI

Rs. Cross

Sector	1986-87		Cumulative upto June 1987			% of
	No. of Projects	Ammont sanctioned	No. of Projects	Amount sanctioned	Desburse-ments	diesburse-ments to sanctions
Private	428	620.65	1765	2684.58	1856.18	69.1%
%	77.0%	72.8%	69.5%	66.4%		
Joint 62	93.35	221	534.74	364.12	68.0%	
%	11.1%	10.9%	8.7%	13.2%		
Public	40	93.71	254	443.83	324.96	73.2%
%	7.2%	11.0%	10.0%	11.0%		
Cooperative	26	45.31	301	379.43	341.28	89.9%
%	4.7%	5.3%	11.8%	9.4%		
	556	853.02	2541	4042.58	2886.54	

Note: % are percentage to totals.
Source: IFCI, Annual Report, 1986-87, p. 52.

SECTORWISE ASSISTANCE SANCTIONED BY IFCI

(TABLE 2.3)

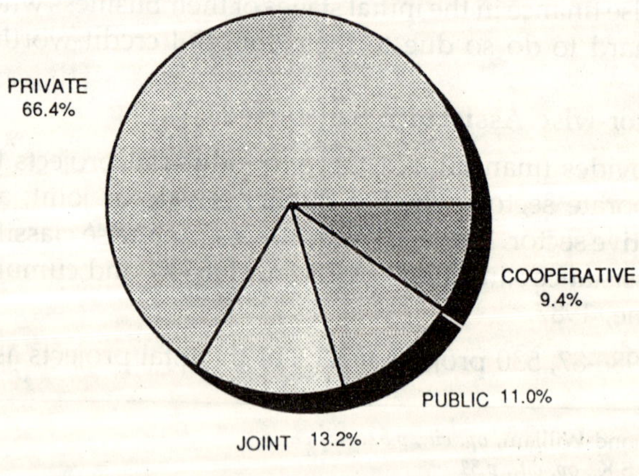

in the corporate sector were sanctioned Rs. 807.71 crores which is 94.7% of the total assistance sanctioned. The share of cooperative sector was Rs. 45.31 crores (5.3% of the total assistance sanctioned) to 26 projects (4.7% of the total projects assisted).

Cumulatively, the corporate sector accounts for 90.6% of IFCI's total assistance portfolio as on June 30, 1987; the share of private, joint and public sectors being 66.4%, 13.2% and 11.0% respectively. The share of cooperative sector is 9.4% in the total assistance sanctioned to 11.8% of the total projects assisted upto June 30, 1987; as out of 2541 projects assisted, 2240 projects (88.2%) are in the corporate sector. This indicates that the assistance portfolio of IFCI is lop-sided in favour of private corporate sector.

However, the amount disbursed as a percentage of sanctions is very high in the cooperative sector i.e., 89.9% as against an average of about 70% in the corporate sector. Sugar and textile cooperatives have been the major beneficiaries of IFCI's assistance in the cooperative sector.

IV. Industry-wise Assistance Sanctioned:

IFCI's financial assistance is spread over a wide range of industries including:

1) Basic industries, viz. basic metal industries, basic industrial chemicals, fertilizers, cement, mining, power generation etc.
2) Capital goods industries, viz. machinery and accessories, electrical machinery and appliances, transport equipment etc.
3) Intermediate goods industries, viz., chemical products, non-ferrous metal industries, iron and steel etc.
4) Consumer goods industries, viz. sugar, food products, cotton, woollen and jute textiles, paper and other miscellaneous industries and
5) Service industries, viz., hotels, medical services, shipping etc.

The industry-wise distribution of assistance sanctioned during 1986-87 and cumulatively as on June 30, 1987 according to use- based classification of products is given in **Table 2.4.**

Table 2.4

Industry-wise classification of Assistance Sanctioned by IFCI.

Crores Rs.

Category industries	No. of Projects (1986-87)	Amount sanctioned (1986-87)	% to total sanctioned (1986-87)	No. of Projects (Cumulative as on 30th June, 1987)	Amount sanctioned (Cumulative as on 30th June, 1987)	% to total sacntions (Cumulative as on 30th June, 1987)
Basic industries	122	249.30	29.2% (47.7)	555	1406.77	34.8
Capital goods industries	108	219.29	25.7% (10.8)	423	609.65	15.1
Intermediate goods industries	108	175.09	20.5% (23.5)	479	770.37	19.0
Consumer goods industries	196	186.63	21.9% (16.4)	1020	1174.89	29.1
Service industries	22	22.71	2.7% (1.6)	64	80.90	2.0
	556	853.02		2541	4042.58	

Note: Figures in ( ) denote % for 1985-86.
Source: IFCI, Annual Report, 1986-87, p. 58

INDUSTRY-WISE CLASSIFICATION OF ASSISTANCE SANCTIONED BY IFCI

(TABLE 2.4)

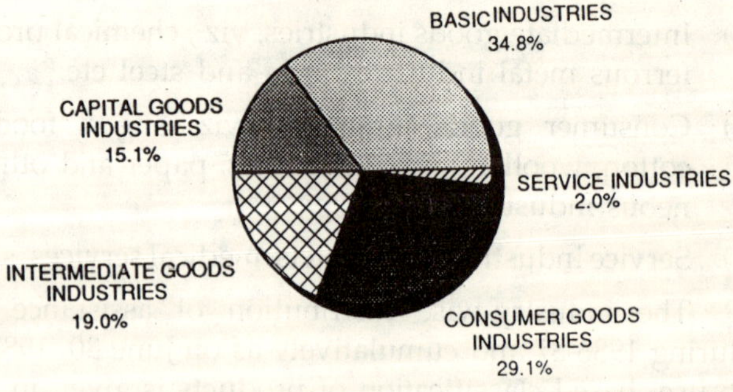

A phenomenal increase of 250.3% can be noticed from the Table 2.4, in the share of assistance claimed by Capital Goods Industries in 1986-87, as its share in the total assistance sanctioned by IFCI went upto 25.7% from 10.8% in 1985-86.

In general, industries of high national priority and other selected industries of importance (generally known as Appendix-1 industries to Industrial Policy Statement of February 2, 1973 as amended from time to time) accounted for 78.9% of the total IFCI's assistance sanctioned during 1986-87. By and large, over 80% of IFCI's assistance has gone to such industries over the past decades. Textiles, cement, chemical and chemical products, sugar, fertilizers, pesticides, iron and steel and electrical machinery and appliances etc. have been the major beneficiaries of IFCI's assistance.

V. Purpose-wise Assistance Sanctioned:

IFCI provides financial assistance either singly or jointly with other term lending institutions for the following purpose:

a) setting-up of new industrial projects,

b) expansion of existing units or for diversification into new lines of activity and

c) renovation and modernisation of the existing units.

Apart from the industries which are specifically listed by the Government as enjoying priority, the projects which come under the priority criteria for IFCI's financing operations are:

a) Employment-oriented and labour intensive projects,

b) Export oriented projects,

c) Projects proposed to be set up in notified less-developed districts/areas,

d) Projects promoted by new or technician entrepreneurs and

e) Projects which contemplate harnessing indigenous technology.

Table 2.5 gives a purpose-wise classification of assistance sanctioned by IFCI in 1986-87 and cumulatively upto June 30, 1987.

Table 2.5

Purpose-wise assistance sanctioned by IFCI

Crores Rs.

	1986-87			Cumulative upto 30th June 1987	
Type of Project	No. of Projects	Amount sanctioned	% to total sanctioned	Ammount sanctions	& to total sanctioned
New Projects	203	514.51	60.3	2683.03	66.4
Expansion or Diversification	40	69.70	8.2	620.70	15.3
Moder-nisation	135	128.71	15.1	313.90	7.8
*Other purposes	178	140.10	16.4	424.95	10.5
	556	853.02		4042.58	

*Other purposes include meeting over-run in the cost of projects, rehabilitation etc.

Sources: IFCI, Operational Statistics, 1986-87. p. 24.

IFCI, Annual Report, 1986-87, p. 45.

PURPOSE-WISE ASSISTANCE SANCTIONED BY IFCI

(TABLE 2.5)

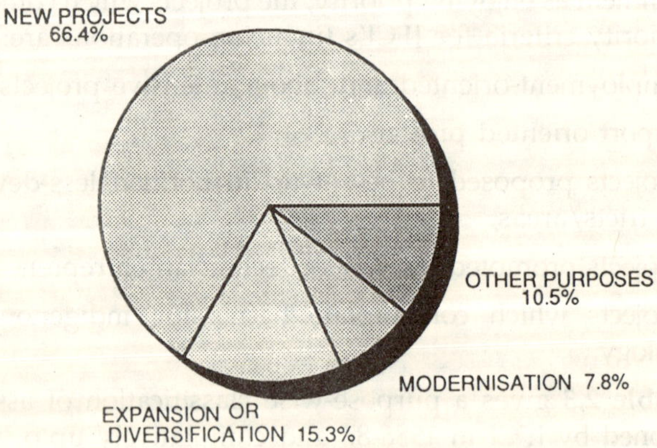

In 1986-87, out of 556 projects assisted by IFCI, 203 projects were new projects, and of these, 26 projects were those which were promoted by new technician entrepreneurs. Also, out of 556 projects assisted, export-oriented and import substitutive projects numbered 27. During the year, 47 projects assisted involved foreign collaboration and/or technology transfer from abroad. IFCI provided 15.1% of the total assistance for modernisation purpose which went to 135 projects under various modernisation schemes, viz., Soft Loan Scheme, Textile Modernisation Fund Scheme and Jute Modernisation Fund Scheme. The Equipment Finance Scheme of IFCI for acquiring equipment either indigenously or from abroad also evolved considerable response and 45 units were sanctioned assistance under the scheme, which was more than double that of 1985-86.

A look at the cumulative figures as on June 30, 1987, indicates that, in general, about two-third of the financial assistance provided by IFCI has gone to new projects. The share of assistance given to expansion, diversification or modernisation of the existing units amounts to about 23% of the total cumulative assistance.

The foregoing paragraphs provide an insight into the Project Financing Operations of IFCI as reflected in the various forms and purposes for which finance is made available covering a wide range of industries all over the country.

Promotional Activities:

All activities of IFCI, in a way, are promotional or developmental in nature. However, activities other than the project financing operations, which are termed as 'Promotional Activities' have come to occupy a place of major significance over the years. This is because no amount of fiscal and financial incentives alone can bring success in industrialisation efforts, unless other inputs like resourceful entre-preneurship, latest and efficient technical know-how, professionalised management, well motivated and skilled manpower coupled with project counselling facilities and extension services are available at every stage during the life cycle of a project. Therefore, the endeavour of IFCI in the area of promotional activities is on providing these non-financial inputs and supportive measures so as to:

a) fill up gaps in the institutional infrastructure and provide a base for accelerating the overall process of industrial growth,

b) dispersal of industries to backward areas to induce balanced regional development,

c) provide consultancy services and guidance in identification, promotion and execution of projects to the new, tiny, small-scale or medium-scale entrepreneurs,

d) broadening of entrepreneurship, improving the technological base of the industry and helping in the development and upgradation of managerial skills and

e) improve the productivity of human and material resources to accelerate the process of industrialisation in the country in its multi-faceted form.

Various activities testifying IFCI's promotional or catalytic role include:

1) Development of backward areas through direct financial assistance to projects being set up in such areas,
2) Participation in the Industrial Potential Surveys of backward areas,
3) Technical consultancy services through Technical Consultancy Organisations,
4) Risk Capital Assistance through Risk Capital Foundation,
5) Management Development through Management Development Institute,
6) Development of Entrepreneurship,
7) Support for Rural Development Programmes,
8) Subsidies and loans granted under Promotional Schemes,
9) Promotion of Research Studies etc. and
10) Merchant Banking Services.

Resources for Financing Promotional Activities:

The promotional activities of IFCI are being financed either out of Benevolent Reserve Fund (BRF) or Interest Differential Funds (IDFs).

BRF was created in 1972-73 in pursuance of amendment to the IFC Act, 1948[5] in 1972 for the purpose of meeting certain special objectives such as:

a) Meeting cost of feasibility studies, project reports, market and techno-economic surveys,
b) assisting projects promoted by new entrepreneurs and technologists,
c) promoting research in financial and industrial management by creation of Chairs in Universities and other academic institutions and
d) meeting the cost of training the personnel of financial institutions etc.

Since the creation of the funds in 1972, a sum of Rs. 762 lacs have been transferred to it out of the profits of IFCI against which a sum of Rs. 484 lacs have been utilized upto June 30, 1987.

IDFs represent the moneys received from the Government of India out of the interest payable by IFCI in terms of agreements entered into between IFCI, Kreditanstalt-Fur-Wideraufbau (KFW), Government of India and the Government of Federal Republic of Germany, in connection with the DM Lines of Credit made available to IFCI by KFW.

Upto June 30, 1987, IFCI had received a sum of Rs. 1964.10 lakhs, against which Rs. 1665.34 lakhs had been utilised on various promotional activities.

Table 2.6 shows the allocation and utilization of BRF and IDFs upto June 30, 1987.

Table-2.6

Allocation and utilisation of BRF and IDF's upto June 30, 1987,

Rs. lakhs

Fund	Total Allocations	Total Utilization	Balance
BRF	762.00	484.00	278.00
IDFs	1964.10	1665.34	298.76
Total	2726.10	2149.34	576.76

Source: IFCI, Operational Statistics, 1986-87, p.71.

5 Sec. 32B, IFC Act (Amendment, 1972) 1948, as amended up to date, 1987, p. 25.,

Table: 2.7 gives a summary of the amounts utilised by IFCI on various promotional activities which have been mentioned earlier, for the year 1986-87 and cumulatively upto June 30, 1987.

This account provides only a bird's-eye view of the promotional aspect of IFCI's operations. The same has been dealt with at length in the later chapters.

The information in the preceeding few pages gives an idea of the project financing operations and promotional activities of IFCI. It would not be inconsistent in this connection to analyse the relative position of IFCI amongst other financial institutions in the country over the past four decades.

Table 2.7

Amount utilised by IFCI on Promotional Activities:

Rs. lakhs

Sl. No.	Nature of Activities supported by IFCI	1986-87	Cumulative upto June 30, 1987
1.	Promotional Schemes	30.08	252.58
2.	Industrial Potential Surveys	1.09	9.25
3.	Support for Technical Consultancy Services	.27	56.48
4.	Support for Risk Capital Assistance through RCF	213.00	982.92
5.	Support for Management Development Activities of MDI etc.	149.44	630.53
6.	Support for Entrepreneurship Development	47.28	108.01
7.	Promotion of Research etc.	1.90	35.91
8.	Orientation Programmes and assistance to state-level institutions	—	4.30
9.	Support for international conferences and seminars	3.00	10.00
10.	Others (utilised for direct financing of projects)	—	59.36
	Total	446.06	2149.34

Source: IFCI, Annual Report, 1986-87, p. 87

IFCI vis-a-vis other financial institutions:

IFCI is the oldest in the battery of financial institutions in India and provides financial assistance to eligible industrial concerns either singly or jointly with other financial institutions like IDBI, ICICI, UTI, GIC, LIC, IRBI and SFCs and SIICs/SIDCs. (A brief introduction of these institutions was given in Chap.1).

Table 2.8 gives assistance sanctioned by all financial institutions from 1982-83 to 1986-87 and also the cumulative assistance sanctioned and disbursed upto March, 1987. The percentage share of each institution in the total assistance sanctioned and disbursements as a percentage of cumulative sanctions for each institution have also been calculated in the table.

Few critical observations have been noted as under:

1) Though IFCI is the longest established financial institution of India, yet it contributes even less than 10% of the aggregate sanctions made by all financial institutions; IFCI's share being a meagre 9.3% on cumulative basis.

2) Comparing the asistance sanctioned by the three all-India Development Banks, viz., IDBI, IFCI and ICICI, the share of IFCI is the lowest, i.e. 9.3% as that of IDBI is 39.5% and ICICI is 14.2% in the aggregate of cumulative sanctions by all financial institutions.

3) IFCI's disbursements as a percentage of sanctions on cumulative basis is 70%, which is lower than the corresponding figures for every other financial institution, which are: IDBI 75.6%, ICICI 73.5%, LIC 79.7%, UTI 76.8%, GIC 73.0%, IRBI 71.5% and SFCs 71.8%, with the only exception of SIDCs where it is 67.5%.

The essence of the above discussion is that though IFCI's operations over the past four decades have grown with the progress and development of Indian Industry, the tasks that lie ahead are both varied and challenging. Newer demands of the changing socio-economic environment may not only call for substantial step-up in the efforts for resource mobilisation and recycling of funds to keep pace with the growth in volume of

Table 2.8

Assistance Sanctioned and Disbursed by all financial institutions

Rs. Crores

Sl.	Institution	SANCTIONS					Cumulative upto March 1987	Cumulative disbursements upto March 1987	% of cum. bursements to cum. sanctions
		1982-83	1983-84	1984-85	1985-86	1986-87			
1.	IDBI	1800.23	2317.47	3454.18	3738.82	4656.26	23232.06	16749.72	75.6%
		(1282.23)	(1766.08)	(2558.38)	(2561.17)	(3332.27)	(16022.04)	(12108.63)	
	%	39.7	42.9	45.3	38.7	40.8	39.5		
2.	IFCI	230.22	321.91	415.43	499.24	798.05	3748.54	2626.58	70%
	%	7.1	7.8	7.4	7.6	9.8	9.3		
3.	ICICI	392.06	507.55	620.69	708.24	1118.28	5733.10	4215.22	73.5%
	%	12.1	12.3	11.0	10.7	13.7	14.2		
4.	LIC	212.83	255.61	332.13	509.13	504.83	N.A.	N.A.	79.7%
		(136.53)	(166.81)	(219.87)	(383.63)	(363.83)	(2044.79)	(1629.34)	
	%	4.2	4.1	3.9	5.8	4.5	5.0		
5.	UTI	127.46	165.79	357.27	696.59	465.02	2204.89	1694.32	76.8%

(Contd. Table)

(Contd. Table)

Rs. Crores

Sl.	Institution	SANCTIONS 1982-83	1983-84	1984-85	1985-86	1986-87	Cumulative upto March 1987	Cumulative disbursements upto March 1987	% of cum. bursements to cum. sanctions
	%	3.9	4.0	6.3	10.6	5.7	5.4		
6.	GIC	92.70	108.49	144.08	153.00	153.27	876.35	638.96	73%
	%	2.9	2.6	2.6	2.3	1.9	2.2		
7.	IRBI	62.26	69.45	110.79	75.22	148.86	572.03	408.72	71.5%
	%	2.0	1.7	1.9	1.1	1.8	1.4		
8.	SFCs	611.57	644.91	743.12	1009.07	1206.28	6092.95	4371.64	71.8%
	%	19.0	15.7	13.3	15.3	14.8	15.0		
9.	SIDCs	296.64	364.59	477.94	526.96	571.29	3250.06	2193.33	67.5%
	%	9.1	8.9	8.4	7.9	7.0	8.0		
	Total	3231.67	4115.58	5647.57	6613.12	8157.15	40544.75	29886.74	

Note: i) % are percentages to total.

ii) Figures in ( ) indicate assistance net of inter institutional flows and are counted for the purpose of total assistance.

Source: IDBI, Report on Development Banking in India, 1986-87 p. 69, Appendix 1.

assistance but also require realignment of policies and priorities for allocation of resources with the complex needs of development financing.

While a general outline of IFCI's operations has been given in this chapter, the developmental or promotional role of IFCI has been discussed at length in the following chapters. Tracing as a backdrop, the exercise of identification of backward areas and the incentives given by the Government and the financial institutions for their development, the study proceeds to analyse (i) IFCI's direct financial assistance to projects set up in backward areas, and (ii) various promotional activities undertaken by IFCI, either singly or jointly with other financial institutions, as supportive measures for accelerating the process of industrialisation in less-developed areas of the country.

3

Identification of Backward Areas and Incentives for their Development

India is a large country having apparant disparities in levels of development in different regions. This is so because the regions differ in their history, their resource endowment, the level of infrastructural development and the attitude of inhabitants to development opportunities. However, with the growth of industry, technology, communication and spread of education, people become aware of the developments in other parts of the country. Quite naturally then, the prevailing pattern of regional imbalances and backwardness becomes unacceptable, and there is an urge to correct these inequalities by putting more emphasis on industrial development of those areas which have hitherto been less privileged. But, for a developing nation like ours, industrial development is not a spontaneous or a smooth process, and this is particularly true about the less developed regions of the country, where there are scarcities of capital, infrastructure facilities and resources — both human and material. It is therefore necessary for the political and the administrative system to take note of such problems if the country is to achieve balanced regional development. That is why accelerated development of backward areas with a view to reducing regional imbalances has been one of the important national objectives of planning in India. Successive five year plans have visualised and drawn attention to the problem of development of backward areas, and it would not be inconsistent in this regard to trace out as a background what the initial Five Year Plans say in this respect.

The First Five Year Plan (1951-56) recognised that if industrial development in the country is to proceed rapidly and in a balanced manner, greater attention will have to be paid to the development of those states and regions which have so far remained backward. It pointed out that there are large potentialities of industrial development in several states (other than those which were relatively developed) and it was desirable to give increasing preference to such areas in the matter of location of more industrial undertakings.[1] The plan however did not talk explicitly about the problem of regional inequalities or of backward area development except in the context of industrial location, and did not outline any specific programme or provision for the development of backward areas.

The Second Plan document stated that in any comprehensive plan of development, it is axiomatic that the special needs of the less developed areas should receive due attention. The pattern of investment should be so devised as to lead to balanced regional development. Resource constraints would limit the extent to which this can be done but as development proceeds and large resources become available for investment, the stress on development programmes should be on extending the benefits of investment to under-developed regions.[2] More specifically, the plan proposed that the objective of more balanced development should be attained by

(a) programmes for setting up decentralised industrial production,

(b) consideration of the need for regional balance in the location of new enterprises and

(c) steps to promote greater mobility of labour and organise schemes of migration and settlement from more to less densely populated areas.[3] However, the bold statements of Second Plan found no ways to be translated into action in any effective manner.

The problem of balanced regional development received much greater attention in the Third Five Year Plan, when for the first time, the plan document devoted a separate chapter on the subject. It stated that "a large country with extensive natural resources viewing each phase of its development in the perspective of a long term plan, has the means not only to realise a high and sustained rate of growth but also to enable its less

1 First Five Year Plan, p.442, Para 49.
2 Second Five Year Plan, Chap. II, p.33.
3 *Ibid.*, p.37.

developed regions to come up to the level of the rest.[4] The plan document stated that "there are several important features in the Third Plan which enlarge the possibilities of development in areas which have in the past been relatively backward"[5] and then goes on to list almost all the major sectors of development, for instance development of agriculture, extension of irrigation and power supply to rural areas, develoment of transport and communications, development of village and small industries and so on. The Plan reiterated the policy of using industrial location decisions as instruments for promoting balanced regional development. It also pointed out the need to pay attention on education and training, availability of competent administrative and technical personnel and on entrepreneurship development in backward areas.

Similar views were expressed in the Industrial Policy Resolution, 1956, and other subsequent statements on Industrial Policy emphasising that in order that industrialisation may benefit the economy of the country as a whole, it is important that disparities in levels of development between different regions should be progressively reduced.[6]

By and large the approach outlined upto the Third Plan Period was very general. The concern for balanced regional growth and backward area development was articulated only in qualitative terms and no systematic and quantitative analysis of the problem had been attempted. This clearly indicates that even after 20 years of attaining independence, very little was done to achieve this important national objective.

The Estimates Committee (1974-75) in their sixty-ninth report have put this problem in a proper perspective when they stated, "The Committee are concerned to note that although the problem of development of backward areas and removal of regional imbalances has been engaging the attention of Government from the beginning of the First Five Year Plan, yet no concrete and

---

4 Third Five Year Plan, Chap.IX.

5 Ibid.

6 Industrial Policy Resolution, 1956, Abstracted from Report on Industrial Dispersal, NCDBA, p.7.

concerted measure was initiated in this behalf till 1968."[7] The Fourth Plan placed renewed emphasis on regional balance and development of backward areas and it was in September 1968 that the Committee of National Development Council in its meeting held on 13th September, 1968 reviewed in detail the problems of regional disparities. In purusance of the decisions taken at this meeting, the Planning Commission appointed two Working Groups popularly known as

(i) Pande Committee, for identification of backward areas; and
(ii) Wanchoo Committee for suggesting fiscal and financial incentives for industrial development in backward areas.

Identification of Backward Areas: Pande Committee:

In any strategy aiming at the development of specific areas, the areas/regions proposed to be developed should be identified first. The task of identifing industrially backward areas was taken up for the first time by the Pande Committe under the Chairmanship of Shri B.D. Pande. The committee submitted its report in February, 1969 and recommended that the following criteria be applied in aggregate for the purpose of identification of industrially backward states and Union Territories:

i) Per capita income,
ii) Per capita income from industry and mining,
iii) Number of workers in registered factories,
iv) Per capita annual consumption of electricity,
v) Length of surfaced roads in relation to population and the area of the State,
vi) Railway milege in relation to the population and the area of the State.

Table 3.1 gives the index of industrial backwardness as indicated by % variations (All India Average = 100) given by Pande Committee. On this basis it was recommended that the following States and Union Territories having indices below All-

---

7 Estimates Committee, Sixty Ninth Report, Lok Sabha Secretariat, New Delhi, p.13.

Table 3.1

Index of Industrial Backwardness
(All India Average = 100)

State	I. No.	State	I. No.
Nagaland	28	Kerala	111
Jammu & Kashmir	59	Karnataka	118
Orissa	72	Haryana	120
Uttar Pradesh	76	Punjab	137
Assam	78	Maharashtra	146
Madhya Pradesh	80	Gujrat	147
Rajasthan	81	Tamil Nadu	154
Bihar	85	West Bengal	160
Andhra Pradesh	87		

Source: Report of the Working Group on Identification of Backward Areas, 1969, Statement I-B, pp. 18-19.

India Average should be considered industrially backward and qualify for special treatment by way of incentives for industrial development:

States: Andhra Pradesh, Assam, Bihar, Jammu & Kashmir, Madhya Pradesh: Nagaland, Orissa, Rajasthan and Uttar Pradesh. Union Territories All, except Delhi and Chandigarh. Subsequently, Meghalaya, Himachal Pradesh, Sikkim, Tripura, Manipur, Goa, Arunachal Pradesh have been added to the list as they have been given status of States.

The Pande Committee also recommended criteria for identification of backward districts in backward States/Union Territories:

a) Districts should be outside a radius of about 50 miles from larger cities and large industrial projects,

b) Poverty of people as indicated by low per capita income starting from the lowest to 25% below the state average,

c) High density of population in relation to utilisation of

productive resources and employment opportunities as indicated by: (25% below the State Average be considered as backward)

i) Low % of population engaged in secondary and tertiary activities,

ii) Low % of factory employment,

iii) Non and/or underutilisation of economic and natural resources,

iv) Adequate availability of electric power, water, transport and communication facilities or likelihood of their availability within next one or two years.

The group also suggested that taking into account the constraints on resources, it would be desirable initially to select only 20-30 backward districts from industrially backward states which may qualify for special treatment by way of incentives for industrial development.

Wanchoo Committee:

This Committee was appointed by the Planning Commission under the Chairmanship of Shri N.N. Wanchoo to suggest fiscal and financial incentives for industrial development in backward areas. The committee submitted its report in April, 1969, and recommended several special fiscal and financial incentives like higher development rebate, exemption from income tax, corporate tax, payment of import duties and excise duties for a specific period and grant of financial assistance on concessional terms etc. to be offered by:

i) Central Government (ii) State Governments and (iii) Financial Institutions.

The recommendations of the two working groups were considered in a meeting of the National Development Council in September 1969 and the main decisions taken were:

i) The criteria to be adopted for selection of industrially backward districts in the States and Union Territories may be settled by the Planning Commission in consultation with the financial institutions and the State Governments in the light of the two sets of criteria recommended by the Pande Working Group; and

ii) Concessions to be offered by financial and credit institutions for financing industries in backward areas should be available to selected backward areas in all the States and Union Territories.

Both these decisions had far reaching operational implications on the basic objective of development of backward areas to reduce regional imbalances and have been appraised hereunder.

According to the former decision, the Planning Commission held deliberations with Reserve Bank of India and other financial institutions like IDBI, IFCI and ICICI etc. for evolving a set of criteria for the purpose of demarcating backward districts in all the States/Union Territories, whether identified as backward or not by the Pande Committee. Eventually, the State Governments were requested by the Planning Commission to indicate districts which could be deemed as backward on the basis of the criteria finalised by it, and also indicated that only those districts with indices well below the state average were to be selected as backward. These criteria were:

1) Per Capita production of food grains/commercial crops,
2) Ratio of agricultural workers to population,
3) Per Capita industrial output (gross),
4) Number of factory employees per lakh of population or number of persons engaged in secondary and tertiary activities per lakh of population,
5) Per Capita consumption of electricity,
6) Length of surfaced roads and railway mileage in relation to population and
7) Districts which are industrially backward should possess a minimum level of infrastructure facilities essential for industrial development.

The 'either-or' nature of some of the above criteria provided plenty of room for manipulation by interested State Governments. The actual selection process of backward districts was not based on the Planning Commission's criteria. In fact, only four States — Andhra Pradesh, Bihar, Himachal Pradesh and Maharashtra — followed the above criteria in toto. All others modified the criteria to suit their own convenience giving non-availability of the data or local circumstantial reasons as the excuse. Ironically, West Bengal which got 13 out of its 16 districts declared as backward, did not adopt any of the criteria suggested by the Planning Commission. The West Bengal's classification of districts was based solely on the per capita district income.[8] West Bengal had been placed on the top as the most developed state according to Pande Index.

The major lacuna of the Planning Commission's criteria as also the Pande Committee's criteria was that the backwardness of a district was to be measured in terms of the distance from State averages and not national averages. What is more, unlike the Pande Committee which stipulated a distance of 25% from the State averages in respect of some of the indicators, the Planning Commission did not stipulate precisely the distance from the State average to qualify for backward status for a district. The only indication was that districts with indices 'well below' the State averages should be selected as backward. Consequently, the obvious view taken was that all the districts with indices below (and not 'well below') the State average could be selected as backward. Accordingly, in most States, all districts with indices below the State average were selected to qualify for concessional finance facilities; also, in the case of a few States like Assam, Himachal Pradesh, Jammu & Kashmir, West Bengal, Madhya Pradesh, some districts above the State average had also been selected as backward, as a special case. So, what is 'well below the average' is anybody's guess now. The anomaly is clear from the fact that with the use of State Averages, even the developed districts of a backward state which were much more backward than the so-called backward districts of a developed state, could not be classified as 'backward'. The result was that

8 Seminar Paper on Strategies for the development of backward areas Do they widen inter-state disparities by N. Parmeswaran Nair and K.K. George, IDBI publication of Seminar Papers, pp. 164-165.

many backward states have lesser percentage of their districts declared as backward as compared to some of the most developed states. The glaring examples are of West Bengal (13 out of 16 districts backward), Tamil Nadu (9 out of 16 districts backward), Gujarat (10 out of 19 districts backward) and Maharashtra (13 out of 26 districts backward). These four States are those which were classified by the Pande Committee as the top four developed States of the country and they have got more than half of their districts declared as backward.

On the other hand, Bihar — whose rank in the industrial development is only 10th according to the Pande Panel Index — has the lowest percentage of the districts (16 out of 31 distt.) eligible for the package of incentives.

Thus, for identification of backward districts, no objective and uniform criteria were followed, as though it was done with an elastic yardstick. It has favoured the more developed states against the less developed states. With this non-selective and indiscriminate approach, 247 (now the number of backward districts stands at 301; as they have been reorganised) districts in the country were selected as industrially backward to qualify for concessional finance facilities from the financial institutions. This constituted almost two thirds of all the districts in the country and covering about 70% of the land area.[9] In selecting larger number of districts as backward, the Planning Commission had clearly gone against the recommendations of both the Pande and Wanchoo Working Groups. Pande group had suggested that taking into account constraints on resources, it would be desirable initially to select about 20-30 backward districts from backward states which may qualify for special incentives. Wanchoo Group had also opined that in view of the vast size of the country with major portion of it as backward, it would not be possible to select too many regions for development, and suitably concentrated programme should be drawn up for maximum impact depending upon the resources available instead of thinking in terms of a very massive and widespread programme. Therefore it seems that promoting 247 districts was

---

9 This aspect has been again discussed later in this chapter with supportive data.

trying to do everything under the sun. Similar views had been expressed in the Estimates Committee (1974-75) Report. "In the present situation of constraints of resources and availability of entrepreneurial skill as well as administrative and organisational resources of the States, it would have been far better if the recommendation of the Pande Group had been accepted and had been concentrated in a limited number of districts by giving them liberal incentives so that in the backward states, there would have been atleast one district/area where significant economic development had taken place which would have served as an example to other areas." [10] These were one aspect of implications with regard to the identification of backward areas. The other aspect relates to the incentives and concessions to be offered by the Central and the State Governments and the financial institutions for the development of industrially backward areas.

The important concessions/facilities offered by the Centre for the industrial units located/proposed to be located in specified backward districts/areas included (i) Central Investment Subsidy, (ii) Transport Subsidy for hill and remote areas, (iii) Facilities for procuring machinery on hire-purchase basis, (iv) Preferential treatment for import of machinery, raw materials and components and (v) Income Tax reliefs in the form of deduction of 20% of taxable profits for computation of assessable income.

The several schemes of incentives and concessions offered by the State Governments pertained to provision of essential infrastructure facilities like land, power, water, raw materials etc. at concessional rates, subsidising the cost of preparation of feasibility reports, provision of interest-free loans and marketing assistance, exemption from State sales tax and octroi duties, besides providing technical guidance and training programmes for new entrepeneurs.

The all-India financial institutions viz. IDBI, IFCI and ICICI introduced in 1970, special schemes of concessional finance for all new and existing units in the identified industrially backward

10 Estimates Committee Report, 1974-75, Sixty-ninth Report, Lok Sabha, New Delhi.

areas. The concessions extended were in the form of lower interest rates, longer initial moratorium period, longer repayment period, reduced commitment charges, lower underwriting commission for shares and debentures and participation in the risk capital.

What follows in the next few pages is a brief appraisal of the efficacy of two more important of these several incentives i.e., Central Investment Subsidy Scheme and the Concessional Finance Scheme of financial institutions as a measure to achieve balanced regional development through the development of backward areas.

Central Investment Subsidy Scheme:

The Central Capital Investment Subsidy Scheme was initiated in August 1971. Keeping aside the recommendations of the Pande Working Group regarding selection of only 20-30 districts in industrially backward States/Union Territories for special incentives, instead, the State Governments were requested to select two districts/areas from each of the State identified as industrially backward and one district/area from each of the other States to qualify for the Scheme. Initially under this scheme an investment subsidy amounting to 10% of the fixed capital investment subject to a ceiling of Rs. 5 lakhs for new and existing units undertaking substantial expansion was provided. Subsequently in June 1972, the scope of the scheme was further extended so as to enlarge its coverage by increasing the number of districts/areas from 2 to 6 from each of the identified backward state and from 1 to 3 from each of the other states. From March, 1973, the rate of subsidy was also increased from 10% to 15% of the fixed capital investment subject to a ceiling of Rs. 15 lakhs. The number of districts eligible for the Central Subsidy thus increased from 44 in 1971 to 101 in 1973. With effect from 1.1.1977, the existing units could be eligible to subsidy for the purpose of expansion if additional investment is not less than 10% of the existing investment.

Table 3.2 gives the pattern of distribution of funds under the Central Subsidy Scheme. The disbursements under this scheme seem to be highly skewed in favour of the developed states. For

Table 3.2

State-wise and Year-wise reimbursements made under Central Investment Subsidy Scheme upto 1979

(Rs. Lakhs)

Sl.	State/U.T.	1972-73	1973-74	1974-75	1975-76	1976-77	1977-78	1978-79	Total	% of total
1.	Andhra Pradesh			61.47	79.68	158.46	258.76	132.08	690.45	12.1
2.	Assam		2.50	1.91	18.55	33.64	26.14	56.19	128.97	2.3
3.	Bihar			12.74	2.00	19.95	45.95	36.99	117.61	2.1
4.	Gujrat		.56	15.26	73.41	90.20	64.11	186.37	429.92	7.5
5.	Haryana				12.61	8.96	94.66	43.35	159.59	2.8
6.	Himachal Pradesh			23.67	28.42	12.88	105.09	23.98	194.05	3.4
7.	J & K				2.59	47.03	27.18	70.81	147.61	2.6
8.	Karnataka	10.25		18.35	24.98	115.01	154.01	87.90	400.60	7.0
9.	Kerala			29.84	28.30	19.31	129.28	71.01	277.73	4.8
10.	Madhya Pradesh			12.76	40.58	140.25	156.78	34.03	284.39	5.0
11.	Maharashtra		48.11	70.40	101.22	86.00	218.12	144.31	668.16	11.7
12.	Manipur	.18					6.24		6.43	.1
13.	Meghalaya			5.95	3.67	4.64	5.05		19.31	.3
14.	Nagaland			3.77			34.63		38.41	.7
15.	Orissa			8.16	1.68	12.23	11.21	28.95	62.29	1.1
16.	Punjab		.59	11.11	22.06	45.45	65.36	45.48	190.45	3.3
17.	Rajasthan	1.33	2.31	35.67	50.40	81.76	182.84	132.90	487.21	8.3

(Contd. Table)

(Contd. Table)

(Rs. Lakhs)

Sl.	State/U.T.	1972-73	1973-74	1974-75	1975-76	1976-77	1977-78	1978-79	Total	% of total
18.	Sikkim					1.34			1.34	.1
19.	Tamil Nadu		4.57	144.65	104.73	238.32	292.78	198.47	883.52	15.5
20.	Tripura						4.84	14.05	18.89	.3
21.	Uttar Pradesh			28.39	7.59	54.38	19.09	37.02	146.46	2.6
22.	West Bengal		.18	4.40	5.60	32.33	4.47	63.32	107.30	1.9
23.	Andeman & Nikobar					.36		4.42	4.78	.1
24.	Dadra & Nagar Haveli						8.37	9.69	18.06	.3
25.	Arunachal Pradesh							9.19	9.19	.2
26.	Goa, Daman & Diu				1.46	21.66	66.35	95.25	184.72	3.3
27.	Lakshdweep									
28.	Mizoram						5.50		5.50	.1
29.	Pondicherry		.08		.19	2.70		24.23	27.21	.5
	Total	11.76	58.90	385.46	599.71	1116.99	1996.00	1541.19	5710.01	

Source: "Capital Investment Subsidy Scheme as an instrument for industrialisation of backward areas -- An exploratory view" -- by Ajay Dua, paper read at Seminar on Industrial Development of Backward Areas, Bombay, 1980, organised by IDBI (NCDBA Report on Industrial Dispersal, 1980, p. 21) (Some difference in the totals are due to approximations)

example, four of these states namely Tamilnadu, Maharashtra, Gujarat and Karnataka accounted for about 42% of the total subsidy disbursed with their respective shares being 15.5%, 11.7%, 7.5% and 7%. Out of the states identified as industrially backward by the Pande Group, only Andhra Pradesh and Rajasthan received 12.1% and 8.3% of the total subsidy disbursed respectively. The share of other backward states like Assam, Bihar, Orissa and Jammu & Kashmir has been very small.

Table 3.3 gives a more vivid picture of the subsidy disbursed as shared between the developed and the backward states. Out of total disbursements of Rs. 57.10 crores made till 1978-79, over 55% had gone to the developed states. All the backward states together could receive only 44.8% of the total subsidy disbursed till 1978-79. The year-wise distribution also shows that for the initial years, the utilisation of the subsidy was very limited and that too highly in favour of the developed states. Another fact with regard to the disbursement of Central Subsidy is that cumulatively upto 1978-79, only 15 districts out of 101 eligible districts accounted for over 56% of the subsidy disbursed; and out of these 15 districts, only 3 districts were in backward states.[11] This further substantiates the fact that the benefits of the Central Subsidy accrued to a smaller number of districts with a definite bias towards developed states.

Concessional Finance Scheme:

A still more relevant analysis from the point of view of this work is to appraise the efficacy of Concessional Finance Scheme introduced in 1970 by the all-India term-lending financial institutions in which IFCI was a participant alongwith IDBI and ICICI. The scheme covered all the 247 districts declared as backward to qualify for concessional finance facilities from these financial institutions. A state-wise list of such districts is given in **Table 3.4**.

Under the Concessional Finance Scheme, IDBI, IFCI and ICICI provided concessional assistance upto Rs. 3 crores (loan assistance upto Rs. 2 crores and underwriting assistance upto Rs.

11 Abstracted from Report on Industrial Dispersal, NCDBA, 1980, Para 4-19.

Table 3.3

Share of Developed and Backward States in the Total Reimbursement of Investment Subsidy (1972-79)

Rs. Lakhs

Year	Developed States		Backward States		
	Amount	% to Total subsidy	Amount	% total subsidy	Total subsidy
1972-73	10.25	87.2	1.51	12.8	11.76
1973-74	54.09	91.8	4.81	8.2	58.90
1974-75	191.01	49.6	194.45	50.4	385.46
1975-76	363.11	60.6	236.60	39.4	599.71
1976-77	638.37	57.2	478.62	42.8	1116.99
1977-78	1022.79	51.4	973.21	48.6	1996.00
1978-79	870.44	56.6	670.75	43.4	1541.19
Total	3150.06	55.2%	2559.95	44.8%	5710.01

Source: "Capital Investment Subsidy Scheme as an instrument for industrialisation of backward areas : An Exploratory view" : by Ajay Dua, Paper read at Seminar on Industrial Development of Backward Areas, Bombay, 1980, organised by IDBI (Seminar Papers published by IDBI, p. 305)

SHARE OF DEVELOPED AND BACKWARD STATES IN REIMBURSEMENT OF INVESTMENT SUBSIDY

(TABLE 3.3)

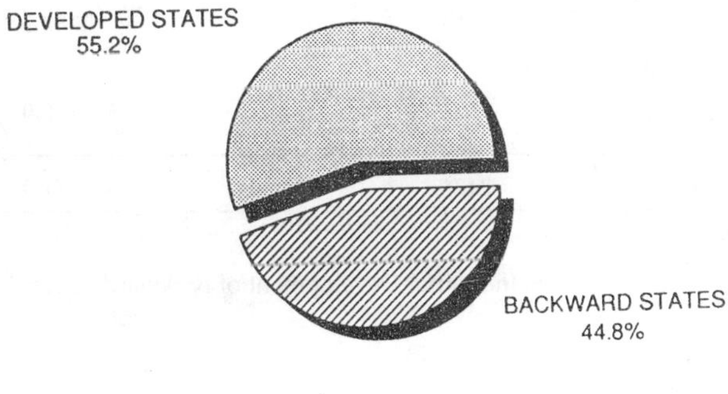

Table 3.4

State-wise list of industrially backward districts selected for concessional finance from the financial institutions

State	No. of Backward Districts	% of backward area to the total area of the state
Andhra Pradesh	14	72.4
Assam	7	77.4
Bihar	16	47.2
Gujrat	10	67.2
Haryana	4	50.0
Himachal Pradesh	7	88.0
J & K	10	100.0
Karnataka	11	66.7
Kerala	5	42.3
Madhya Pradesh	36	87.0
Maharashtra	13	54.7
Manipur	5	100.0
Meghalaya	3	100.0
Nagaland	3	100.0
Orissa	8	61.0
Punjab	5	38.9
Rajasthan	16	61.9
Tamil Nadu	9	64.4
Tripura	3	100.0
Uttar Pradesh	38	68.4
West Bengal	13	82.5
U.T. excluding Delhi and Chandigarh	7	100.0
	247*	71.3

*including Sikkim.

Source: Annexure p. 266, Industrial Development of Backward Areas, IDBI, 1980.

1 crore) to new projects as well as to expansion, diversification, renovation and rehabilitation programmes of the existing units in these backward areas. The concessions offered were in the form of lower interest rate, (about 2% lower than the normal lending rate), a reduced commitment charge which could be waived in exceptional cases, a reduction of 50% in the underwriting and guarantee commission, a longer initial moratorium period upto 5 years against the normal practice of 2-3 years, longer amortisation period of 15-20 years as against the normal repayment period of 10-15 years and participation in the risk capital on a selected basis. Besides this, IDBI also provided concessional refinance facilities through State Financial Corporations and Banks to small and medium sized projects in the specified backward areas.

Table 3.5 gives a state-wise distribution of concessional finance by the three all-India financial institutions upto 1979. The total disbursements under concessional finance amounted to Rs. 77840.10 lakhs. The amount diverted to the developed states was Rs. 42038.05 lakhs and that shared by the backward states was Rs. 35802.05 lakhs.

Table 3.6 which gives the figures of the disbursement of concessional finance in percentages for each state brings out the crux of the problem more clearly. This shows that about 54% of the concessional finance flowed to units in those states which were not considered backward by the Pande Committee; the share of all the backward states put together being only 46%. Amongst the developed states also, four of these states namely, Tamil Nadu, Maharashtra, Karnataka and Gujarat accounted for 38.8% of the total concessional assistance. It is worth noting that these four states are the same which claimed a high 42% share of the total Central Investment Subsidy also. Amongst the backward states, only Andhra Pradesh and Uttar Pradesh received 11.8% and 9% of the total concessional assistance respectively. The least developed of the backward states continued to lag behind accounting for a meagre share of about 10% altogether.

Table 3.5

State-wise Disbursement of Concessional Finance as on 31.12.1979

(Rs. Lakhs)

States	**IDBI**	**IFCI**	**ICICI**	**Total**
Developed States				
Gujrat	4977.70	448.54	665.21	6091.45
Haryana	1438.08	472.49	154.88	2065.45
Karnataka	5107.94	864.37	895.14	6867.45
Kerala	2390.71	391.49	381.95	3164.15
Maharashtra	4329.39	2038.05	1995.89	8363.33
Punjab	1959.96	448.50	433.74	2842.20
Tamil Nadu	6999.23	1009.14	939.04	8947.41
West Bengal	2630.71	398.51	667.39	3696.61
Sub-Total	29833.72	6071.09	6133.24	42038.05
Backward States				
Andhra Pradesh	7063.42	1047.93	1053.99	9165.34
Assam	2757.47	194.96	282.36	3234.79
Bihar	1681.39	178.89	141.15	2001.43
Himachal Pradesh	781.19	128.55	142.07	1051.81
J & K	1424.54	61.00	118.12	1603.66
Madhya Pradesh	2367.81	272.87	363.31	3003.99
Manipur	15.07	—	—	15.07
Meghalaya	411.74	73.95	23.79	509.48
Nagaland	76.50	50.00	—	126.50
Orissa	495.42	110.64	54.65	660.71
Rajasthan	3276.42	547.42	501.94	4325.78
Tripura	114.84	52.25	31.66	198.75
Uttar Pradesh	4476.17	1965.14	543.43	6984.74
U.Ts.	1554.39	487.84	877.77	2920.00
Sub-Total	26496.37	5171.44	4134.24	35802.05
Total	56330.09	11242.53	10267.48	77840.10

Source: Abstracted from Table 4.4, p. 23 and Annexure IV. 3, p. 75, Report on Industrial Dispersal, NCDBA 1980.

Table 3.6

Percentage share of States in the Disbursement of Concessional Finance upto 31.12.1979

Sl.	States	%
	Developed States	
1.	Gujrat	7.8
2.	Haryana	2.7
3.	Karnataka	8.8
4.	Kerala	4.1
5.	Maharashtra	10.7
6.	Punjab	3.6
7.	Tamil Nadu	11.5
8.	West Bengal	4.7
		53.9
	Backward States	
9.	Andhra Pradesh	11.8
10.	Assam	4.2
11.	Bihar	2.6
12.	Himachal Pradesh	1.4
13.	J & K	2.1
14.	Madhya Pradesh	3.8
15.	Manipur	Neg.
16.	Meghalaya	0.6
17.	Nagaland	0.2
18.	Orissa	0.8
19.	Rajasthan	5.6
20.	Tripura	0.3
21.	Uttar Pradesh	9.0
22.	U.Ts.	3.7
		46.1

Source: Derived from Table 5.

SHARE OF DEVELOPED AND BACKWARD STATES IN DISBURSEMENT OF CONCESSIONAL FINANCE

(TABLE 3.6)

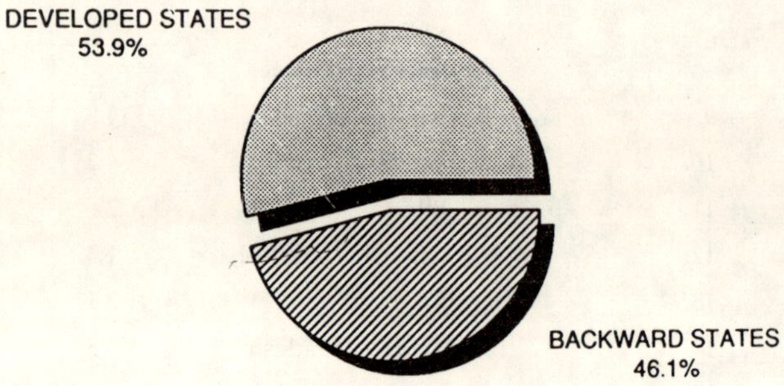

A district-wise analysis[12] of the disbursals made by IDBI, IFCI and ICICI on concessional terms to units in backward areas also revealed that 22 out of the 247 eligible districts accounted for about half of the total disbursals, and out of these, only 12 districts claimed 33% of disbursals,[13] indicating highly uneven distribution of concessional assistance.

Table 3.7 gives an institution-wise disbursement of concessional finance, which shows that all the three financial institutions viz IDBI, IFCI and ICICI diverted a higher percentage of their concessional assistance in favour of the developed states as compared to the States identified as backward.

Another point of consideration is that backward districts obtained finance from the all-India institutions on concessional terms as well as normal terms. Out of the total assistance sanctioned by these institutions upto 1979, the share of backward areas had been only about 40% and out of this, only about half of the assistance was on concessional terms.[14]

Table 3.8 further testifies this fact that the share of backward areas in the total disbursements of all-India financial institutions had been only about 40% out of which only about 60% on an average was under concessional terms. This percentage share of backward districts in total disbursement can be compared with the fact that these districts are about two-third of all the districts, cover about 70% of the area of the country and about 60% of the population. Thus, neither on a population nor on an area basis, backward districts got as much as the other non- backward districts. Also, a significant proportion of the finance going to these districts was not on concessional terms.

Hence the facilities provided under Concessional Finance and Central Investment Subsidy Schemes, the two most important segments of the schemes of incentives, could not be channelised in the manner it was envisaged. The distribution of benefits was highly skewed and accrued mainly to a small

12 Annexure IV-3, Report on Industrial Dispersal, NCDBA, 1980.

13 Para 4.24, Report on Industrial Dispersal, NCDBA, 1980.

14 Concessional Finance from all-India Development Banks, Paper read by Sh. K.S.V. Menon in the IDBI Seminar. Industrial Development of Backward Areas, IDBI, 1980, p.251.

Table 3.7

Institution-wise percentage share in the Disbursement of Concessional Finance

Financial Institution	% share Developed States	Backward states
IDBI	52.8	47.2
ICICI	59.7	40.3
IFCI	54.0	46.0
Total	53.9	46.1

Source: Para 4.21, p. 14, Report on Industrial Dispersal, NCDBA, 1980.

Table 3.8

Flow of Concessional Finance to Backward areas as percentage of total disbursements of All-India Financial Institutions.

	1976-77	1977-78	1978-79
Share of Backward Areas in the total disbursements % of which	35.6	40.4	44.2
Portion under concessional terms %	64.7	64.4	57.6

Source: Para 4.22, p. 14, Report on Industrial Dispersal, NCDBA, 1980.

number of districts/areas, and these too, predominantly located in industrially advanced states. In this connection, the Sixth Plan (1980-85) observed that "Regional imbalances in industrial development have not been corrected to the extent required.....even within the state, industries have tended to gravitate towards existing centres, the backward areas remaining substantially backward. The schemes of concessional finance and Central subsidy benefited the advanced states more than the industrially backward states,"[15] and called for closer monitoring and evalu-

15 Evaluation Report on concessional finance and other incentives in industrially backwards areas, Programme Evaluation Organisation, Planning Commission, 1981, Para 1.5, p.1.

ation of the schemes. At the time of the formulation of the Sixth Plan, it was felt that the working of these various programmes needed to be reviewed and a suitable strategy for the development of backward areas formulated.

Therefore, the Planning Commission set up the National Committee on the Development of Backward Areas (NCDBA) and entrusted it with the task of examining the validity of concepts of backwardness, review the working of existing schemes for stimulating industrial development in backward areas and recommend an appropriate strategy for effectively tackling the problem as well as suggest remedies. The committee organised series of seminars and conducted several studies covering a large variety of problems of backward area development and submitted the results of its deliberations in the form of eleven reports in 1980-81. The Programme Evaluation Organisation of the Planning Commission also undertook an Evaluation Study of the various incentive schemes in industrially backward areas and submitted its report in November, 1981. In the light of the recommendations of the reports by NCDBA and other reviews, the entire scheme of incentives for development of backward areas was revised by the Government of India from 1st April, 1983.

The specified backward areas were classified into three categories, known as category A, B and C depending upon the degree of backwardness. Category 'A' districts, now 134 in all, include 91 No-industry districts, which have no medium or large-scale industrial units. Category 'B' covers 54 those districts, minus districts included in category A, where industrial projects were entitled to the earlier scheme of Central Investment Subsidy. Category C includes those 113 districts in which the industrial projects were earlier entitled only to concessional finance from financial institutions, but they have now been made eligible for Central Investment Subsidy also. Thus, now in all 301 districts are declared backward out of 412 total districts in the country.[16]

The schemes of incentives for projects in backward areas have also been considerably liberalised based on this categori-

16 As in June, 1987. Refer Appendix I at the end.

sation. Central Investment Subsidy ranging from 10%, 15% and 25% of fixed capital investment subject to a maximum ceiling of Rs. 10 lakhs, Rs. 15 lakhs and Rs. 25 lakhs respectively is available for projects coming up in Category C, B and A districts respectively. From 1st April, 1985, the ceiling of Rs. 25 lakhs has been raised to Rs. 50 lakhs, at the rate of 25% of fixed capital investment, for encouraging industries in hill districts under Category A. Several other incentives given by the Central Government include tax concessions, assistance for infrastructural development of growth centres, concessions for industries promoting ancillarisation and projects under MRTP/FERA etc. in notified backward areas.

The scheme of concessional finance by the financial institutions has also been revised in 1983 and made more comprehensive with a thrust on providing graded scale of incentives to attract investment in No-Industry districts and other relatively more backward regions. Concessional assistance on aggregate basis from the financial institutions for industrial projects to be set up in backward districts is available as under:

Districts	Loan Assistance	Underwriting Assistance
A	5 Crores	2.5 Crores
B	3 Crores	1.5 Crores
C	2 Crores	1.0 Crores

The nature of concessions is similar to those provided earlier, i.e. lower interest rate, 50% reduction in underwriting commission, relaxed norms relating to promoters' contribution, nil or reduced commitment charge, participation in the equity capital and additional concessional assistance for infrastructure development and Industrial Estates.

The basket of incentives announced by the Government and the financial institutions in 1983 has given an impetus to the share of financial assistance attracted by the backward regions.

This fact has been verified in **Table 3.9** which gives the total assistance sanctioned by the three all-India development banks, IDBI, IFCI and ICICI during 1983-1987. The backward regions which could not claim more than 40% of the assistance from these institutions have now been able to attract about half of their sanctions on an average. However, even this proportion cannot be regarded too good as compared to the proportion of backward regions in the country as a whole.

Table 3.9

Total financial assistance sanctioned by IDBI, IFCI & ICICI

(Rs. Crores)

Year	Backward areas	Non-backward areas	Total	% of backward ward areas in total sanctions
1983-84	1414.5	1686.8	3101.3	45.6%
1984-85	2125.1	1933.1	4058.2	52.4%
1985-86	2249.6	2417.4	4667.0	48.2%
1986-87	2737.2	3323.0	6060.2	45.2%

Source: Compiled from Report on Development Banking in India, IDBI -- 1986-87, 1985-86.

Therefore, it has been increasingly recognised that while fiscal and financial incentives have their own role in inducing the development of backward areas, there are a number of other factors which facilitate establishment of industrial projects in such areas. These include identification of project ideas, providing consultancy services for preparation of feasibility studies and project reports, search and development of entrepreneurial/ managerial talents etc. Guided by these considerations, the financial institutions have also undertaken certain supportive steps, as a part of their promotional activities to bridge the gaps in the institutional infrastructure and fill the lacunae in enterprise and management in the less-developed areas.

The following chapters analyse the role of Industrial Finance Corporation of India (IFCI) in channelising its funds to the development of backward areas as also the several promotional measures undertaken by it as are regarded necessary for the accleration of the process of industrialisation in the developing areas.

4

IFCI's Assistance to Backward Areas: Financial Aspect

Since its establishment in 1948, Industrial Finance Corporation of India was expected to take keen interest in the industrial development of less developed states/areas so that a more balanced economic development is brought about. This is evident from one of the earliest directives issued by the Government (issued on 21.8.1948) that In its operations, the Corporation should assist, as far as may be practicable, the industrial development of backward provinces and areas in order that such regions may attain a more balanced economic growth. However, in implementing the above directive, IFCI had to function within the terms of its Charter. According to section 6(2) of the IFC Act, 1948, the Board in discharging its functions shall act on business principles, due regard being paid by it to the interest of industry, commerce and general public.[1] In other words, IFCI was required to strike a balance between financing projects located in an industrially less developed area and their economic and commercial viability. Therefore, the phrase as far as may be practicable in the Central Government's directive was suitably exploited by IFCI, in the sense that it could not afford to ignore business principles, and, viability of the project apparently remained the over-riding consideration in providing financial assistance to projects. With the result that in the pre-1970 period, the share of backward areas in the total assistance sanctioned by IFCI was a meagre 26% on an average as shown in **Table 4.1** which gives the percentage share of backward areas in the total assistance sanctioned by IFCI on an yearly basis. But the responsibility for this lop-sidedness cannot be put squarely on IFCI itself, as there had been no clear indications from the side of the Government as to which regions or areas were to be treated as backward. In fact, the first attempt in the direction of identification and classification of backward areas was done only during 1969-70

1 Sec. 6 (2), IFC Act, 1948, as amended up to date, 1987, p.10.

Table 4.1

Percentage share of Backward Areas in the total Assistance Sanctioned by IFCI

(Yearly Basis) Rs. Crores

Year ended 30th June	Total Assistance Sanctioned	Assistance Sanctioned to Backward Areas	% share of Bachward Areas
1948-1970	325.65	84.64	26.0
1970-71	26.66	5.27	19.8
1971-72	36.93	13.17	35.7
1972-73	41.64	19.90	47.8
1973-74	35.46	14.17	40.0
1974-75	32.09	17.26	53.8
1975-76	47.77	23.32	48.8
1976-77	92.14	59.41	64.5
1977-78	107.21	55.10	51.4
1978-79	151.88	64.12	42.2
1979-80	149.81	68.97	46.0
1980-81	198.45	96.65	48.7
1981-82	256.56	126.74	49.4
1982-83	264.75	157.83	59.6
1983-84	353.62	242.42	68.5
1984-85	450.64	272.59	60.5
1985-86	579.45	323.57	55.8
1986-87	853.02	426.39	50.0
Cum. upto June'87	4042.58	2109.87	52.2%
Pre 1970 Period			26.0%
Post 1970 Period			54.4%
1970-83			50.1%
Cum. upto June, 1983			46.6%
1984-87			58.7%
1948-87			52.2%

Source: Compiled from the Annual reports of IFCI

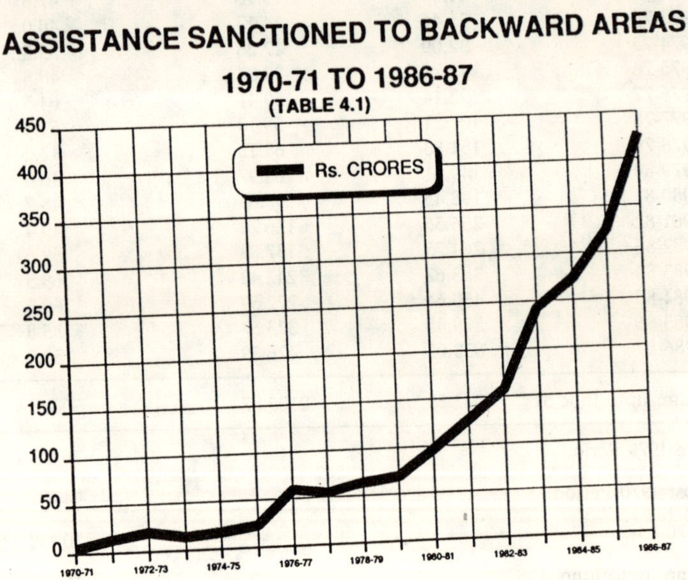
ASSISTANCE SANCTIONED TO BACKWARD AREAS
1970-71 TO 1986-87
(TABLE 4.1)
Rs. CRORES
450
400
350
300
250
200
150
100
50
0
1970-71
1972-73
1974-75
1976-77
1978-79
1980-81
1982-83
1984-85
1986-87

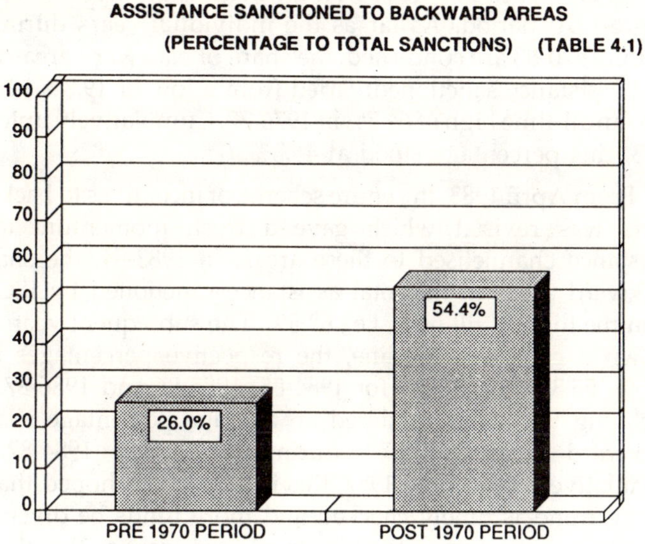
ASSISTANCE SANCTIONED TO BACKWARD AREAS
(PERCENTAGE TO TOTAL SANCTIONS) (TABLE 4.1)
100
90
80
70
60
50
40
30
20
10
0
26.0%
54.4%
PRE 1970 PERIOD
POST 1970 PERIOD

as has already been discussed. So in 1970, IFCI joined hands with other financial institutions in undertaking the scheme of concessional assistance to the backward areas in the country. Since then, the share of backward areas in the total assistance sanctioned by IFCI has registered a definite increase which is evident from the figures in **Table 4.1.**

IFCI's financial assistance to projects in backward areas which was a meagre 26% of its total sanctions in pre-1970 period more than doubled to 54.4% in post-1970 period. During the period 1970-1983 this was 50.1% on an average, nearly twice that of pre-1970 period. As far as the individual years during the period 1970-83 are concerned, the share of backward areas in the total assistance sanctioned varied from a low of 19.8% in 1970-71 to an all-time high of 64.5% in 1976-77. Cumulatively upto June 1983, this percentage stood at 46.6%.

From April 1983, the entire scheme of incentives to backward areas was revised which gave a fresh momentum to the assistance channelised to these areas. In 1983-84, the share of backward areas in the total assistance sanctioned by IFCI has been the highest till now, i.e., 68.5%. The subsequent years have shown a consistent decline, the respective percentages being 60.5%, 55.8% and 50.0% for 1984-85, 1985-86 and 1986-87. This declining trend has rendered an average percentage share of backward areas as 58.7% during the period 1984-87, and cumulatively upto June 1987, this is 52.2%. It is hoped that this falling trend is timely checked and more funds be diverted to projects being set up in the less developed areas so that they can also be lifted upto the level of the rest and be a beneficiary in the country's developmental process.

A more comprehensive picture emerges from **Table 4.2** which gives the state-wise pattern of assistance sanctioned by IFCI to projects set up in less developed areas during the entire period of its operations till now, i.e., cumulatively upto June 1987. From the figures of the Table, following observations are made:

i) Out of a total 412 districts in India, 301 are declared backward, which means 73% of districts in India are backward.

(TABLE 4.2)

PERCENTAGE OF BDs IN TOTAL DISTRICTS

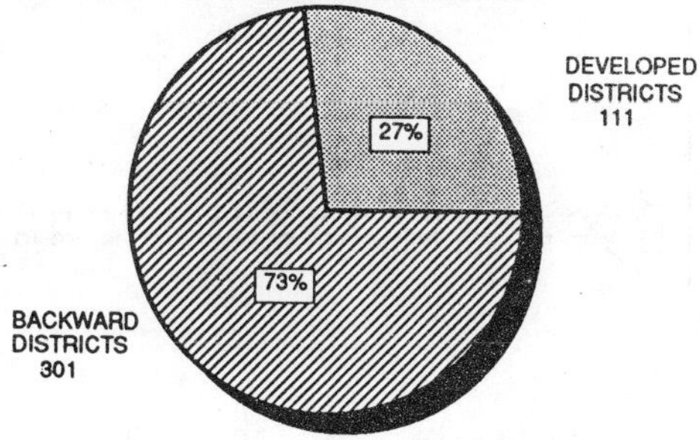

PERCENTAGE OF FINANCIAL ASSISTANCE TO BACKWARD AREAS OUT OF CUMULATIVE TOTAL SANCTIONS

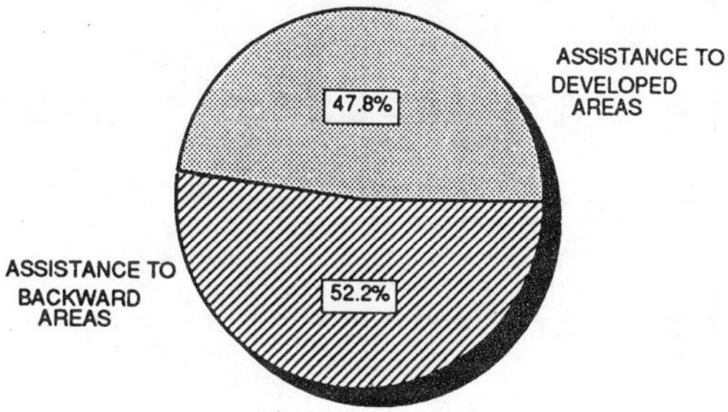

SHARE OF DEVELOPED AND BACKWARD STATES IN ASSISTANCE TO BACKWARD AREAS

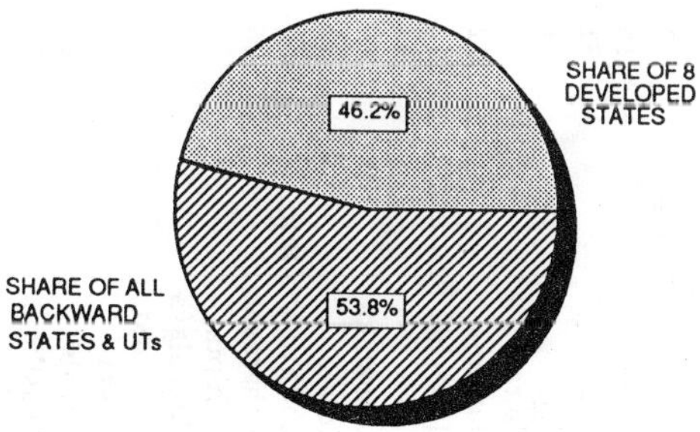

Table 4.2

State-wise Distribution of Assistance Sanctioned to Projects setup in Less Developed Areas (1948-87)

Rs. Crores

State	Total Districts	B.D.	B.D. Covered	Proj. in B.D.	Amt. Sanc.	% to total Sanc.	Amt. Disbursed
Andhra Pradesh	23	19	14	129	259.04	12.3	162.24
Arunachal Pradesh	9	9	1	1	.16	Neg.	.16
Assam	10	10	8	28	36.81	1.7	26.10
Bihar	31	17	10	25	21.45	1.0	22.88
Goa	1	1	1	14	15.91	.7	12.66
Gujrat	19	11	10	87	214.78	10.2	126.38
Haryana	12	7	4	37	58.04	2.8	40.55
Himachal Pradesh	12	12	6	29	39.95	1.9	32.51
J & K	14	14	5	18	21.65	1.0	9.24
Karnataka	19	11	11	98	146.90	7.0	118.02
Kerala	12	7	6	32	43.63	2.1	28.54
Madhya Pradesh	45	41	18	76	163.81	7.8	105.08
Maharashtra	26	14	13	121	184.33	8.7	141.59
Manipur	6	6	--	--	--	--	--
Meghalaya	5	5	2	4	5.25	.2	3.24
Nagaland	7	7	2	3	2.09	.1	1.45
Orissa	13	8	7	28	65.40	3.1	47.72
Punjab	12	6	6	55	106.69	5.1	77.17
Rajasthan	26	16	12	80	167.92	8.0	113.38
Sikkim	4	4	1	2	1.90	.1	1.35
Tamil Nadu	16	12	8	87	126.69	6.0	102.82
Tripura	3	3	2	2	2.63	.1	1.56

(Contd. Table 4.2)

(*Contd. Table 4.2*)

Rs. Crores

State	Total Districts	B.D.	B.D. Covered	Proj. in B.D.	Amt. Sanc.	% to total Sanc.	Amt. Disbursed
Uttar Pradesh	56	41	37	144	312.77	14.8	219.16
West Bengal	16	13	9	65	92.90	4.4	72.32
Andeman & Nikobar	2	2	1	1	.91	Neg.	.91
Chandigarh	1	--	--	--	--	--	--
Dadra & Nagar Haveli	1	1	1	3	2.14	.1	1.28
Daman & Diu	2	--	--	--	--	--	--
Delhi	1	--	--	--	--	--	--
Lakshdeep	1	1	--	--	--	--	--
Mizoram	3	2	--	--	--	--	--
Pondicherry	4	1	--	--	16.12	.8	8.42
Total	412	301	196	1184	2109.87	100%	1476.73

Source: Compiled from Table 29, p. 52, IFCI Operational Statistics, 1987.

ii) Out of a total 2541 projects assisted by IFCI till June 1987, 1184 projects were in backward districts, i.e., 46.6% of the projects assisted by IFCI were in less developed regions of the country.

iii) Out of a total financial assistance of Rs. 4042.58 crores sanctioned by IFCI till June 1987, a sum of Rs. 2109.87 crores were santioned of which 70% had been disbursed to projects which were established in backward areas. In other words, 52.2% of the total assistance sanctioned by IFCI has gone in favour of the backward regions of the country.

Alternatively, 53.4% of the total projects assisted by IFCI account for 47.8% of the total financial assistance sanctioned by it which has been channelised to the mere 27% of the relatively developed regions of the country. Obviously, the less-developed areas deserve a much higher share in the quantum of assistance to give an impetus to their industrial development.

iv) There are 301 backward districts in the country out of which only 196 backward districts have been the beneficiaries of IFCI's assistance. Therefore, as many as 105 backward districts in the country are such where IFCI has not extended its helping hand during the entire four decades of its functioning.

v) The number of backward districts in relatively developed states[2] (like Gujarat, Haryana, Karnataka, Kerala, Maharashtra, Punjab, Tamilnadu and W. Bengal) is 81 out of total 301 BDs which implies that only 27% of the BDs are in developed states. The number of BDs in backward states is 220, implying that 73% of the total BDs are in backward states.

vi) In sharp contrast to the revelation in point (v), IFCI sanctioned financial assistance to the tune of Rs. 973.96 crores upto June 1987 to the projects in backward districts of the

---

2 W. Bengal, Tamilnadu, Gujarat, Maharastra, Punjab, Haryana, Karnataka and Kerala are the 8 states classified as developed by Pande Index. Also, according to the list of NIDs as per the latest classification; Tamil Nadu, Punjab and Haryana have no NIDs, Gujarat, Karnataka and Maharashtra have only one NID each and the rest have very few. Apart from these states, the number of NIDs is quite large in other states of the country, particularly in the North-East region, M.P. & U.P.

eight developed states, which means that 46.2% of the total assistance to backward areas was shared by the BDs of the developed States. This assistance was diverted to 582 projects in the BDs of developed states which amounts to 49.2% of the total projects assisted in backward areas. On the other hand, all the backward states together could attract only 602 projects (50.8% of total 1184 projects) in their backward districts accounting for Rs. 1135.91 crores (53.8% of assistance sanctioned to backward areas).

vii) The lesser industrially advanced of the industrially backward states like Assam, Himachal Pradesh, Jammu & Kashmir, Orissa and Bihar together account for a meagre 8.7% of IFCI's assistance to backward areas on a cumulative basis, the respective shares of these states being 1.7%, 1.9%, 1.0%, 3.1% and 1.0%.

viii) Andhra Pradesh and Uttar Pradesh are the only two states considered industrially backward whose less developed regions have attracted a sizeable proportion of IFCI's assistance, the respective shares being 12.3% and 14.8%.

ix) North-East regions, the least industrially developed regions of the country, together claim an insignificant 2.2% of IFCI's assistance to backward areas.

x) Only six states namely Andhra Pradesh, Gujrat, Karnataka, Maharashtra, Tamilnadu and Uttar Pradesh have drawn 59% of IFCI's assistance to 666 projects covering 93 backward districts of the country on a cumulative basis till June, 1987; leaving 41% of the assistance to be shared by 518 projects in 103 backward districts spread over remaining 19 States and 5 Union Territories.

The crux of the problem is crystal clear. Not only that almost half of the IFCI's total assistance has gone in favour of projects located in relatively industrially advanced areas on an aggregate basis, but also even in the distribution of assistance to backward areas, unduly high proportions have been sanctioned to the BDs of developed states. In addition to this, there has been an uneven distribution of assistance amongst different states. With such a pattern of distribution of assistance, skewed highly in favour of developed areas, one can not expect much towards the achievement of the objective of development of backward areas to reduce regional disparities in development.

It seems that the foregoing paragraphs present quite a gloomy picture of IFCI's assistance to backward areas on a cumulative basis. However, with the new scheme of incentives implemented from 1983, the situation has slightly improved during the recent past.

Table 4.3 gives a state-wise distribution of assistance sanctioned by IFCI to backward areas during 1983-84 and 1986-87. **Table 4.4** presents the data of IFCI's assistance to such areas classified according to the categories of backward districts. A look at these two sets of figures brings out the following observations on an yearly basis:

i) In 1983-84, out of 337 projects assisted by IFCI, 187 were in backward areas. Out of the total assistance sanctioned of Rs. 353.62 crores, 68.5% (Rs. 242.42 crores) was received by the less-developed areas. 43.8% of this amount was diverted to projects in backward districts of the developed states and 56.2% shared by the BDs of backward states. The share of category. A BDs was too small i.e. only 23 projects were sanctioned a sum of Rs. 26.97 crores, in other words, 12.3% of projects given a share of 11.1% in assistance to backward areas. The rest was divided between category B and C districts.

ii) In 1984-85, 220 projects assisted by IFCI were in backward areas out of 418 projects. A sum of Rs. 272.59 crores (60.5% of the total Rs. 450.64 crores) was sanctioned to them. The backward districts of developed states got only 38.4% of the assistance whereas the BDs of backward states shared the rest 61.6% of the sanctions. The number of projects assisted in category A districts more than doubled, i.e. 49 projects were sanctioned Rs. 87.03 crores (32% of the assistance to backward areas).

iii) In 1985-86, the number of projects assisted by IFCI declined. Out of 365 projects assisted 185 were those in backward areas. The share of these areas in the total assistance also declined to 55.8% (Rs. 323.57 crores out of Rs. 579.45 crores).

As if this was not enough, the BDs of developed states attracted 47% of the backward area assistance and all the BDs of backward states together could claim 53% of the sanctions. The number of projects assisted in category A districts also decreased to 40 accounting for 28% of the assistance to backward areas.

iv) In 1986-87, the share of backward areas in the total sanctions has further gone down to 50% (Rs. 426.39 crores out of Rs. 853.02 crores), which is even lower than the cumulative average of 52.2%. Out of 556 projects assisted, 296 were in less- developed regions, of which 76 belonged to category A districts and were sanctioned a sum of Rs. 127.05 crores, i.e. about 30% of the assistance to backward areas. Despite the fall in the percentage of IFCI's assistance to backward areas, the BDs of developed states could grab only 37.4% of the assistance and the rest 62.6% was shared by the BDs of backward states.

From the analysis of the above facts relating to the channelisation of IFCI's assistance to backward areas during the years 1983-84 to 1986-87, following trends can be noticed:

i) Backward areas have been able to attract a higher percentage of projects in the recent years. In post-1983 period, 53% of the projects assisted by IFCI were in backward areas as compared to 46.6% on a cumulative basis (1948-1987).

ii) During 1983-87, 41.6% of IFCI's assistance to backward areas was taken away by the BDs of developed states whereas 58.4% was received by the BDs of industrially backward states. This situation is a shade better as compared to the respective percentages of 46.2% and 53.8% for the entire period of IFCI's operations. This is indicative of a considerate attitude towards the backward districts of backward states, which is required still more if regional disparities are to be reduced and these areas are to participate in industrial development.

iii) Another favourable indication is given by the rise in the percentage of projects assisted by IFCI in category A districts which includes 91 NIDs and other special hill regions. In 1983, category A districts accounted for 12.3% of the projects

Table 4.3

State-wise Distribution of Assistance Sanctioned to backward areas (1983-84 to 1986-87)

(Rs. Crores)

State	1983-84			1984-85			1985-86			1986-87		
	Total Sanc.	Sanc. in BD	% Sanc. in BD	Total Sanc.	Sanc. in BD	% Sanc. in BD	Total Sanc.	Sanc. in BD	% Sanc. in BD	Total Sanc.	Sanc. in BD	% Sanc. in BD
Andhra Pradesh	61.92	36.73	15.2	45.79	28.91	10.6	33.49	20.18	6.2	143.30	85.69	20.1
Arunachal Pradesh	.16	.16	.1	--	--	--	--	--	--	--	--	--
Assam	2.30	2.00	.8	3.20	3.20	1.2	2.17	2.17	.7	8.87	8.87	2.1
Bihar	4.12	3.01	1.2	4.76	2.26	.8	7.42	.23	.1	15.33	2.14	.5
Goa	--	--	1.25	1.25	.5	--	--	--	4.15	4.15	1.0	
Gujrat	48.86	35.02	14.4	34.13	20.28	7.4	89.61	38.77	12.0	98.00	48.24	11.3
Haryana	20.91	11.88	4.9	6.42	3.90	1.4	23.85	11.37	3.5	29.67	9.68	2.3
Himachal Pradesh	2.53	2.53	1.0	5.71	2.1	4.95	4.95	1.5	7.17	7.17	1.7	
J & K	2.52	2.52	1.0	7.66	7.66	2.8	1.55	1.55	.5	7.54	7.54	1.8
Karnataka	13.88	11.07	4.6	24.71	14.55	5.3	13.76	6.31	1.9	28.30	17.40	4.1
Kerala	7.86	3.10	1.3	16.28	12.91	4.7	5.82	5.04	1.6	15.87	11.60	2.7
Madhya Pradesh	20.93	19.33	8.0	23.11	20.51	7.5	25.78	25.47	7.9	58.00	52.90	12.4
Maharashtra	33.30	11.91	4.9	65.88	25.03	9.2	83.99	34.86	10.8	112.40	29.60	6.9
Meghalaya	--	--	--	--	--	--	.80	.80	.2	1.71	1.71	.4
Nagaland	.16	.16	.1	1.41	1.41	.5						
Orissa	17.27	13.75	5.7	20.61	7.36	2.7	6.87	1.20	.4	21.76	12.04	2.8
Punjab	15.06	13.37	5.5	17.81	9.12	3.4	39.20	27.18	8.4	44.87	14.72	3.4
Rajasthan	16.89	14.95	6.2	25.51	22.79	8.4	46.83	36.73	11.3	28.32	25.37	5.9
Sikkim	1.00	1.00	.4	--	--	--	.90	.90	.3	--	--	--

(Contd. Table 4.3)

(Contd. Table 4.3)

(Rs. Crores)

State	1983-84			1984-85			1985-86			1986-87		
	Total Sanc.	Sanc. in BD	% Sanc. in BD	Total Sanc.	Sanc. in BD	% Sanc. in BD	Total Sanc.	Sanc. in BD	% Sanc. in BD	Total Sanc.	Sanc. in BD	% Sanc. in BD
Tamil Nadu	23.27	14.70	6.1	32.41	11.09	4.1	49.00	9.30	2.9	45.57	20.80	4.9
Tripura	--	--	--	--	--	--	--	--	--	1.47	1.47	.3
Uttar Pradesh	48.32	36.72	15.1	84.81	64.57	23.7	115.12	75.13	23.2	153.14	52.24	12.3
West Bengal	8.41	5.21	2.1	21.33	7.81	2.9	21.93	19.20	5.9	15.07	7.62	1.8
Andeman & Nikobar	--	--	--	.30	.30	.1	--	--	--	--	--	--
Chandigarh	--	--	--	.41	--	--	--	--	--	.75	--	--
Dadra & Nagar Hav.	--	--	--	.61	.61	.2	.76	.76	.2	.65	.65	.2
Delhi	.65	--	--	5.17	--	--	4.18	--	--	6.32	--	--
Pondicherry	3.30	3.30	1.4	1.36	1.36	.5	1.47	1.47	.5	4.79	4.79	1.1
Total:	353.62	242.42	100%	450.64	272.59	100%	579.45	323.57	100%	853.02	426.39	100%

Source: Compiled from the Operational Statistics, IFCI, 1984-87.

Table 4.4

Assistance Sanctioned to Projects in Backward Areas Classified according to Category of Backward Districts

(1983-84 to 1986-87)

(Rs. Crores)

Category of BD	1983-84		1984-85		1985-86		1986-87	
	No. of Projects	Amount Sanctioned	No. of Projects	Amount Sanctioned	No. of Projects	Amount Sanctioned	No. of Projects	Amount Sanctioned
A	23	26.97	49	87.03	40	91.92	76	127.05
B	102	135.35	97	97.75	68	132.32	128	189.54
C	62	80.10	74	87.81	77	99.33	92	109.80
Total:	187	242.42	220	272.59	185	323.57	296	426.39

Source: Compiled from the Annual Reports of IFCI (1983-84 to 1986-87)

with 11% of financial assistance sanctioned whereas in 1987, 25.7% of the projects involved 30% of the assistance to backward areas. Therefore, during these four years, the least developed areas of the country have experienced a two-fold rise in the number of projects assisted and a little less than three times increase in the financial assistance sanctioned by IFCI.

iv) Notwithstanding these healthy trends, the share of backward areas in the total quantum of assistance sanctioned by IFCI has drastically gone down from 68.5% in 1983-84 to 50% in 1986-87. During 1983-87, 1985-86 was the least favourable year from the point of view of IFCI's assistance to backward areas, when the number of projects, the share of backward areas in the total assistance as well as the shares of backward districts in developed and less-developed states, all registered a deterioration. For an institution like IFCI, which has four decades of operational experience to its credit, it is imperative that a proper balance is maintained between the quantum and the quality of distribution of assistance flowing to backward areas on one hand, and, the proportion of such areas in the country as a whole on the other, if the national objective of developing backward areas to reduce regional disparities is to be achieved. IFCI has still to go a long way to meet this criterion.

However, it is worth noting in this regard that though IFCI's assistance in the development of backward areas in only like one of the many rivers flowing to the sea, yet it would not be an exaggeration to term IFCI as the pioneer development bank making wishful gains during the entire period of its operations.

Table 4.5 gives the total assistance sanctioned by the three All-India Development Banks, viz., IDBI, IFCI and ICICI cumulatively upto March, 1987, as shared between the backward and the non-backward areas of the country. The total quantum of assistance sanctioned by IFCI is least as compared to the other two development banks, yet the quality of its distribution in favour of backward areas appears to be the best. 52% of IFCI's total assistance has gone to the less-developed regions of the country whereas this share in case of IDBI and ICICI has been only 43.9% and 43% respectively on a cumulative basis.

Table 4.5

Institution-wise Total Assistance Sanctioned Cumulative upto 31st March, 1987

(Rs. Crores)

Name of the Institution	Total Assistance Sanctioned			
	Backward Area	Non-Backward Areas	Total	% share Backward Areas in total
IDBI	9654.4	12313.0	21967.4	43.9%
IFCI	1959.2	1789.3	3748.5	52.2%
ICICI	2180.7	2894.0	5074.7	43.0%

Source: Compiled from Report on Development Banking in India, IDBI, 1986-87.

INSTITUTION-WISE % SHARE OF BACKWARD AREAS IN TOTAL CUM.ASSISTANCE SANCTIONED
(TABLE 4.5)

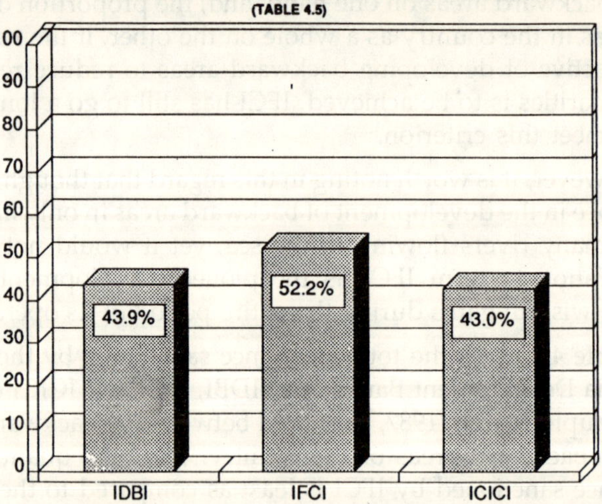

Thus it can be said that throughout the entire span of IFCI's operations, its assistance to backward areas has been unevenly distributed, concentrated in a few states, tilted more in favour of the backward districts of the developed states; yet when the three All-India Development Banks are compared, IFCI ranks at the top in so far as the share of less-developed areas in the cumulative assistance sanctioned individually by IDBI, IFCI and ICICI is the highest in IFCI's case.

Apart from this financial role, IFCI has undertaken several supportive measures in collaboration with other financial institutions as also individually on its own, as a part of its developmental or promotional role. Often such measures can not be quantified. What matters is their impact in inducing industrial activity so as to develop industrially backward areas and accelerate the process of industrialisation in the country as a whole.

5

Industrial Potential Surveys

Entrepreneurial Role of Development Banks:

The promotional role of development banks is occupying a place of major significance now-a-days in their functional charter. *"Most development banks in their public declarations and policy statements generally express their intention to 'promote', 'encourage' or 'stimulate' development in one sector or another. Used in this broad sense, the word "promotion covers a wide range of activities, from studies of industrial structure to financial packaging, from project formulation to influencing business to adopt new practices and Governments to adopt new policies — so broad a range of activities, that promotion' loses precise meaning. In the narrower, more conventional sense, promotion is the process of enterprise creation. It involves the formulation and development of a proposal, the mobilisation and organisation of the various elements that are needed to give life to it, and, finally, its execution. Promotion is, in fact, carrying out of the entrepreneurial function."*[1] Though the primary role of a development bank is that of a purveyor of long term finance, which is the hard core of its functions, yet experience has proved that for developing nations like India, industrial advancement requires not only the financial incentives but also various other kinds of inputs like well-developed infrastructure, entrepreneurship and efficient management, technical know-how and skilled manpower etc., therefore, the development banks have acquired the additional 'entrepreneurial role' to provide some of these necessary ingredients. This entrepreneurial or catalytic role of development banks involves undertaking several promotional or supportive measures with an aim to fill up vital information gaps and create institutional structure to broaden the technological, managerial and entrepreneurial base for promotion and growth of industries, especially in the less developed regions of the

---

1 Diamond William, 2nd IFCI Silver Jubilee Memorial Lecture, The Inter-play between Financial Institutions and Economic Development, Compendium of IFCI Silver Jubilee Memorial Lectures, p.37.

country so that a more balanced economic development of the nation can take place.

The promotional aspect of IFCI's functioning began with that of its contemporary financial institutions around 1970. Two decades of Independence had already passed when the industrially backward areas were identified for the first time. The financial institutions, including IFCI, promptly started schemes for providing concessional finance and other incentives to such areas but simultaneously realised that monetary benefits alone would do very little to initiate the process of growth in these regions. They were also aware of the fact that the problems in the nascent stage were essentially of non-financial character requiring a detailed study of factors that have prevented growth and of factors that could promote growth. Therefore, considerable amount of preparatory work was required to be done before actual schemes for industrial promotion could be suggested. This work was promotional and supportive in nature and comprised evaluation of resources in the less-developed regions, identification of new project ideas, preparation of preliminary feasibility and detailed project reports, search for managerial and entrepreneurial talents and extension of managerial, technical and financial assistance to prospective entrepreneurs both during project implementation and project follow-up.

Thus, while providing concessional finance for activising the process of industrialisation of backward areas has been one part of the strategy of these institutions, the other part has been to identify industrial potential and project opportunities in such areas and create 'entrepreneurial interests' for the implementation of identified projects.[2]

Industrial Potential Surveys of less-developed States:

The first endeavour of all-India Financial Institutions in following up this 'promotional strategy' was to have, in 1970 and onwards, Industrial Potential Surveys of backward states and Union Territories for the purpose of identifying specific project ideas in the light of resource endowments, infrastructure facilities and

2 IFCI Brochure on Backward Areas Development Scheme, 1986, pp.23-24.

prospective demand for implementation over a period of next 5-10 years. These surveys were carried out by the study teams under the supervision and guidance of a Committee of Direction comprising senior officers of Goverment of India, Reserve Bank of India, the three development banks, IDBI, IFCI and ICICI and Agricultural Refinance Corporation. The study teams comprised mostly officers of participating financial institutions, concerned lead banks and state-level institutions. Since the initiation of the survey work in May, 1970, industrial potential surveys of all the States/Union Territories identified as backward had been completed by 1976-77. These surveys provided a useful background material regarding the development potential of the backward areas and identified a number of resource-based, market-oriented and foot-loose industries which could be taken up for implementation in the near future. In order to facilitate implementation of identified project ideas in an intensified manner, the follow up work was allocated on a geographical basis among IDBI, IFCI and ICICI as under:

	Area to be covered
IFCI	Delhi, Chandigarh, Haryana, Himachal Pradesh, Punjab, Rajasthan, Madhya Pradesh.
ICICI	Andhra Pradesh, Gujrat, Karnataka, Maharashtra, Tamil Nadu.
IDBI	Remaining States and Union Territories.

It is point worthy to note here that the Estimates Committee in their sixty-ninth report (1974-75) stated that "The surveys are of general nature and can at best serve as only the starting point for detailed investigation for establishment of industries in the specified backward areas. As already more than four years have elapsed since this work was initiated, the follow-up in the form of detailed analysis and technical studies to identify the specific industry and the location thereof should be undertaken by high-powered teams, comprising competent technical personnel who should be asked to submit their reports as per time bound programme.[3]

3 Estimates Committee (1974-75), Sixty Ninth Report, Lok Sabha Secretariat, New Delhi, p.36.

This observation of the Committee indicated several critical points:

1) There was a need to carry out more specific project identification exercises in the specified backward areas, i.e. at the district-level, for setting up industries in such areas. This in turn required involvement of State-level institutions, since it is they who can be expected to have a clearer idea of the local resources and other factors influencing the development and the project identification.

2) Such district surveys involving detailed analysis and technical studies should be undertaken by competent technical personnel.

3) Much time had already elapsed and there was a need to carry out this survey work under the guidance of high-powered teams so that delays could be minimised and procedures streamlined.

All these elements paved the way for the financial institutions to evolve a new integrated strategy[4] to handle this promotional work which had the following aspects:

i) identification of inter-related functions comprising the promotional work;

ii) providing a mechanism for effective decision-making; and

iii) creating an institutional machinery to perform the identified-functions.

The functions which comprised the promotional work were similar to those conceived earlier, i.e., identification of project ideas, preparation of preliminary and detailed project reports, training and development of potential entrepreneurs, upgrading their technical and managerial skills etc.

The responsibility of the performance of these functions in a coordinated way was entrusted to the Inter-Institutional Groups (IIGs) set up at the state-level. IIGs serve as the decision making organ with regard to the various promotional functions

4 Based on the article of Shri V.V. Bhatt, Financial Institutions and Technical Consultancy Services, Economic & Political Weekly, Bombay, November, 1981.

and therefore their members comprise of representatives of the IDBI, IFCI, ICICI, SFCs, SIDCs and the leading commercial banks. Twenty three IIGs have since been set up working practically in all the states.

While IIGs provide the mechanism for decision-making and coordination in respect of the various types of promotional work, the need to have an institutional machinery which could perform the technical tasks of identification, appraisal and implementation of the projects was served by the setting up of Technical Consultancy Organisations (TCOs) in various states. So far, 18 TCOs have been set up by the financial institutions in joint collaboration. (detailed discussion on TCOs follows in the next chapter).

Survey of No-Industry Districts:

With this framework, the all-India financial institutions, including IFCI, are now directing their efforts towards systematic development of backward areas based on their local resource endowment, adopting district as a unit for intensive study. To start with, out of 134 identified No-Industry/Special Region Districts (NIDs), 30 NIDs were selected for intensive developmental efforts in close consultation with the respective State Governments. Later on 17 more NIDs were added to the list. Besides these 47 NIDs, industrial potential surveys were commissioned in respect of two more NIDs by the state-level institutions.

Under this Institutional Intensive Developmental Efforts Programme for NIDs, the initial work of identifying industrial opportunities as also the extent of essential infrastructure required to be provided in these districts was assigned to the Technical Consultancy Organisations. The job assigned to the TCOs in this respect involved:

i) identification of industrial opportunities in respect of few (not less than 5, the exact number may vary depending upon the inherent strength of the district) medium and large scale units;

ii) assessment of market potential and preparation of detailed project profiles in respect of identified projects;

iii) identification of infrastructural gaps and requirements and

iv) selection of entrepreneurs and their matching with the projects.

A list of all the 49 NIDs selected for intensive developmental efforts[5] alongwith the names of the TCOs to whom the job has been assigned and the lead responsibility agreed to be taken up by IDBI, IFCI and ICICI is given in Annexure 5.1.

IFCI has the lead responsibility for monitoring the developmental efforts of NIDs in Rajasthan, Madhya Pradesh, Himachal Pradesh, Punjab and Haryana. The lead responsibility of ICICI extends to Karnataka, Gujarat, Maharashtra, Goa, Daman and Diu, Dadra & Nagar Haveli and the entire North-East region. The NIDs in all other states and UTs are under the lead of IDBI.

By the end of the year 1986-87, reports relating to industrial potential surveys in respect of 45 NIDs had been received from the various TCOs. Based on these reports, 122 project ideas involving an investment of Rs. 362.83 crores and an estimated direct employment potential for about 19,591 persons had been cleared by the screening committee comprising senior executives of IDBI, IFCI and ICICI.[6] These project ideas were passed on to the concerned Governments/State level promotional agencies for taking further steps and follow up action towards their implementation. Entrepreneurs had been identified for 22 project ideas and implementation plans are at various stages of finalisation.

As a further follow-up action, IDBI, IFCI and ICICI have agreed mutually that the lead institution amongst them can consider commissioning the Techno-Economic Feasibility Reports (TEFR) once an entrepreneur is identified for taking up and implementing a project idea, provided the entrepreneur agrees to pay atleast 25% of the consultancy charges of the TCOs. In case an entrepreneur prefers an approved consultant other than a TCO for the preparation of TEFR, the institutions can subsidise the cost of preparation of TEFR to the extent of 50%, thus extending their helping hand towards speedy implementation of the projects.

5 Upto 1987.

6 As per the Annual Report of IFCI, 1986-87, p.91.

In addition to the 49 NIDs covered, industrial potential surveys in respect of four districts in Haryana (Jind, Mohinder Garh, Bhiwani and Hissar) have also been completed through National Industrial Development Corporation, the expenditure on which has been shared by various financial institutions including IFCI. The intention is to cover all NIDs in a phased manner under the 'Institutional Intensive Developmental Efforts Programme' for NIDs, as also additional districts that can be covered in consultation with State Governments under the programme, the cost of which is shared by IDBI, IFCI and ICICI.

Thus, the promotional role of IFCI, in so far as the industrial potential surveys of backward states and No-Industry Districts are concerned, has been designed in collaboration with other financial institutions. IFCI itself has utilised Rs. 9.25 lakhs out of the Benevolent Reserve Fund, cumulatively upto June, 1987, for this purpose. However, such promotional work can not be precisely quantified in monetary terms, and has to be judged in its efforts in creating a suitable climate for enterprise creation. Till June, 1987, surveys of only 45 NIDs have been completed, and there is a long way to go when such suveys in respect of all the 91 NIDs and other backward regions in the country would be accomplished and industrial opportunities identified. The day is still farer when the impact of these surveys would be visible in the form of industrial advancement of these regions and there would be no NIDs any longer.

ANNEXURE 5.1

List of NIDs taken up for Intensive Development Efforts

Lead Institution and State	NIDs	No.	TCO
IFCI			
Himachal Pradesh	Kengra, Mandi, Shimla	3	HIMCON
Rajasthan	Jaisalmer, Churu, Barmer, Sirohi*	4	RAJCON
Madhya Pradesh	Dhar, Guna, Sidhi, Jhabu, Bhind, Mandla, Rajgarh, Chhatarpur	8	MPCON
	Chindwara, Panna, Narsinghpur	3	APITCO
IDBI			
Bihar	Purnea, Bhojpur, Nalanda, Khagaria	4	BITCO
J & K	Doda, Kupwara, Rajouri, Pulwamma, Udhampur	5	J & KITCO
Orissa	Balasore, Bolangir, Boudh Khondmel*	3	ORITCO
U.P.	Hamirpur, Jalaun, Uttar-Kashi	3	UPICO
W. Bengal	Cooch Behar, Jalpaiguri, Malda, Bankura, Darjeeling	5	WEBCON
Sikkim	East district (Gangtok) South district	2	WEBCON
Kerala	Wynad, Idukki	2	KITCO
ICICI			
Gujrat	Dangs	1	GITCO
Karnataka	Bidar	1	TECSOK
Assam	Lakhimpur	1	NEITCO
Meghalaya	East Garo Hills	1	NEITCO
Manipur	Chandel, Tamenglong	2	NEITCO
Tripura	South Tripura	1	NEITCO
		49	

* Indicates industrial potential survey commissioned by state-level institution.
Source: Backward Area Development Scheme, IFCI Brochure, pp. 48-49.

6

Development Of Institutional Infrastructure: Technical Consultancy Services

The strategy for achieving an accelerated growth rate in the industrial sector calls for considerable organisational inputs, innovative measures and a lot of initiative, at various levels of policy making and project execution, on the part of concerned functionaries, particularly in less developed areas where certain identified gaps exist and need to be filled. IFCI, in collaboration with other national-level financial institutions and banks, or on its own, has tried to fill up a number of gaps in the institutional infrastructure to provide technical consultancy services, risk capital assistance and facilities for professionalised management. This and the following two chapters cover three important aspects of IFCI's promotional role in this regard in:

i) sponsoring Technical Consultancy Organisations to provide technical and other guidance to projects particularly in tiny, small and medium sector,

ii) setting up of Risk Capital Foundation to help the entrepreneurs in raising a part of promoters' equity contribution in respect of projects promoted by them and

iii) setting up of Management Development Institute and its wing Development Banking Centre to provide training in modern management techniques to entrepreneurs and executives of industry, conduct entrepreneurship and management development programmes for the staff and executives of development finance institutions and undertake research studies in the areas of management and development banking.

Technical Consultancy Organisations (TCOs):

It has been observed in the previous chapter that as a part of the new strategy to handle promotional work for the development of backward areas, Inter-Institutional Groups (IIGs) were set up at the state level to function as the decision-making organ of the financial institutions. IIGs comprised of senior officials of the national and state-level financial institutions and banks empowered to take decisions on behalf of their respective institutions. While the IIGs represent the decision-making body, the TCOs serve as their promotional and functional arms with regard to various types of promotional activities to be undertaken for developing less-developed areas.

The rationale of setting up of institutions like TCOs was based on the premise that:

— Proper identification, formulation and planning of the project are very crucial for their successful implementation and operation,

— New entrepreneurs need considerable guidance, counselling and extension services, whatever be the size of the project,

— Available consultancy services in the country looked to big assignments pertaining to highly capital intensive industries and were not readily prepared to take up assignments for tiny, small and medium scale entrepreneurs,

— Big consultancy firms were located in few highly industrialised metropolitan cities, and there were no such facilities available in less-developed areas of the country, and

— State-level financial institutions who did not have the requisite consultancy services available to appraise the technical aspects of the projects submitted to them for assistance found it too costly to build their own technical expertise, and needed institutions like TCOs to serve their requirements.

Therefore, the national-level financial institutions decided to set up, in a phased manner, well-equipped, autonomous Technical Consultancy Organisations (TCOs) with a view to providing low cost but quality consultancy services from concept to commissioning of the projects to tiny, small and medium-scale entrepreneurs.[1] The first TCO was established in Kerala in 1972,

1 IFCI, Promotional Activities, 1984, p.15.

followed by seventeen others in the past 15 years. The TCOs in the country have been set up on regional basis, normally each one covering one or in some cases more than one state, so that practically entire country has been covered by the services of TCOs. Of the 18 TCOs in India[2] at present, nine are under the lead of IDBI, five under IFCI, three under ICICI and one sponsored by the Government of Karnataka.

The objective of TCOs is to provide under one roof a total package of consultancy services, which include:

1) Preparation of feasibility and project reports and other pre-investment investigations,
2) Conducting market research studies and surveys for specific industry or product,
3) Providing technical and administrative guidance on formulation, implementation and operation of the projects,
4) Providing marketing intelligence and technical advice to existing units with regard to their schemes of diversification, modernisation and more efficient operations,
5) Conducting diagnostic studies for rehabilitation of sick projects, and implementation and nursing of programmes for revival of sick units,
6) Identifying potential entrepreneurs and undertaking activities for their training and development by organising EDPs,
7) Taking up turn-key assignments relating to the setting up of functional industrial complexes,
8) Carrying out Industrial Potential Surveys of No-Industry Districts and other less developed areas to identify their industrial potential which would serve as a basis for undertaking developmental work in such areas and
9) setting up of information cells and data banks relating to industrial and economic activities.

Thus, the objectives of TCOs are quite comprehensive and cover a wide range of developmental activities expected of a pro-

2 Annexure 6.1 at the end of the chapter gives details of the geographical distribution and the lead sponsoring institution of the 18 TCOs in the country.

motional agency. However, the resources of the TCOs both human and financial do not seem to match with this. The TCOs have been organised as small organisations with limited set up and expertise and having recourse to Technical Consultancy Service Centres (TCSCs) and the larger development banks for help in case of large complicated projects. As such, the professional consultant staff of a TCO, on an average, does not exceed ten,[3] with nearly a similar number of supporting staff. The authorised share capital of each TCO is Rs. 20 lakhs, (except that of UPICO, which is Rs. 2 crores) while the paid up share capital varies from Rs. 5 to 15 lakhs for different TCOs. Besides the lead sponsoring institution, the other all-India institutions, state-level institutions and banks also subscribe to the share capital of the TCOs. The joint participation of various financial institutions in pooling financial resources for TCOs is welcome, however, the prescribed authorised share capital of the TCOs appears to be too small considering the heavy responsibilities that they have to shoulder with regard to promotional work.

IFCI has participated in the growth and development of all TCOs (except the one in Karnataka) which have been sponsored jointly by the national and state-level financial institutions and banks. **Table 6.1** shows IFCI's contribution to various TCOs[4] towards their paid-up share capital, and, deficits and non-recurring expenditure as at 30th June, 1987. Out of IFCI's total contribution of Rs. 56.05 lakhs upto 30th June, 1987 to all TCOs, Rs. 33.37 lakhs (i.e. 59.5% of the total) has been made towards 5 TCOs which are under IFCI's lead. Also, out of IFCI's contribution to the share capital, and, deficits and non- recurring expenditures of various TCOs, 59.7% and 58.8% respectively have gone to the 5 TCOs under IFCI's lead, and the rest has been shared by other TCOs in the country.

As IFCI has participated in setting up of all the TCOs in collaboration with other financial institutions, it is relevant to

---

3 The older TCOs like KITCO have 18 professionals while the more recent ones have only eight. Singh V.S., Development Banking in India, p.336.,

4 The table shows IFCI's contribution to 16 TCOs. The seventeenth TCO NECON was incorporated in 1987, to which IFCI contributed Rs. 1.00 lakh towards its share capital in 1987-88. IFCI, Operational Statistics, 1987-88, p.80.

Table 6.1

IFCI's Contribution to TCOs towards their paid-up Share Capital, deficits and non-recurring expenditure, as at 30th June, 1987

Rs. Lakhs

Sl. No.	Name of TCO	Amounts paid towards Share Capital	Deficits & non-recurring exp.	Total
1.	HIMCON	8.25	1.49	9.74
2.	RAJCON	5.10	1.71	6.81
3.	MPCON	7.65	1.53	9.18
4.	NITCON	2.60	1.22	3.82
5.	HARICON	2.60	1.22	3.82
6.	KITCO	2.40	1.36	3.76
7.	NEITCO	1.47	.64	2.11
8.	BITCO	1.42	.70	2.12
9.	APITCO	1.50	.68	2.18
10.	UPICO	1.37	--	1.37
11.	J & KITCO	1.35	.20	1.55
12.	ORITCO	1.25	.30	1.55
13.	WEBCON	1.27	--	1.27
14.	GITCO	2.51	.02	2.53
15.	ITCOT	1.25	.45	1.70
16.	MITCON	1.87	.67	2.54
	Total	43.86	12.19	56.05

Note: No. 1 to 5 TCOs are under IFCI's lead.
Source: IFCI, Operational Statistics, 1986-87, p. 74.

have a glance on the overall activities and operations of the TCOs and thereby visualise their impact on fostering consultancy culture in the country.

Tables 6.2 and **6.3** give assignment-wise and TCO-wise summary of operations respectively of all the TCOs in the country as reflected by number of assignments handled by them since inception of each TCO upto 30th June, 1987. While the overall performance of TCOs may not be assessed only in terms of number of assignments completed by them, because qualitative aspects of their performance are even more significant, all the same, the feasibility studies, project reports, pre-investment studies, industrial potential and area-development surveys, market surveys, rehabilitation studies, appraisal of projects and other assigments which aggregated to over 23,000 upto 30th June, 1987, do bear testimony to the ongoing thrust being built by the TCOs in the area of consultancy to the small and medium industrial projects. Of these more than 80% of the assignments relate to the projects in the village, tiny, small and ancillary sector of industries.[5]

In the field of entrepreneurship development, the TCOs in most of the states function as nodal agencies for carrying out Entrepreneurship Development Programmes (EDPs). All the TCOs together had conducted upto 30th June, 1987, 591 EDPs benefitting 16,685 new entrepreneurs and had rendered counselling and extension services to them towards the implementation of their identified projects.

Besides preparation of feasibility studies, project reports and project profiles, which constitute over 75% of the consultancy assignments handled by the TCOs; one of the thrust areas to

---

5 IFCI, Promotional Activities, 1984, p.16.In fact, in the conference of Managing Directors of TCOs held in March, 1987, under the aegis of IDBI, an important decision taken was, that while each TCO was free to evolve its own operational plans and strategies, it was to be ensured that the share of small scale industry in a TCO's total consultancy business was not to be less than 75% number-wise and 35% consultancy-income wise. This was decided as a policy matter to enable TCOs to maintain their commercial viability, retaining at the same time, their focus on providing consultancy services to small entrepreneurs in areas and at a price, which other consultants might not be able to offer. IFCI, Annual Report, 1986-87, p. 94.

Table 6.2

Summary of Operations of all TCOs

Nature of Assignments		No. of assignments completed since inception of each TCO and upto 30th June, 1987
I	Pre-investment Consultancy Assignments	
	— Feasibility studies/Project reports etc.	10055
	— Industrial potential/area development surveys	425
	— Market surveys	435
	— Project profiles	7605
	— Preliminary fact finding studies	92
	— Appraisals	988
	— Others	1626
	Sub Total (I)	21226
II	Post-investment consultancy assignments	
	— Diagnostic studies	697
	— Rehabilitation of sick units	405
	— Others	851
	Sub Total (II)	1953
III	Turnkey assignments/Functional Industrial Complexes	56
	Grand Total (I+II+III)	23235
	Entrepreneurship Development Programmes	591
	Persons trained	16685

Source: Annual Report, IFCI, 1986-87, p. 92.

Table 6.3

Operations of TCOs Cumulative upto 30th June, 1987

Sl. No.	Name of TCO	Pre-investment Assignment	Post-investment Assignment	Others	Total	EDPs conducted	Persons Trained
1.	APITCO	934	40	—	974	73	2104
2.	BITCO	991	121	2	1114	9	232
3.	GITCO	1272	1227	13	2512	—	—
4.	HARICON	71	19	—	90	3	89
5.	HIMCON	1293	16	—	1309	20	352
6.	ITCOT	1037	31	—	1068	9	320
7.	J & KITCO	995	17	—	1012	6	95
8.	KITCO	1905	47	13	1965	73	2071
9.	MPCON	2680	15	—	2695	118	2640
10.	MITCON	233	70	—	303	17	432
11.	NEITCO	1773	11	16	1800	46	1394
12.	NITCON	591	27	—	618	4	83
13.	ORITCO	579	32	2	613	26	760
14.	RAJCON	695	67	—	762	17	390
15.	TECSOK	3648	103	2	3753	72	2557
16.	UPICO	1694	57	—	1751	86	2885
17.	WEBCON	835	53	8	896	12	281
		21226	1953	56	23235	591	16685

Source: IFCI, Operational Statistics, 1986-87, p. 75.

which the TCOs have been recently paying increasing attention in line with the objectives of the Seventh-Five-Year Plan is taking up integrated programmes for technological upgradation and modernisation of select-ed segments of the existing small scale industrial sector. Under these programmes, in-depth studies[6] of specific sub-sectors of small-scale industry prominent in various states have been taken up so as to identify their modernisation needs and draw up package of services accordingly for implementation of modernisation programmes.

Apart from these activities, some of the TCOs have initiated diversifying their operations to establishment of Functional Industrial Complexes and undertaking technical consultancy assignments on a turn-key basis, i.e., right from the conception of the project idea to the successful implementation of the project. The idea of setting up functional industrial complexes was first promulgated by KITCO for promoting small entreprises on a viable basis in certain districts of Kerala. Each such complex constitutes ten to twenty five small units, manufacturing similar or related products, based on common raw materials, process and market; and these units are linked to a large 'mother unit' which would procure materials and equipment, provide know-how and quality control mechanism and arrange for the marketing of the products. The technical services related to project formulation, identification and training of entrepreneurs and project implementation would be provided by the concerned TCO. Cumulatively upto 30th June, 1987, 56 such assignments have been completed by seven TCOs in the country.[7] It is desirable that such activities be taken up by all the TCOs on a much wider scale as promotion of industrial complexes can be instrumental in providing industrial opportunities to small

---

6 Modernisation studies on paint, ceramics and mini-cement industries in Gujrat, refractory industry in Bihar, drugs and pharmaceuticals industry in West Bengal, engineering industry in Karnataka, switch/control gear and Mangalore tile industry in Andhra Pradesh etc. can be cited as few examples of such studies undertaken by the respective TCOs of these states. IDBI, Annual Report, 1986-87, p.66.

7 GITCO and KITCO completed 13 assignments each, NEITCO and WEBCON undertook 16 and 8 assignments respectively and 2 assignments each have been accomplished by BITCO, ORITCO and TECSOK. Refer Table 6.3 of this chapter.

entrepreneurs of rural and backward areas at a scale which would be economical with respect to technical, financial, marketing and other supporting services.

Over the years, the TCOs have registered a remarkable progress in their operations. The number of assignments handled and the total consultancy business of all the TCOs together, both have gone up by more than two and a half times during the period 1981-82 to 1985-86. Whereas the number of consultancy assignments completed by the TCOs rose from 1010 in 1981-82 to 2786 in 1985-86, their consultancy business increased from Rs. 142 lakhs in 1981-82 to Rs. 363 lakhs in 1985-86.[8] The field in which the TCOs have made a more than six times progress during this period is entrepreneurship development, as evidenced by the fact that 137 EDPs were conducted by the TCOs in 1985-86 in which 3778 new entrepreneurs were given training as against 22 EDPs organised in 1981-82 in which 560 persons were trained.[9] From the point of view of financial viability also, the functioning of the TCOs has improved over the years to a significant extent. Though the TCOs were envisaged to function on business principles and become financially self supporting, they were not able to earn profits in the initial years of their gestation period and as such the participating institutions contributed to meet their operating deficits. However, now almost all the TCOs are not only in a position to meet their current costs but also generate modest surpluses. The overall surpluses generated by the TCOs have in fact increased from Rs. 3.31 lakhs in 1981-82 to Rs. 12.68 lakhs in 1985-86 reflecting improved viability of their operations.[10] To give impetus to the consultancy operations of the TCOs, the sponsoring institutions extend their support by assigning them research studies, project appraisals and techno-economic surveys to be conducted by them on their behalf and also utilise their services for monitoring the progress of their assisted units. In addition to this, under various promotional schemes, IFCI and

8 IDBI, Annual Report, 1981-82, p.71.
IFCI, Operational Statistics, 1985-86, p.63.
IFCI, Annual Report, 1986-87, p.93.

9 Ibid

10 Ibid.

PROGRESS OF TCOs (1981-82 TO 1985-86)

NO. OF CONSULTANCY ASSIGNMENTS COMPLETED

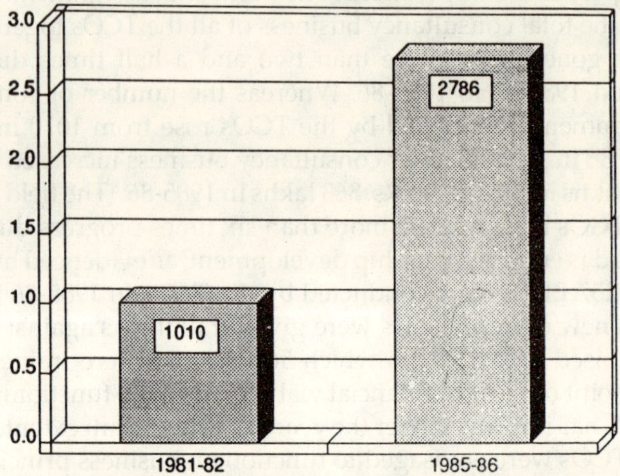

PROGRESS OF TCOs (1981-82 TO 1985-86)

CONSULTANCY BUSINESS (RS. LAKHS)

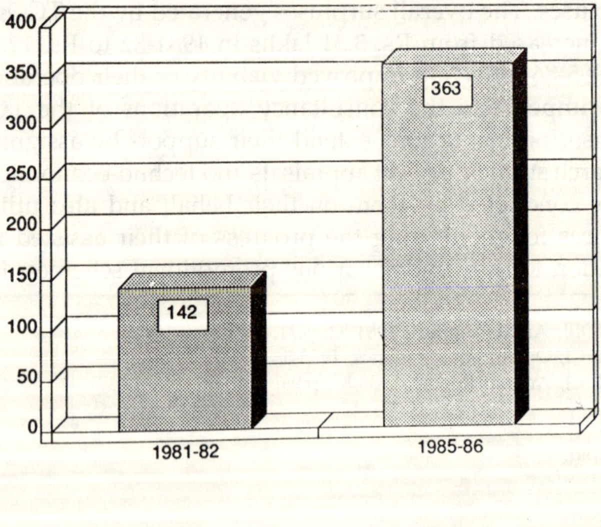

PROGRESS OF TCOs (1981-82 TO 1985-86)

NO. OF EDPs CONDUCTED

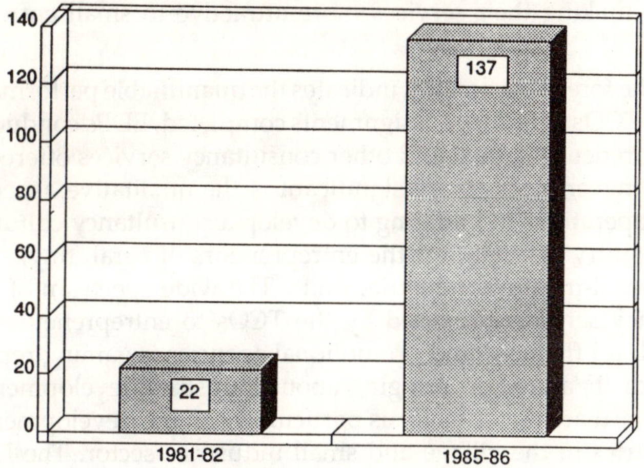

PROGRESS OF TCOs (1981-82 TO 1985-86)

NO. OF ENTREPRENEURS TRAINED

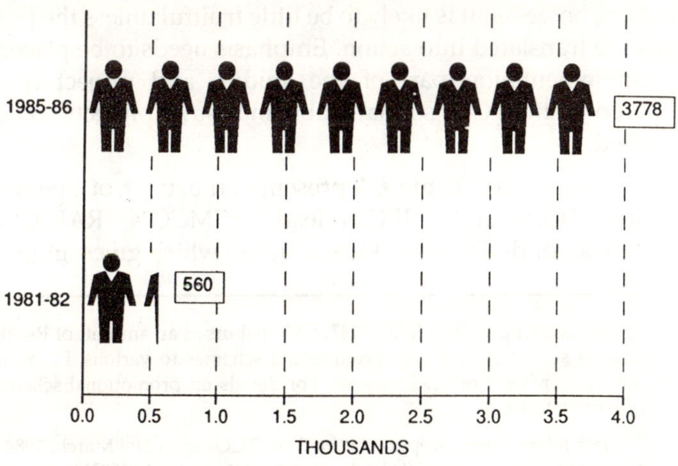

IDBI subsidise the cost of assignments received by the TCOs,[11] thus passing on the benefit of the subsidy to the entrepreneurs from tiny, small and ancillary sectors on one hand, and on the other, adding to the remunerative consultancy business of the TCOs making their services more attractive to small entrepreneurs.

The foregoing account indicates the quantifiable performance of the TCOs in terms of assignments completed, EDPs conducted, entrepreneurs trained and other consultancy services offered by them, nevertheless more significant is the qualitative aspect of their operations in initiating to develop a consultancy culture in the country specially for the entrepreneurs of rural, tiny, small and small-medium industrial units. The wide spectrum of consultancy services provided by the TCOs to entrepreneurs and state-level financial and promotional agencies is gaining reputation for its accent on bringing about industrial development of backward areas and its focus particularly on the development of industries in the village and small industries sector. The EDPs conducted by them for training the entrepreneurs provide motivation and create awareness amongst them and thus energise the hitherto untapped human resource to take up self-employment ventures. The need for the kind of developmental consultancy work in which the TCOs are engaged is beyond question, however, it is likely to be little fruitful unless the project plans are translated into action. Emphasis needs to be placed on the implementation part of the studies and project reports prepared by the TCOs so that viable industrial projects could be launched.

In this context, **Table 6.4** presents an extract of operations of three TCOs under IFCI's lead[12] HIMCON, RAJCON & MPCON all of declared backward states, which gives an idea as

---

11 Cumulatively up to 30th June, 1987, IFCI disbursed an amount of Rs. 186.10 lakhs as subsidies under its promotional schemes to various TCOs in the country in respect of 5175 projects. For details on promotional schemes of IFCI, refer to Chap. 11.

12 The data relates from inception of the three TCOs upto 31st March, 1984. The other two TCOs under IFCI's lead, viz. NITCON and HARICON commenced their operations from September, 1984, and September, 1985 respectively.

Table 6.4

Summary of Operations of three IFCI sponsored TCOs — HIMCON, RAJCON and MPCON (Since inception upto 31st March, 1984)

Sl. No.	Item	HIMCON	RAJCON	MPCON
1.	Year of commencement of business	1977	1978	1979
2.	Number of Assignments (involving investment) completed	513	310	696
3.	Estimated investment contemplated in respect of (2) above (Rs. crores)	124.34	52.23	354.04
4.	Employment Potential (No. of persons)	23447	9393	16057
5.	No. of projects implemented out of (2) above	89	73	337
6.	Actual investment made in respect of (5) above (Rs. crores)	18.16	7.43	22.02
7.	Employment created as a result of (5) above	3649	2573	4630
8.	Other assignments completed	61	73	39

Source: Extracted from IFCI, Promotional Activities, 1984, pp. 16-17.

to the extent to which the assignments completed by the TCOs have been implemented. The figures from the table reveal that there is a wide gap between the number of consultancy assignments completed by the TCOs and those that have actually been translated into viable projects. On an average, not more than one-third of the number of assignments completed have been implemented,[13] with the result that the gap between the contemplated investment and the employment potential in respect of identified projects, and, the actual investment made in respect of such projects and the employment created as a consequence of this is still wider. (Actual investment made and employment created is not more than 15% - 25% of the contemplated in case of different TCOs). The conspicuous conclusion emerging from these findings is that there is a need to find out ways for a more effective implementation of the projects for which the TCOs have provided technical consultancy services.

The rationale of setting up the chain of TCOs in the country was to fortify the institutional structure concerned with the development of industrially backward areas and to fill the distinct gap in the services available to the small and relatively inexperienced entre-preneurs who need institutional help from the stage of project conception to project formulation and implementation. As majority of the TCOs have been in operation for over a decade now or are nearing completion of a decade of functioning,[14] their level of operations, though progressing in quantum, cannot be considered satisfactory and points out to the wide scope for improvement and extension in their services to bring about effective implementation of the identified projects.

---

13 For example, in the Annual Report of RAJCON, 1985, it is reported that about 130 projects for which consultancy services were provided by RAJCON had been implemented upto 1985. (The total no. of assignments completed upto 1985 stood at 541, which means about 24% of the assignments have been implemented.) RAJCON, Annual Report, 1985, pp. 8-9. The Chairman's speech of RAJCON at the 9th Annual General Meeting (p. 2) reports that about 150 projects had been implemented upto 1986 (total no. of assignments completed till 1986 being 710, which implies a cumulative implementation rate of about 21% only).

14 Except MITCON, NITCON, HARICON and NECON which were set up in 1982, 1984, 1985 and 1987 respectively.

To extend the geographical coverage of the TCOs' services it would be desirable that apart from the centrally placed offices in the cities, branch offices of the TCOs/Consultancy Cells be opened in as many districts as possible, so that there could be close follow-up and monitoring of the projects coming up in the backward areas. This becomes more essential in case of projects promoted by new and small entrepreneurs who lack adequate experience and require the guidance and expertise of technical and financial consultants at every stage of project execution. The branch offices of the TCOs in turn should empanel Field Officers to conduct spot surveys on the performance of the projects already implemented and to identify the difficulties faced by those entrepreneurs who have not been able to launch their projects in the scheduled time so that appropriate remedial measures could be chalked out. In addition to this, the Field Officers should establish a good rapport with the local organisations working at the village and block level which will enable them to know the problems and needs of the local entrepreneurs more closely. This kind of information can serve as a useful feedback for improving the qualitative aspect of the TCOs' services and identifying the thrust areas, which may differ from state to state and even within different regions of a state. Accordingly, entrepreneurship development programmes and industrial consultancy/awareness campaigns can be devised by the TCOs suited to the requirements of the local entrepreneurs and the kind of industrial activities that could be undertaken particularly in the village and small industries sector depending upon the locally available resources. Such an exercise would help building a nexus between the training and placement in the EDPs conducted by the TCOs and likely to result in an increasing percentage of the trained entrepreneurs being able to set up viable industrial projects. A follow-up of this kind requires a lot of energy in terms of money, time and other overheads, yet it is unavoidable to ensure success. The catalytic role of all-India development banks like IFCI[15] through the Promotional Schemes,[16]

---

15 IDBI also operates various promotional schemes under which TCOs are subsidised for the consultancy fees on behalf of the beneficiary industrial units.

16 For details of Promotional Schemes of IFCI, Refer to Chap. 11.

which are operated by the TCOs for providing consultancy fee subsidies for projects in tiny, village small and ancillary sectors, would also be more fruitful when the TCOs would avail the subsidies offered to the maximum possible extent thus creating as well as reinforcing the desired thrust in these sectors and encouraging educated/skilled unemployed youth from backward areas to avail themselves of the services of TCOs.

While suggesting ways for making services of the TCOs more effective in the effort of industrialising backward areas, it would be improper to overlook the fact that the nature of the role assigned to the TCOs is promotional and their function is consultancy. Therefore, their services are essentially complementary to that of other financial and promotional institutions, like State Financial Corporations (SFCs) State Industrial Development Corporations (SIDCs/SIICs), Commercial and Regional Rural Banks, National and State Small Industrial Development Corporations (NSIC, SSIDCs) etc. entrusted with the responsibility of providing financial assistance, infrastructure facilities, for e.g. construction of industrial sheds and undertaking various other supportive activities like procurement of raw materials, machinery and equipment, providing marketing assistance etc. for the development of industries in the village and small sector. The way to speedy implementation of the identified projects lies in the coordinated and integrated efforts of all the institutions which provide different—technical, financial and infrastructural -- but equally essential assistance for the industrial development of less-developed areas.

Directory Of Industrial Consultants

The usefulness of industrial, technical and management consultants as a reservoir of diverse skills and experience in promoting sound industrial enterprises hardly needs to be emphasised. Apart from entrepreneurs wishing to set up industrial projects, Government and other institutional agencies involved in industrial promotion, financing and development, often need independent advice from experts outside their own organisation, who could assist in the efforts of these institutions to strengthen their capabilities in port-folio analysis and monitoring and supervision of the projects assisted by them. But the problem that often arises is how to locate and identify a suitable consultant. The consultancy profession in India is comparatively new and the consultants are not expected to advertise themselves. In the circumstances, the all-India financial institutions, viz., IDBI, IFCI and ICICI felt that it would be useful to collect and compile information on the industrial consultancy services available in the country in the form of a Directory for instant reference by different types of clients, entrepreneurs, institutions, Government agencies etc. engaged in the process of industrialisation. Accordingly, with the joint endeavours of IDBI, IFCI and ICICI, a Directory of Industrial Consultants was prepared and first published in 1980, which is kept revised and updated. The total number of consultants empanelled in the Directory stood at 654 as on the 30th June, 1987. Full particulars including the field of specialisation of these technical and non-technical industrial consultants as also of research laboratories affiliated to Central/State Government/Council of Scientific and Industrial Research etc. are contained in the Directory to serve as a guide about the technical, industrial and management consultancy services available in the country.

Annexure 6.1

List of Technical Consultancy Organisations

Sl.	TCO	Name of TCO	Year of establishement	Area of Operation	Lead sponsoring financial institution
1.	APITCO	Andhra Pradesh Industrial & Technical Consultancy Organisation Ltd.	1976	Andhra Pradesh	IDBI
2.	BITCO	Bihar Industrial & Technical Consultancy Organisation Ltd.	1974	Bihar	IDBI
3.	GITCO	Gujrat Industrial & Technical Consultancy Organisation Ltd.	1978	Gujrat	ICICI
4.	HARICON	Haryana Industrial Consultants Ltd.	1985	Haryana, Delhi	IFCI
5.	HIMCON	Himachal Consultancy Organisation Ltd.	1977	Himachal Pradesh	IFCI
6.	ITCOT	Industrial & Technical Consultancy Organisation of Tamil Nadu Ltd.	1979	Tamil Nadu	ICICI
7.	J & KITCO	Jammu & Kashmir Industrial and Technical Consultancy Organisation Ltd.	1977	Jammu & Kashmir	IDBI
8.	KITCO	Kerala Industrial and Technical Consultancy Organisation Ltd.	1972	Kerala	IDBI
9.	MPCON	Madhya Pradesh Consultancy Organisation Ltd.	1979	Madhya Pradesh	IFCI
10.	MITCON	Maharashtra Industrial and Technical Consultancy Organization Ltd.	1982	Maharashtra, Goa Daman & Diu	ICICI
11.	NEITCO	North Eastern Industrial & Technical Consultancy Organisation Ltd.	1973	Arunachal Pradesh Assam, Meghalaya	IDBI
12.	NECON	North Eastern Industrial Consultants Ltd.	1987	Nagaland, Tripura Manipur, Mizoram	IDBI
13.	NITCON	North India Technical Consultancy Organisation Ltd.	1984	Punjab	IFCI
14.	ORITCO	Orissa Industrial & Technical Consultancy Organisation Ltd.	1976	Orissa	IDBI
15.	RAJCON	Rajasthan Consultancy Organisation Ltd.	1978	Rajasthan	IFCI
16.	TECSOK	Technical Consultancy Services Organisation of Karnatka	1976	Karnataka	Govt. of Karnataka
17.	UPICO	Uttar Pradesh Industrial Consultants Ltd.	1974	Uttar Pradesh	IDBI
18.	WEBCON	West Bengal Consultancy Organization Ltd.	1979	W. Bengal, Sikkim Andaman & Nicobar Islands	IDBI

7

Development of Institutional Infrastructure: Risk Capital Assistance

One of the objectives of national policy has been to lay increasing emphasis on encouragement to new entrepreneurs, particularly professionals and technologists with practical experience of industry, for starting small and medium scale industrial ventures since they represent a reservoir of entrepreneurial talent which the country needs very much. But the practical problem confornted by them is to find sources for meeting their requirements of seed or risk capital in order to meet the institutional norms of minimum financial stake in the project, due to "inadequacy of institutional arrangement for provision of promoters' equity capital."[1] For the medium, medium-large and large scale projects, where the minimum 10 to 15% promoters' contribution to the project cost itself works out to a very significant amount, the entrepreneurs could not think of taking up such an industrial venture, unless they have some positive encouragement by provision of some part of risk capital assistance. These considerations led IFCI to sponsor the Risk Capital Foundation (RCF)[2] in 1975, as an institution to provide special risk capital assistance on soft terms to new entrepreneurs, setting up medium and medium-large scale projects[3] as a modest step to remove one of the financial constraints to the growth of new entrepreneurship.

---

1 This has been indentified as one of the important constraints to teh growth of new entrepreneurs by the Committee on "Development of small and medium entrepreneurs" set up by the Government of India in 1973. (Extracted from the first Annual Report of RCF, 1976).

2 Risk Capital Foundation (RCF) has been renamed as Risk Capital and Technology Finance Coporatation Ltd. (RCTC) w.e.f. 12th January, 1988.

3 Contemporary to this, in 1976, IDBI introduced the "Seed Capital Scheme" for the benefit of the small-scale entrepreneurs to enable them to raise a portion of equity to be treated as promoters' contribution for their projects.

Risk Capital Foundation

Risk Capital Foundation was registered as a society under the Societies Registration Act, 1860, and was inaugurated on the 10th March, 1975 by the then Minister of Industry and Civil Supplies, Government of India, with the main objective to encourage technologists and professionals to promote sound and viable medium-sized industrial projects by giving them loans on soft terms to enable them to provide a part of the equity capital as promoters' contribution.

The assistance granted by RCF is normally considered for projects costing between Rs. 2 crores and Rs. 15 crores and is limited to 50% of the promoters' contribution to the equity of the project as may be stipulated by a financial institution, subject to upper limits in respect of any project as under:

— Where there is only one promoter applicant	Rs. 15 lakhs
— where there are 2 promotor applicants	Rs. 25 lakhs
— where there are 3 or more promoter applicants	Rs. 30 lakhs.
where the cost of project does not exceed	Rs. 10 crores.

For projects costing between Rs. 10 crores and Rs. 15 crores, the upper limit can be enhanced to Rs. 40 lakhs, provided the assistance to any one promoter does not exceed Rs. 15 lakhs.

RCF grants assistance in the form of interest-free personal loans (which carry a nominal service charge of 1% to 3% p.a. depending upon the period of the loan) to be repaid by the promoters out of their personal income including income from dividends. The repayment schedule for the loan is fixed having regard to the repayment capacity of the beneficiary, age and other factors. The loan from RCF is required to be secured by the pledge of shareholdings of the promoters in the promoted company, acquired out of own resources as well as out of assistance provided by RCF. Apart from personal loans, RCF also considers in suitable cases, to extend a part of assistance by way of subscription to equity shares of the promoted company in its own name with suitable buy-back arrangements with the promoters.

The entire resources of RCF are provided in the nature of grants and interest free loans by IFCI out of its Benevolent Reserve Fund and KFW Interest Differential Funds allocated by Government of India to the IFCI. IFCI also funds the deficits of RCF in meeting its administrative expenses whenever necessary. Cumulatively upto 30th June, 1987 IFCI had provided Rs. 982.92 lakhs by way of grants and interest-free loans to RCF.[4] The total funds allocated by IFCI upto 31st December, 1987 to RCF were Rs. 1150 lakhs (Rs. 11.50 crores) comprising Rs. 4.20 crores as grants and Rs. 7.30 crores as interest free loans.[5]

The following paragraphs give an account of the operations of RCF in order to highlight the economic contribution of the projects promoted by entrepreneurs assisted by RCF.

RCF's Operations:

Since inception upto 31st December, 1987, RCF has provided assistance to 234 promoters for setting up 137 projects in various parts of the country. The net cumulative sanctions of RCF upto 31st December, 1987 amounted to Rs. 1601.28 lakhs of which Rs. 1244.18 lakhs had been disbursed to 194 promoters for setting up of 115 projects. **Table 7.1** gives an yearly break-up of sanction and disbursements of RCF from inception in 1975 to 1987. A more vivid picture emerges from the data given in **Table 7.2,** reflecting RCF's growth in perspective through its entire period of operations till 1987. The progress of RCF's operations was rather slow in the initial period of five years. Upto 31st December, 1979, RCF had sanctioned assitance to 39 promoters of the order of Rs. 149 lakhs for 23 projects. Out of this, Rs. 94 lakhs were disbursed to 25 promoters for setting up 16 projects. The next five years, 1980-84, witnessed a more than two to three times growth in RCF's operations in every respect. The amount sanctioned went up by more than three times to Rs. 534 lakhs. This was in respect of 85 promoters for setting up 52 projects. For the same period, the amount disbursed increased by more than three and a half times to Rs. 358 lakhs to 65 promoters for 41 projects. The amount of risk capital assistance provided by RCF has tremendously gone

4 IFCI, Operational Statistics, 1986-87, p. 70.

5 As per Annual Report of RCF, for the year ending 31st December, 1987, p.15.

Table 7.1

Risk Capital Assistance by RCF
1976 - 1987

Year (Jan-Dec)	Sanctions			Disbursements		
	Amount (Rs. lakhs)	No. of Promoters	No. of Projects	Amount (Rs. lakhs)	No. of Promoters	No. of (Rs. lakhs)
1976	25.90	9	5	6.75	1	1
1977	27.50	4	4	21.55	6	4
1978	28.39	10	5	16.75	4	3
1979	67.20	16	9	49.39	14	8
1980	63.85	14	8	52.20	14	7
1981	82.50	13	10	76.85	15	10
1982	65.00	10	7	66.35	12	7
1983	83.14	14	7	59.74	8	7
1984	239.49	34	20	102.39	16	10
1985	217.87	31	18	173.50	25	13
1986	302.84	36	19	267.77	37	20
1987	410.00	43	25	350.94	42	25
Total	1601.28	234	137	1244.18	194	115

Source: Compiled from the Operational Statistics, IFCI, 1986-87 and the Annual Reports of RCF.

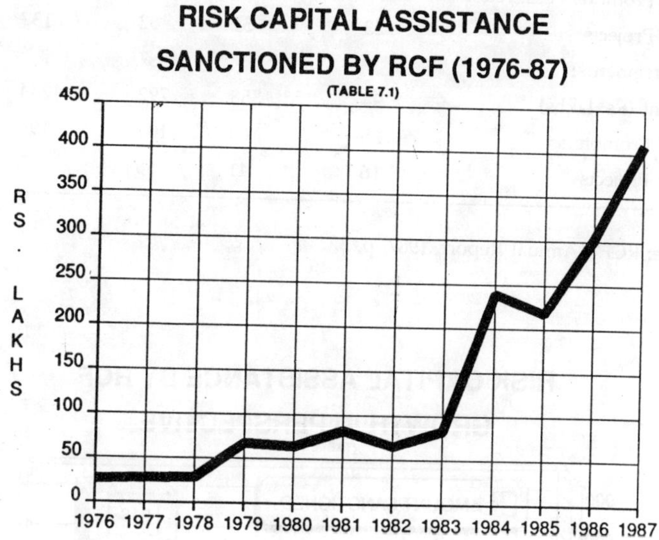
RISK CAPITAL ASSISTANCE
SANCTIONED BY RCF (1976-87)
(TABLE 7.1)
RS. LAKHS
0
50
100
150
200
250
300
350
400
450
1976
1977
1978
1979
1980
1981
1982
1983
1984
1985
1986
1987

Table 7.2

Risk Capital Assistance by RCF: Growth in Perspective

	1975-79 (5 years)	1980-84 (5 years)	1985-87 (3 years)	1975-87 Cumulative
Sanctions:				
Amount (Rs. lakhs)	149	534	918	1601
No. of Promoters assisted	39	85	110	234
No. of Projects	23	52	62	137
Disbursements:				
Amount (Rs. lakhs)	94	358	792	1244
No. of Promoters	25	65	104	194
No. of Projects	16	41	58	115

Source: RCF's Annual Report, 1987, p. 3.

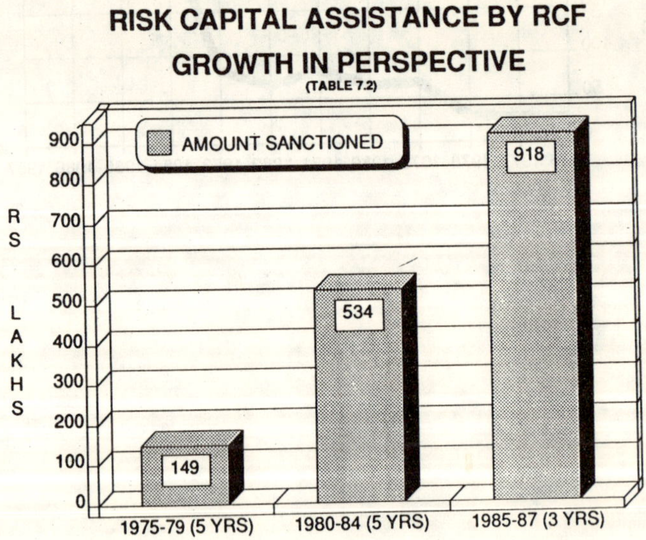

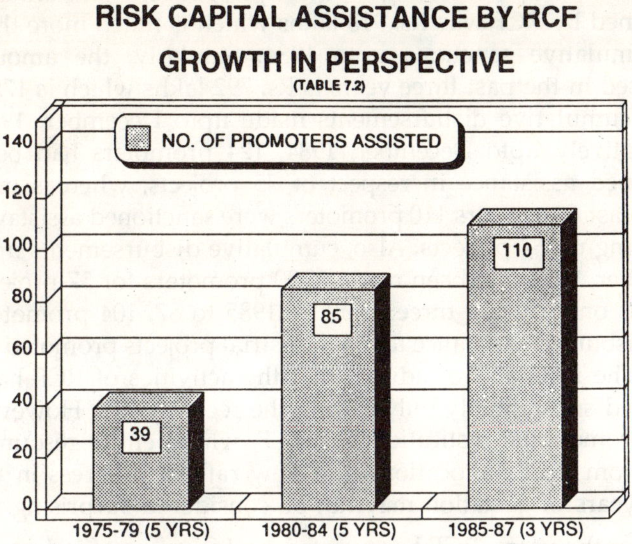
RISK CAPITAL ASSISTANCE BY RCF
GROWTH IN PERSPECTIVE
(TABLE 7.2)
NO. OF PROMOTERS ASSISTED
140
120
100
80
60
40
20
0
39
85
110
1975-79 (5 YRS)
1980-84 (5 YRS)
1985-87 (3 YRS)

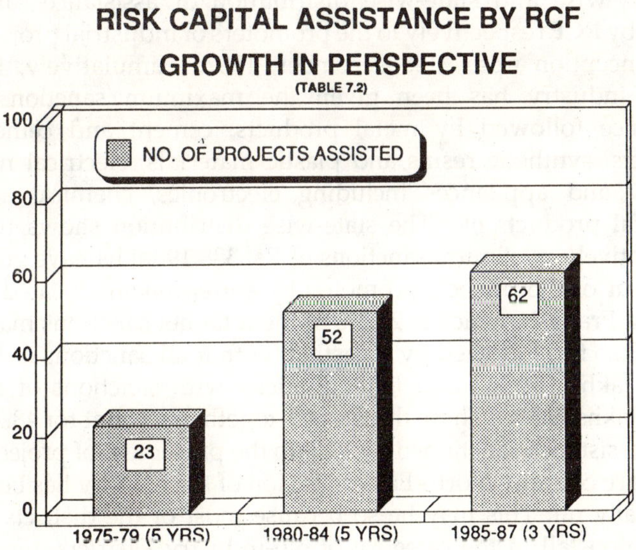
RISK CAPITAL ASSISTANCE BY RCF
GROWTH IN PERSPECTIVE
(TABLE 7.2)
NO. OF PROJECTS ASSISTED
100
80
60
40
20
0
23
52
62
1975-79 (5 YRS)
1980-84 (5 YRS)
1985-87 (3 YRS)

up in the recent past. During the three years 1985-87, the amount sanctioned by RCF was Rs. 918 lakhs which is much more than the cumulative sanctions upto 1984. Similarly, the amount disbursed in the past three years is Rs. 792 lakhs which is 175% of the cumulative disbursements made upto December, 1984. Cumulatively upto December, 1984, 124 promoters had been sanctioned assistance in respect of 75 projects, whereas only during last three years 110 promoters were sanctioned assistance for setting up 62 projects. Also, cumulative disbursements upto December, 1984 had been made to 90 promoters for 57 projects whereas only during three years — 1985 to 87, 104 promoters were disbursed assistance for 58 industrial projects promoted by them. The facts above indicate that the activities of RCF have increased substantially only during the recent years. However, for a promotional institution like RCF, whose entire resources come from IFCI's allocations, the slow rate of progress in the initial years of gestation may not be considered surprising.

Over the years, RCF has assisted a wide range of industries in various parts of the country. **Table 7.3** and **Table 7.4** give an industry-wise and state-wise distribution of assistance sanctioned by RCF respectively to the promoters of industrial projects since inception upto 31st December, 1987. Cumulatively, the textile industry has been given the maximum sanction of assistance followed by metal products, cement and cement products, synthetic resins and plastic materials, electrical machinery and appliances including electronics, chemical and chemical products etc. The state-wise distribution shows that cumulatively maximum sanctions of Rs. 388.19 lakhs have gone in favour of the projects promoted by entrepreneurs located in Andhra Pradesh, which is 24.2% of the total net sanctions made by RCF so far, followed by Rajasthan with total sanctions of Rs. 231.92 lakhs (14.5%) and Uttar Pradesh with sanctions of Rs. 151.50 lakhs (9.5%). These three states together account for 48.2% of the assistance sanctioned by RCF to the promoters of projects. The share of entire North-Eastern region of the country has been practically nil. This may be so because most of the districts in this region fall in the category of No-Industry Districts due to entire area being the hill area where it is difficult to set up medium and large scale industrial projects. Out of RCF's total

Table 7.3

Industry-wise distribution of Assistance Sanctioned by RCF to the promoters of industrial projects since inception upto December, 1987.

Sl.	Industries of	No. of Projects	No. of Projects	Amount (Rs. lakhs)	%
1.	Food Products	3	2	32.00	2.01
2.	Textile	31	17	185.00	12.6
3.	Wood Products	5	3	19.60	1.2
4.	Paper and Paper Products	6	5	30.85	1.9
5.	Leather Products	1	1	7.50	.5
6.	Rubber Products	1	1	5.00	.3
7.	Basic Industrial Chemicals and Gases	11	6	55.75	3.5
8.	Fertilizers & Pesticides	6	4	62.00	3.9
9.	Synthetic Resin & Plastic Material	21	9	144.74	9.0
10.	Synthetic & other fibres	11	4	53.00	3.3
11.	Chemical & Chemical Products	16	11	131.99	8.2
12.	Cement & Cement Products	18	13	146.74	9.2
13.	Non-Metallic Mineral Product	11	7	63.50	4.0
14.	Iron, Steel & Ferro Alloys	21	11	101.79	6.4
15.	Non-ferrous Metal Industry	2	1	10.00	0.6
16.	Metal Products	17	10	152.05	9.5
17.	Machinery & Accessories	3	3	22.50	1.4
18.	Electrical Machinery & Parts	20	11	143.32	8.9
19.	Transport Equipment & Parts	14	7	109.75	6.8
20.	Misc. Manufacturing Industry	13	9	102.20	6.4
21.	Electricity & Gas	2	1	16.00	1.0
22.	Hotel	1	1	6.00	.4
		234	137	1601.28	

Source: 12th Annual Report of RCF, 1987, p. 18.

Table 7.4

State-wise distribution of Assistance Sanctioned by RCF to promoters of projects since inception upto December 31, 1987.

Sl.	State/UTs	No. of Projects	No. of Projects	Amount (Rs. lakhs)	%
1.	Andhra Pradesh	54	36	388.19	24.2
2.	Assam	1	1	15.00	.9
3.	Bihar	3	3	18.50	1.2
4.	Gujrat	13	9	99.00	6.2
5.	Goa	2	1	8.00	.5
6.	Haryana	16	9	132.99	8.3
7.	Himachal Pradesh	13	6	94.40	5.9
8.	Karnataka	12	6	79.40	4.9
9.	Madhya Pradesh	7	4	59.00	3.7
10.	Maharashtra	22	13	111.25	6.9
11.	Orissa	6	4	33.00	2.1
12.	Punjab	12	8	72.13	4.5
13.	Rajasthan	41	20	231.92	14.5
14.	Tamil Nadu	3	1	25.00	1.6
15.	Uttar Pradesh	18	10	151.50	9.5
16.	West Bengal	3	2	20.00	1.2
17.	Andman & Nicobar	1	1	6.00	.4
18.	Delhi	2	1	6.00	.4
19.	Pondicherry	5	2	50.00	3.1
		234	137	1601.28	

Source: RCF's 12th Annual Report, 1987, p. 19.

assistance sanctioned cumulatively upto 31st December, 1987, two third amount has been provided to the promoters for setting up 88 industrial projects (out of a total of 137) in the less-developed states of the country. It is worth noting that out of 137 projects assisted by RCF, 112 are located in the declared backward districts of the country.[6] This indicates that RCF has been paying due attention while providing assistance to the promoters of industrial projects to the industrial development of the backward areas.

Upto 31st December, 1987, RCF has provided risk capital assistance to 234 promoters for setting up 137 medium or medium-large scale industrial projects. **Table 7.5** gives the economic contribution of these projects in terms of (i) expected employment potential of the projects, (ii) investment catalysed as indicated by the total cost of the projects and (iii) the annual sales value envisaged at the optimum level of production of these projects. These 137 projects set up with the help of RCF's assistance to the promoters' equity are expected to generate employment for about thirty-three thousand persons and mobilise investment of over Rs. 611 crores in the industrial arena of the country. The projects are expected to have an annual sales value of the order of Rs. 827 crores at the optimum level of their production. Thus RCF has been making modest effort in encouraging technologists and professionals to take up industrial activity and develop them into first generation entrepreneurs in order to enlarge the technological entrepreneurial base in the country.

RCF's Assistance to First Generation Entrepreneurs in Rajasthan:

In this context, data has been collected[7] in respect of all the projects located in a particular state — Rajasthan — whose promoters have received risk capital assistance from RCF upto 31st December, 1987, for starting their industrial ventures.

6 The figure has been compiled from the Annual Reports of RCF from 1976 to 1987.

7. The data has been personally collected from the RCF office, Janpath, New Delhi I gratefully acknowledge the help rendered to me by teh staff of RCF.

Table 7.5

Economic Contribution of the Projects Promoted by Entrepreneurs Assisted by RCF during 1976-1987.

Year	Employmen Potential of Projects (No. of persons)	Investment Catalysed (Total cost of projects) (Rs. Crores)	Annual Sales Value at the optimum level of Production of projects (Rs. Crores)
1976	1186	12.36	18.48
1977	1382	12.64	16.08
1978	1507	9.46	18.06
1979	2365	22.11	33.65
1980	2518	31.11	33.76
1981	3173	44.95	58.91
1982	3781	42.79	62.07
1983	2089	34.15	48.62
1984	3525	107.66	154.55
1985	3832	68.24	102.42
1986	3938	97.41	100.70
1987	3690	128.43	179.68
	32986	611.31	826.98

Source: RCF's 12th Annual Report, 1987, p. 14.

Rajasthan is a less-developed state and has been the second major beneficiary of RCF's assistance to promoters of industrial projects. Table 7.6 presents the statement of such industrial projects in a classified manner. An analysis of this data reveals the following important aspects:

i) In aggregate, RCF's total assistance cumulatively upto 31st December, 1987, to the promoters of projects located in Rajasthan has been Rs. 231.92 lakhs of which Rs. 203.92 lakhs has already been disbursed.

ii) This assistance has been sanctioned to 20 projects, out of which 2 were additional loans (of this, one was later on clubbed with the earlier request by the same applicant).

iii) The promoters who have received assistance from RCF are mostly engineers, professionals, post-graduates or graduates having long experience in the relevant industry.

iv) All the projects are located in the declared backward districts of Rajasthan. However, majority of these have been set up in districts of Alwar and Udaipur.

    Proximity to Delhi in the former case and availability of adequate infrastructure facilities due to industrial estates in the latter, seem to be the probable reasons for this locational pattern.

v) These projects have mobilised investment of over Rs. 77.66 crores in Rajasthan generating employment for approximately 6654 persons. The annual sales value of these projects at their optimum level is over Rs. 111.21 crores.

The facts above indicate the kind of impact that the projects promoted by technologists and professionals with RCF's assistance can have in inducing industrial activity for the development of less-developed areas of the country, as most of the projects whose promoters have availed of RCF's assistance are located in the notified backward districts. It reflects, in turn, the promotional aspect of IFCI's role through RCF in encouraging new entrepreneurs to set up industrial projects as a step forward to the country's industrial progress.

Table 7.6

Statement of Industrial Projects in Rajasthan whose Promoters have received RCF's Assistance since inception upto 31.12.1987 indicating their Economic Contribution

Sl.	Date of Sanction	Name of the Project/ Promoted Company	Names of the promoter with their Qualifications and experience	Loan sanc. (Rs. Lakhs) Amount	Total	Location of the Project and Product to be manufactured	Economic contribution of the Pro. Total cost of the Proj. (Rs. Lakhs)	Empl. gener. (No. of persons	Annual Sales at Opti. level Rs. Lakhs
(1)	(2)	(3)	(4)	(5)	(6)	(7)	(8)	(9)	(10)
1.	11.6.76	Aryavarta Plywoods Ltd.	Sh. I.J. Khosla Sh. S.K. Nayar Sh. R.S. Bassi (Mr. Nayar is a Sh. S.K. Nayar Sh. R.S. Bassi Mechanical Engineer while other two promoters have over 20 years experience in Plywood Industry).	2.55 1.70 .85	5.10	The project is located in Bhiwadi, Distt. Alwar, for the manufacture of flush doors, block doors etc.	111.62	183	222.27
2.	13.12.76	M/s. Banswara Syntex Ltd.	Sh. R.L. Toshniwal (a P.G. in Textiles with 20 years Exp.		6.00	Spinning Mill Project located located in Disst. Banswara for producing synthetic yarn.	366.00	520	823.24
3.	25.7.77	Modern Syntex India Limited	Sh. H.S. Ranka (a Commerce graduate with 14 years experience in textile industry).		7.50	Spinning Mill Project in Distt. Alwar producing synthetic yarn.	360.00	380	763.85

4.	30.10.78	Reliance Chemotex Industries Ltd.	Sh. S.L. Shroff Sh. S.K. Kejriwal (Both Promoters have long experience in textile industry	5.00 5.00	10.00	The Project is located in Madri Ind. Estate Distt. Udaipur, for producing synthetic yarn.	384.00	546	741.28
5.	27.4.79	Jaipur Syntex Ltd.	Sh. M.D. Agarwal Sh. N.K. Agarwal Sh. M.C. Gupta (All are Engineers with long experience).	7.50 5.00 2.50	15.00	Project is located at Behror, Distt. Alwar, for producing synthetic yarn.	410.00	625	841.44
6.	28.5.80	Shree Rajasthan Syntex Ltd.	Sh. V.K. Ladia Sh. S.C. Agarwal (both are textile technologies).	6.00 6.00	12.00	Project is located at Village Udaipura, Distt. Dungarpur for manufacture of polyester viscose blended yarn.	475.00	635	921.00
7.	12.6.81	Perfect Thread Mills Ltd.	Sh. H.S. Bapna Sh. R.K. Lodha Sh. Vipin Lodha (Mr. Bapna is a C.A. while other promoters are P.G. in Management).	10.00 2.50	15.00	Project is located at Amberi, Distt. Udaipur, for manufacturing sewing threads.	200.00	400	469.00
8.	30.11.82	Toto Bubbles India Ltd.	Sh. K. Kapoor Sh. M.M. Malhotra (Mr. Kapoor is C.A. and Mr. Malhotra an Electrical Engineer, both having long experience).	10.00 5.00	15.00	Project is located in Bhiwadi, Distt. Alwar, producing forged hand tools.	200.00	370	282.00

9.	30.11.82	Super Syncotex India Ltd.	Sh. V.S. Sancheti (An Electronics Engineer).		5.00	Project located at Gulabpura, Distt. Bilwara, for producing cotton & polyester viscose blended yarn.	798.00	720	969.00
10.	15.4.83	Shruti Synthetic Ltd.	Sh. N.K. Chhajerh Sh. R.P. Agarwal (Both have over 20 years experience in textile industry).	7.50 7.50	15.00	Project located in Distt. Udaipur, manufacturing polyester viscose blended yarn.	835.00	963	1779.73
11.	4.9.83	Rajasthan Petro Synthetics Ltd.	Sh. O.P. Kedia Sh. S.S. Poddar Sh. G.S. Poddar (Mr. S.S. Poddar is a Civil Engineer, while other two promoters are graduates with over 20 years experience).	7.50 5.00 2.50	15.00	Project located in Distt. Udaipur, manufacturing polypropylene filament yarn.	730.00	132	517.03
12.	31.12.84	Chemcaps Ltd.	Sh. A.K. Mittal Sh. P.C. Goyal Sh. Vinay Mahajan (Shri Mittal is a P.G. in Pharmacy, Shri Goyal a Civil Engineer, while Sh. Mahajan is an Export Partner).	5.00 5.00 5.00	15.00	Project located in Distt. Alwar for manufacturing empty hard gelatine capsules.	409.00	81	166.18

13.	29.4.85	Punsumi India Ltd.	Shri Vishnu Bhargava Sh. Vinesh Bhargava (Former is an M.E. Electronics, while the latter is B.A., LL.B.) (The two were initially sanctioned loans for Rs. 10 lakhs and Rs. 5.62 lakhs respectively; later the amount was reduced by Rs. 50 lakhs on 10th March 1986.)		15.12	The project is located at Bhiwadi, Distt. Alwar, producing aluminium electrolytic capacitators.	400.00	225	490.98
14.	22.7.85	Sudarshan Cement Ltd.	Sh. K.C. Taparia Engineer with 11 years (a industrial experience).		15.00	Project located in Distt. Sirohi manufacturing cement.	360.00	96	201.00
15.	7.10.85	Shree Syntex Ltd.	Additional Loan (Ref. Sl. No. 6)		8.00	(Same as S. No. 11)	303.75	150	525.00
16.	24.12.85	Rajasthan Synthetics Ltd.	Additional Loan (Clubbed with S.No. 11)	7.50		(Same as S. No. 11)			
17.	8.9.86	Kienzle Indian Indian Samay Ltd.	Sh. T.R. Chugh Sh. R.K. Chugh (Former is a Mechanical Engineer and the latter, a commerce graduate, both having long experience in clock industry).	7.85 7.85	15.70	Project located in Distt. Alwar manufacturing quartz timing movements.	490.00	253	624.00

18. 17.3.87	West India Gas Products Ltd.	Sh. B.R. Agarwal Sh. S.C. Chawla (Sh. Agarwal is M.Com., LL.B., AICWA, ACS, and Shri Chawla is a Science Graduate with one year course in fitter trade).	8.00 8.00	16.00	Project located in Mewar Industrial Area Distt. Udaipur, for producing Sulphuric Acid and Single Superphosphate.	320.00	52	166.87
19. 28.5.87	Hi-tech Gears Ltd.	Sh. Deep Kapuria Sh. Digvijay Kapuria (Former is a Chemical Engineer while the latter an Arts Graduate).	4.00 8.00	12.00	Project located in RIICO Ind. Estate, Bhiwadi, Distt. Alwar for producing semi-finished machine gear components.	317.00	211	372.00
20. 28.5.87	Electronic Circuits Ltd.	Sh. S.S. Bhartia (a P.G. in Science and B.E. from U.K.)		7.00	Project located in Bhiwadi, Distt. Alwar for producing printed circuit boards.	297.00	112	246.00
Total				231.92		7766.37	6654	11121.87

This study substantiates that RCF, sponsored by IFCI as a part of its promotional activities, is doing a significant job by providing interest free personal loans to entrepreneurs possessing technical or professional qualifications and/or having reasonable relevant experience in industry or business on soft terms to enable them to make good the shortfall in the promoters' contribution to equity capital of the projects promoted by them, thereby seeking to fulfil the country's objective of broadening the entrepreneurship base.

Here, another aspect of RCF's operational policies and procedures needs consideration. It has often been argued that the criteria for availing assistance from RCF is strict, in the sense that there are several terms and conditions that the entrepreneurs have to comply with, of which only few have been mentioned here as examples. Though the loan from RCF is interet-free, a service charge is levied @1% p.a. for the first five years of loan, @2% between the sixth and the tenth year and 3% p.a. beyond the 10th year of the loan.

In addition, (a) contingent service charges (CSC) @25% of the gross dividend on the equity shares acquired out of the loan from RCF and/or (b) Terminal Service charges (TSC) @10% of the amount of the loan are levied, if the loan is repaid with 10 years and additional 2% for each year beyond 10 years. TSC is, however, reduced by the amount of CSC paid by the borrower out of dividends during the term of loan. Apart from this, the loan from RCF has to be secured against the pledge of shareholdings of the promoters in the promoted project acquired out of their own resources as well as out of the loan from RCF, so that the aggregate face value of such shareholdings shall not be less than double the amount of loan sanctioned by RCF. Also, RCF normally assists only those projects which have been sanctioned financial assistance by IFCI, IDBI or ICICI singly or jointly. Till recently, RCF insisted, besides pledge of shares, the borrowers to take out Mortgage Redemption Insurance Policy (MRIP) as collateral security. However, it was found that the incidence of insurance premia paid by the borrowers was very high and even more than the service charges paid to RCF. This requirement has been waived only after the suggestions received at the Conference of Beneficiaries of RCF in September, 1986. As a matter of policy, RCF does not grant reschedulement of loans, as the same are personal loans and have to be repaid out of the salary, dividened received in the promoted concern on equity holding and other resources of the borrower.

The need to impose these and several other criteria for availing RCF's assistance becomes significant since RCF had been facing difficulties with some of its borrowers due to their inability in repaying the instalments of loans on due dates, as agreed to at the time of execution of Loan Agreements.[8] Out of the cumulative disbursements of Rs. 12.44 crores of RCF upto 31st December, 1987, the total repayments amounted to Rs. 2.52 crores including repayments made by 26 promoters of 12 projects who have repaid their loans of Rs. 103.80 lakhs in full. This leaves an aggregate amount outstanding as on 31st December, 1987 of the order of Rs. 9.92 crores. Though RCF is a promotional agency to provide venture capital to encourage new entrepreneurs, it is neither a lending agency in the normal sense nor a philanthropic organisation. It has to run on business principle at least to the extent that it must get back the loans which it disburses so that its revolving fund remains intact for helping as many deserving entrepreneurs as possible. Since the facility of interest free loans with nominal service charges provided by RCF is unique, it has to be ensured that it is availed of by most deserving cases and therefore strict financial discipline becomes imperative.

Newer Thrusts:

To provide risk capital assistance through a suitable institutional machinery, IFCI had sponsored RCF seeking to strengthen the emphasis of national policy of encouraging new entrepreneurs, particularly the technologists and professionals having industrial experience, to promote industrial projects who are eligible but lack adequate resources of their own. The technology policy of the Government of India lays stress on the development of domestic technology and rapid absorption, adaptation and improvement of imported technology leading to domestic

---

8 As per the Annual Report of RCF, 1987, p.12.

technological innovations crucial to the growth in the emerging competitive national and international environment.

Recognising the need to provide venture capital for technology development for commercial exploitation, for which raising funds through conventional means prove difficult, IFCI has recently formulated a special scheme to meet the specific needs of such technology development. The task of implementation of this scheme called "The Scheme of Technology Finance and Development" has been entrusted to RCF in addition to carrying out of its existing activity of providing risk capital assistance. For this, RCF has been converted into a limited company styled "Risk Capital and Technology Finance Corporation Limited" (RCTC) with effect from 12th January, 1988.

The basic objective of this scheme is to accelerate the pace of technological progress of industry through increasing perception of customer need, innovation and quality. The scheme is specifically designed to extend support to technological innovations and fill the gap in the conventional financial mechanisms to cover the higher risk inherent in such activities.

Under the scheme, risk capital assistance on soft terms would be granted so as to encourage new entrepreneurs, particularly technologists, technocrats and professionals, to set up medium scale industries having distinctive features of exploiting new or improved technology, products, market and service. Assistance will also be provided to eligible projects envisaging upgrading of technology, energy conservation, environmental protection, commercialisation of domestically developed technology, in-house Research & Development, specialised technology training and other supporting infrastructure required for technology development. Preference would be given to viable project proposals having export potential, high priority industries, industries listed in Appendix I to Industrial Policy Statement and industries identified as thrust areas in the current national technological research and development plans.

The financial assistance provided under the scheme will be in the form of conventional loans with concessional 6% p.a. rate of interest during the development period, which may be stepped up thereafter depending on the likely cash generation. The loan has to be secured by a first charge on the fixed assets and the repayment period would normally be 10-12 years with an initial moratorium period of 2-3 years. Assistance in the form of direct equity participation in the project can also be considered with suitable arrangements to enable the promoters to buy-back the equity shares held by RCTC.

RCTC has not only introduced this new scheme of Technology Finance but has also revised its existing scheme of Risk Capital Assistance. While the terms and conditions remain almost the same, preference will now be given to those entrepreneurs who promote risk-oriented projects entailing the use of advanced or complex technology, and adoption of new or improved technology for the manufacture of improved or new products for new usages capable of creating new market segments thereby strengthening the national economy. The revised scheme specifically clarifies that, henceforth, RCTC would normally not extend assistance to promoters of projects engaged in conventional manufacturing activity, or projects based on conventional technology or the traditional service industry (like hotels, shipping etc. except that requests from promoters of hospitals or multi-disciplinary health centres undertaking research in diseases could be considered).[9] Earlier, RCF used to consider requests for financial assistance not only from the professionals and technologists but also from those entrepreneurs who did not possess the technical qualifications in pure academic sense but had long experience in the relevant industry or business. But now, under the revised Risk Capital Assistance Scheme, the promoters must possess the requisite technical or professional prescribed qualifications to be eligible for assistance from RCTC. However, in addition to the facility of interest-free personal loans to the promoters for meeting a part of promoters' equity contribution to the project, the revised scheme now also offers soft loan @6% p.a. (alongwith other terms and conditions) to the company promoted by the entrepreneurs. While the applicants may indicate the form of assistance sought, the discretion of sanctioning assistance in one form or the other or a mix of the two rests with RCTC giving due regard to the merits of each case.

---

9 RCTC, Brochure on Risk Capital Scheme, p.3.

It is yet to be seen how successful the scheme of Technology Finance would prove to be. It is reasonably expected that it will provide new avenues and encouragement to the entrepreneurs engaged in harnessing indigenous technology or using advanced technical know-how for the manufacture of new products for new usages and markets, but it may also disappoint many other aspiring entrepreneurs who may be contemplating projects in traditional manufacturing or service industry and who would have been otherwise eligible. This may also bring a temporary slump in the assistance operations of RCTC due to the initial gestation period of newer scheme and the existing scheme being restricted only to the technocrats and professionals for promoting projects with a fervour for technological advancement and upgradation.

8

Development of Institutional Infrastructure:

Management Development: IFCI's Support for Upgradation of Managerial Skills

Success in modern industry depends upon highly skilled and competent executive management, capable of dealing with complex problems of initial planning and control, production, marketing, personnel and industrial relations, financial management and accounting and manifold aspects of running an industrial organisation. For developing and improving the quality of day-to- day management which is so crucial to the success of any industrial venture, as also with a view to encouraging professionalisation in management, IFCI sponsored 'Management Development Institute' (MDI) in 1973, as a part of its promotional role.

Management Development Institute:

This Institute is an autonomous body registered under the Societies Registration Act, 1860, and is now located in its own campus near Gurgaon, Haryana. The basic objectives of the Institute are:

i) to provide training in modern management techniques to the entrepreneurs, technologists and executives of the industry,

ii) to provide training in various aspects related to development banking to the staff and executives of development finance institutions at the state and all-India level, as also abroad and

iii) to undertake research projects in industrial and business management, development banking and allied subjects.

MDI in fact works as the training arm of IFCI for upgradation of managerial skills as a constituent of IFCI's efforts in the development of institutional infrastructure in the country.

To serve the cause of enriching human capital and development of managerial manpower, MDI organises management development programmes to provide training to the entrepreneurs and professionals in the public, private, joint and cooperative sectors in the industry, commercial and development banks and Government departments. Over the years, MDI has endeavoured to develop a blend of academic and practical orientation in its programmes to promote the application of management science to the day-to-day management of industrial concerns.

Apart from conducting training programmes, MDI also aims at fulfilling the needs of industry in the field of enhancing management skills through research and technical consultancy assistance. Research studies undertaken by MDI[1] are in both macro areas of economic and industrial development as well as in micro areas relevant to a specific industry or economic activity. In this context, mention may be made of the several research studies, conducted by MDI, of the management practices and development needs of certain industries like sugar, textiles, hotel and mining industries, to identify their specific needs of specialised training and consultancy requirements. To follow-up, training programmes for the executives and technologists from units in these industries have been organised, which are tailored to meet the requirements of management to specific functions, such as finance, marketing, personnel, materials management, behavioural sciences etc. in specific industry groups. **Table 8.1** gives an insight into the programmes conducted by MDI for upgradation of managerial skills from its inception in 1973 to 30th June 1987. In all, 561 programmes have been conducted by MDI during the said period, benefitting 13,576 participants, of whom 184 were from other developing countries. In addition to conducting management training programmes, MDI also offers a three-year part-time post-graduate diploma course in Business Administration at New Delhi.

Development Banking Centre (DBC):

During the first couple of years of MDI's activities, a vital gap was felt in providing training to personnel from development finance institutions. Therefore, with the active support of IFCI, MDI set up the Development Banking Centre (DBC) in November, 1977, as a wing of MDI to undertake training, research and

1 Annexure 8.1 at the end of this chapter names some of the research projects completed by MDI (including DBC).

Table 8.1

Management Development Programmes Conducted by MDI (1974-1987)

Classification of Promm.	No. of Programmes									
	1974 to 1979	1980	1981	1982	1983	1984	1985	1986	Jan-June 1987	Tot.
I. General Participation Specific Industry Programmes	30	11	9	12	19	12	15	6	2	116
Financial Management	37	12	12	10	10	11	8	5	2	107
General Management	27	5	8	7	6	5	7	8	3	76
Marketing Management	12	2	2	2	3	7	3	3	--	34
Personnel Management	16	6	8	7	5	6	8	6	1	63
Technical Management	3	--	--	--	--	--	--	--	--	3
II. In-company sponsored Programmes	27	--	3	17	12	4	15	28	13	119
III. Other Programmes organised by outside agencies in campus	--	--	--	--	16	6	8	12	1	43
Total:	152	36	42	55	71	51	64	68	22	561
No. of Participants	4502	934	1104	1323	1412	905	1470	1387	539	13576
No. of foreign participants out of above	77	20	12	6	9	42	18	--	--	184

Source: IFCI, Operational Statistics, 1986-87, p. 82.

technical advisory/assistance activities relating to the organisational and operational areas of development banking. DBC provides exclusive facilities for training in modern development banking techniques to the executives and professionals of various financial, promotional and developmental institutions in India and abroad, as also of commercial banks and Technical Consultancy Organisations. The IPIIP Programmes sponsored by IFCI through the Development Banking Centre deserve a mention in this regard.

IPIIP Programmes: (Identification, Promotion, and Implementation of Industrial Projects)

The rationale of IPIIP Programmes is based on the fact that while proper project identification, planning and formulation are important for their efficient implementation, it is equally important that those concerned with planning and toning up industrial activity should be familiar with the approach to and methodology of the selection, promotion and planned execution of the projects.

The past decade has witnessed increasing accent being placed on the industrial development of backward areas and encouragement to new entrepreneurs and technologists to take up industrial activity. This implies a greater responsibility being placed on the officials of the State Government and State-level financial and developmental agencies engaged in promotional work for developing less developed regions since it is they who are relatively closely associated with such areas. Very often, they have to take upon themselves the role of entrepreneurs by setting up public sector enterprises which are assigned a crucial role in the industrial development of the country. Further, new entrepreneurs and technologists need guidance and counselling for planing and implementation of their projects and look up to the state-level financial and developmental institutions for help.

Thus it has been increasingly recognised that the officers and staff of the Government and promotional agencies as much require certain basic entrepreneurial skills and inputs as the entrepreneur himself, if they are to fulfil their role properly. In their promotional role, they are expected to be more than an entrepreneur, acting as the motivators, coordinators and counsellors for initiating industrial activity in backward regions. Also, while it is necessary that the officers and staff of promotional agencies have a fair knowledge of what the development aspect of banking is, they should also know as to what the promotion of an industrial unit envisages, what are its needs and problems and how these could be solved. Therefore, the need for a better understanding of the various aspects of identification, formulation and implementation of industrial projects was felt on the part of the officials at the state-level in order to facilitate the implementation of industrial development programmes in a more fruitful way. IPIIP Programmes sponsored by IFCI through MDI and Development Banking Centre indicate a modest endeavour to meet these requirements.

Table 8.2 gives an account of the number of training programmes conducted by DBC, of which IPIIP Programmes from a part. So far eight programmes in the IPIIP series have been organised, one each in the states of Andhra Pradesh, Kerala, Madhya Pradesh, Rajasthan, Uttar Pradesh, West Bengal, Orisa and in Shillong covering the North-Eastern Region. The cost of conducting these programmes was subsidised by IFCI. In aggregate DBC has conducted 233 programmes since its incepton in 1977 upto 30th June, 1987, in which 5764 executives and officials participated out of which 352 were from other developing countries.

The Impact:

For industrial development, managerial obsolescence is as bad as the obsolescence of plant and equipment. Productivity of the industry and remedy for industrial sickness lie in the professionalisation of management, continual upgradation of managerial skills and adoption of modern management techniques. With this end in view, MDI and DBC, sponsored by IFCI, provide facilities for management training and human resource development to the executives and professionals of industrial concerns, financial instituions, commercial banks, TCOs and other developmental agencies in India and abroad. The programmes conducted by MDI and DBC have acclaimed international recognition. They have received valuable support and encouragement from the Economic Development Institute (EDI),

Table 8.2

Management Development ProgrammesConducted by DBC (1979-87)

Classification of Promm.	No. of Programmes 1974 to 1979	1980	1981	1982	1983	1984	1985	1986	Jan-June 1987	Tot.
1. General Participation	42	15	15	16	23	23	25	18	6	183
2. IPIIP Programmes	7	1	--	--	--	--	--	--	--	8
3. In-Company sponsored programmes	10	3	2	7	7	4	5	1	3	42
Total:	59	19	17	23	30	27	30	19	9	233
No. of Participants	1771	491	419	587	640	579	648	390	239	5764
No. of foreign participants out of above	101	43	43	75	27	45	18	--	--	352

Source: IFCI, Operational Statistics, 1986-87, p. 82.

Washington, U.S.A., Asian Development Bank (ADB), Association of Development Financing Institution in Asia and the Pacific (ADFIAP), United Nations Industrial Development Organisation (UNIDO), United Nations Development Programme (UNDP), International Labour Organisation (ILO), Asian Productivity Council (APC) etc. Since inception upto 30th June, 1987, MDI including DBC had conducted 794 management development programmes benefitting 19,340 participants of whom 536 were from other developing countries. Cumulatively upto 30th June, 1987, IFCI provided financial support to fund the programmes of MDI and DBC of the order of Rs. 630.53 lakhs, of which Rs. 287.97 lakhs were utilized from the Benevolent Reserve Fund and the rest Rs. 342.56 were met out of Interest Differential Fund.

In the area of consultancy and research, MDI and DBC have accomplished a number of research projects and comprehensive studies in various fields for industrial organisations, financial and developmental institutions at the state and national level. Apart from this, MDI is now poised for significant expansion in its activities and has been selected for a reputed assignment in the field of management training in the country. The Department of Personnel and Training, Government of India, has approved MDI as an agency for conducting an intensive National Managemet Programme with linkages from Harvard University for Government officers belonging to IAS/Group-A services as well as executives of public and private sector organisations, who have potential to acquire top positions. With funds support from IFCI, plans are under way for further development of MDI campus and have a computer centre so as to develop the managerial resources of the country today for meeting the challenges of tomorrow.

The speed of progress of institutions like MDI could be guessed from the information relating to the performance in terms of programmes conducted, participants benefited and the support and acclaim that such efforts receive from other organisations. However, it is very difficult to assess the impact of these programmes in qualitative terms. Undoubtedly, these achievements in the field of enhancing managerial effectiveness and developing managerial skills are general in nature and are not specifically addressed to the problem of development of less-developed areas in the country. None the less, it is important to take steps to see that the advantages following from these flow more to such areas especially in a developing nation like India where 70% of the area are declared backward, since the developed areas already have facilities implied in the efforts and programmes of these institutions. This consideration makes it necessary to discuss a few aspects in relation to the activities and operations of MDI and DBC.

It was way back in 1973, that Mr. Hans Erich Bachem, Member, Board of Management, KFW, Federal Republic of Germany, had expressed in his First IFCI Silver Jubilee Memorial Lecture that "*With the efforts of IFCI's Management Development Institute, the progress of technical and managerial know-how will in the future have positive effects in India's economic development. At the time when Kreditanstalt agreed to the utilisation of Interest Differential Funds for this purpoose, we did so without imposing any restrictive conditions since we believe that IFCI itself knows best how to use scarce funds most effectively. However, we at Kreditanstalt are hoping secretly, that the Institute will soon be in a position to open its door also to the smaller entrepreneurs who need so much advice and training*"[2] MDI has come a long way since 1973, yet no systematic or organised series of programmes have been formulated specifically addressed to the problem of enhancing man-agerial skills of smaller entrepreneurs especially those from relatively less-developed areas of the country, as most of the activities of MDI are concentrated in few big cities. It can be reasonably argued here that it would be difficult, rather practically impossible, for a centrally placed Institute like MDI to reach out far off places and conduct training programmes over there.

It is in this perspective that the 'IPIIP Programmes', the programmes for 'Training the Trainers' and the like can contribute in a wider dispersal of the managerial expertise and experience. IPIIP Programmes conducted for the staff and executives of the State Governments and the state-level financial

2 Bachem Hans Erich, First IFCI Silver Jubilee Memorial Lecture on New Aspects of Development Banking, IFCI, Searchlight on Development Banking : A Compendium of IFCI Silver Jubilee Memorial Lectures, 1984, pp. 26-27.

and developmental agencies appraised them with various aspects of promotion, financing and successful implementation of the projects. The programmes for 'training the trainers' envisage training a core group of personnel of state-level developmental organisations, Technical Consultancy Organisations and other state and district level industrial development authorities, who in turn can conduct management development programmes in the lesser developed remote and rural areas, thus assuming the role of trainer in the conduct of training programmes for small entrepreneurs. If such efforts are undertaken in a big way, they will help decentralise the pool of technical and managerial skills for the benefit of entrepreneurs from industrially backward areas.

Another benefit to be derived from such programmes is that of reducing the faculty cost,[3] which is a major item of expenditure in conducting management development programmes. The state-level developmental and promotional agencies which intend to undertake entrepreneurship development in a big way can get their own team of executives and officials trained beforehand, and become self-sufficient in building a cadre of trained personnel, who in turn can conduct training programmes at the district and block level so as to encourage entrepreneurship from industrially less developed areas. This will help multiply EDPs countrywide at a much faster rate and encourage entrepreneurs to not only get self-employed but also generate employment for few more persons.

Though MDI and DBC have made remarkable progress in their endeavours to serve the cause of development of manage-

---

3 According to an estimate quoted in the paper presented by Dr. M.V. Deshpande and Shri M.V. Panvalkar, "Developing Entrepreneurship : Need for a planned and coordinated effort" , (Para 17, p.45, Proceedings of the Seminar on EDPs published by IDBI, 1980), the cost of one programme was stated to be Rs. 80,000 out of which Rs. 60,000 were to be spent on course material, faculty expenses product identification, preparation of project profiles, monitoring and counselling. EDPs with such fancy budgets cannot become popular in backward areas, also, it is quite unnecessary to spend such huge amounts, when it is possible to conduct an EDP with a modest budget of Rs. 15,000 if the organisation undertaking the programmes has its own faculty.

rial manpower in the public, private, joint and cooperative sectors in the industry, commercial and development banks, Government departments etc., the programmes like 'IPIIP' and 'training the trainers' need to be taken up more enthusiastically due to their inherent potential of reaching out and benefitting small entrepreneurs from lesser developed areas. In this context, it is disappointing to note that with a modest start in 1975, after conducting eight training programmes in the IPIIP series in different states, no IPIIP programme has been conducted since 1980. The reason for inhibitions in conducting training programmes at the regional and state level at different locales[4] for training the personnel of financial and promotional institutions and TCOs has been partly attributed to financial constraints due to additional costs involved in transportation and other overheads. This calls for a more liberal funds support to such promotional efforts from the sponsoring institution (MDI and DBC are sponsored institutions of IFCI) by way of grants and subsidies. In addition to this, suitable incentives -- both monetary and promotional -- should be offered to those executives and officials who have successfully undergone training and are keen to undertake follow-up activities by way of devising further training programmes specially for the small entrepreneurs in the rural and backward areas.

Another set of factors responsible for slow pace of training and entrepreneurial development activities in industrially less-developed areas are both conceptual and practical in nature. A near-absence of entrepreneurial climate conducive to industrial development is the root level problem of backward areas. The operational problems characterised by mass poverty, illiteracy, unemployment, non-availab-ility of infrastructural inputs, narrow linkage with supportive activities like marketing and poor follow-up by the monitoring institutions perpetuate for so long and so deep in the backward areas that efforts to upgrade technical and managerial skills, howsoever well conceived, are likely to be little fruitful. However, one can not be contended by

---

4 The discussion here is based on the views expressed in a personal interview by a senior faculty member of MDI.

blaming the system and situation as sick and stagnant. Dynamic and concerted efforts are needed on the part of all institutions concerned with such promotional work to generate an increasing awareness towards developing technical, managerial and entrepreneurial skills.

The role of these organisations becomes more challenging when entrepreneurs have to be encouraged and developed from rural and industrially less-developed areas. This requires building up an effective support system consisting of Government organisations at the Central and State level, financial and developmental institutions, banks, and above all, the voluntary organizations working in rural and industrially backward areas to act as linkage-agencies for carrying out the entrepreneurial development activities of technical and managerial training institutes. The experience of Xavier Institute of Social Service, Ranchi (XISS)[5] indicates that to have an effective impact of technical, managerial and entrepreneurial development activities, the training Institutes must have a good rapport in the target area either directly or through an organisation working in the same area; for example, a major part of the success of efforts of XISS was shared by Vikas Maitri, an organisation working for the integral rural development of the people of Chotanagpur. Most of the training institutions conducting entrepreneurship and management development programmes are situated in big cities and urban areas because of several infrastructural needs for EDPs which can not be easily arranged in the rural areas. Therefore, in order that the benefits of technical and managerial expertise reach the small entrepreneurs of less-developed areas, the role of local organisations Gram Parishad, Gram Vikas Trust etc. becomes absolutely essential as the linkage agencies to take care of pre-training motivation and identification of the prospective entrepreneurs of the particular area and a good follow-up and feed back. The training institutes can then devise and conduct need-based training programmes for the educated unemployed or skilled youths and expose them to a wide range of industrial

5 Expressed in the paper presented by Shri. A.K. Sinha, XISS, Ranchi, Follow-up and Institutional Supports for EDPs , in the Seminar on EDPs, 1980. IDBI publication of Seminar Papers, pp. 77-79.

opportunities of becoming self-employed and self-reliant as also generating employment for others. The efforts of the regional level organisations for technical and managerial development need to be reinforced by the central-level institutions by assisting them with funds, faculty training and other facilities.

It needs no emphasis that training with all the motivational and managerial inputs alone can not make the prospective entrepreneur successful, unless the other part of the support system functions equally effectively. This covers facilities for concessional finance, incentive schemes, requisite industrial infrastructure and other supportive measures at the initiative of Central and State Governments, financial institutions, banks and other developmental and promotional agencies. A coordinated blend of all these developmental efforts is required to bring about industrial development of the backward areas of the country.

Such a situation is, however, more of an ideal one and difficult to achieve in a short time-span. Immediate and tangible results can not be expected from such promotional efforts. The only immediate satisfaction that could be derived is from initiating to create a development consciousness . To sustain this consciousness and translate into viable projects is the task which the developmental and financial institutions should be poised to take up with more vigour, determination and a sense of commitment.

Annexure 8.1

In the areas of research and consultancy, MDI (including DBC) has completed a number of research projects in various fields, some of them being as follows:

— Some Aspects of Corporate Securities Market.

— Prospects & Policies for Lac in India.

— Dividends and Share Prices of Public Limited Companies.

— Bio-gas Systems in India.

— Techno-Managerial Studies in Selective Collieries.

— Study on Debut Equity Ratio Norms.

— Study for setting up an Off-shore Banking Centre for Financing Economic Development.

— Role of Financial Institutions in Rural Entrepreneurship.

— Market-cum-Feasibility Study Reports for the Establishment of Hotels.

— Study of the Financial Management Systems and Organisational Structure of Himachal Pradesh Cooperative Marketing Development Federation Ltd.

— Study of the Organisational structure, Operation and Financial Management Systems of Haryana State Cooperative Supply Marketing Federation Ltd.

— Study on Organisation and Management Control Systems in the National Cooperative Development Corporation Ltd.

— Assessment of Executive and Non-executive manpower for Rural Electrification Corporation.

— Study on Causes and Incidence of sickness among Small Enterprises, assisted by State-level Institutions and Commercial Banks in the Northern Region.

— Study on the Organisation Structure and evolving a State-level MIS for Rajasthan State Industrial Development & Investment Corporation Ltd.

— Study on Technical Consultancy Services (Focus on Small Industry).

— Institutional Assistance to Small Scale Industries - A case study of selected States of India.

— Organisational Studies for U.P. Financial Corporation, Himachal Financial Corporation and Orissa Financial Corporation.

— Assimilation and Diffusion of Technology in India.

— Alternatives in Fertility Regulating Methods.

— Management of Cooperative Sugar Factories.

— Technology Assessment of Micrographics for use in the National Information System for Science & Technology (NISSAT).

— Study of Hand-woven Wollen Goods Industry in Punjab & Himachal Pradesh.

— Study of Cooperative Handloom Marketing in India.

— Study on Impact of Operations of Selected District Industries Centres (DICs).

— Corporate Plan for Delhi State Industrial Development Corporation Ltd. (DSIDC).

— Study on the Appropriateness of Performance Appraisal Systems for Indian Standards Institute.

— Manpower Planning Study for Neyveli Lignite Corporation.

— Studies of Organisation Set-up of J&K Industrial Development Corporation Ltd.

— Shareholders' Survey - Geographic Distribution.

— Industrial Sickness Management Aspects.

— Inter-firm Comparison Study to be used as a tool for Appraisal and Monitoring of Projects.

— Survey of Training Needs of State-level Financial Institutions in India.

— Impact of Risk Capital/Seed Capital and Special Capital Schemes.

— Study of the Organisational Structure of Development Bodies in the Andaman & Nicobar Islands as also Lakhshadweep Islands.

— Post-harvest System for Apple Crop in Himachan Pradesh.

— Study on Manpower Requirements in Traffic Police Organisation.

— Research Study on District Industries Centres (DICs) for Five States, viz., J&K, U.P., M.P., Haryana and Punjab.

— Problems of Local Entrepreneurs.

— Research Study on Time Management for Executives.

Source: IFCI, Promotional Activities, 1984, pp. 23-24.

IFCI, Annual Reports, 1986-87, pp. 98-99, 1987-88, p. 104.

MDI, Management Journal, Vol. 1, No: 2, July, 1988.

9

Development of Entrepreneurship

Entrepreneur & Development:

An entrepreneur is the most critical factor in the economic development of any region. He plays a very crucial role in widening the country's industrial base, generating self- employment, reducing income inequalities and regional disparities, relieving dysfunctional pressure on urban areas and activising the factors of production leading to the overall economic development. The entrepreneur organises and utilises the various factors and sets productive machinery in action. The availability of entrepreneurs, therefore, is the precondition of economic growth. While discussing factors responsible for economic development, Prof. Schumpeter noted that the supply of entrepreneurs depends on the rate of profit and social climate.[1] Profit induces the prospective entrepreneur to get into the business and start new activities. But this does not necessarily imply that the entrepreneur is concerned only with pecuniary profits. He is basically an innovator, with an achievement motive, which aspires for something more than money. It is for such entrepreneurs to function effectively, that the necessary entrepreneurial culture and a social climate conducive to industrialisation are needed. It is in this context that the entrepreneurship development has to be looked into.

Mere availability of concessional finance and other monetary incentives from the development & financial institution and supply of raw materials and other infrastructure facilities by themselves can not make appreciable impact on the economic development of a region, if the human resources are not developed or reoriented to meet the challenges they face in the industrial arena. Therefore, in an endeavour to fulfil this crucial ingredient to successful industrialisation, the financial and development institutions have taken up entrepreneurship development as an important aspect of their promotional activities.

---

1 Schumpeter J.A., The Theory of Economic Development, Chap. II (III), pp. 74-88, Harvard University Press, 1959 Ed.

Such non-financial incentives assume special significance in the context of the national policy of broad- basing the entrepreneurial cadre and encouraging particularly the tiny, small and medium sector entre-preneurs.

Entrepreneurship Development: Significance of Gujarat EDPs:

Development of entrepreneurship involves identification of potential entrepreneurs, training them and developing in them the characteristics or abilities required for entrepreneurial success and providing support to the trained entrepreneurs in all subsequent stages of actual enterprise building. Entrepreneurship development as an organised programme is of comparatively recent origin which has increasingly questioned the commonly held notion that entrepreneurship, like proverbial leadership is an inborn quality, or to put it differently, an entrepreneur is born and not made.[2] The recent researches and successful experiments in promoting entrepreneurship have shown that entrepreneurship can be developed. The EDP experiences of other developing countries have also revealed that training made a lot of difference in the performance of the entrepreneurs and the EDPs have great scope in increasing the supply of new entrepreneurs to accelerate the process of industrialization.[3]

In India, Gujarat was the first to have come forward with an organised Entrepreneurship Development Programme (EDP) in early seventies as a part of the "Gujarat Experiments".[4] In financing industrial ventures of new entrepreneurs, identifying and developing potential entrepre-neurs and providing infrastructure for accelerated small and medium-scale industry development, the Gujrat Experiments broke new grounds. The Gujrat Experiment carefully integrated three, often separate,

2 Background paper by Dr. P. Asthana, Entrepreneurship Development Programmes (EDPs) Indian Experience presented at the Seminar on EDPs organised by IDBI in 1980. IDBI Publication, pp. 18-19.

3 Ibid.

4 Innovations in Banking: The Gujrat Experiments, Summary Report by Shri V.G. Patel of the World Bank Sponsored Research Study, published by IDBI.

elements in the provision of assistance to small-scale industry, namely, i) provision of finance, ii) identification and training of entrepreneurs and iii) provision of infrastructure facilities.

In an endeavour to remove constraint of finance faced by new entrepreneurs, Gujrat Industrial Investment Corporation and Gujrat State Financial Corporation (GIIC and GSFC) jointly provided loans even up to 100% of the project cost on soft terms under the Techicians' and New Entrepreneurs' Scheme. The task of training and developing new entrepreneurs was implemented through a comprehensive package of entrepreneurship development programmes (EDPs) which included, (i) identifying and selecting those who could be trained as entrepreneurs, (ii) developing their entrepreneurial cap-abilities, (iii) ensuring that each trainee has a viable industrial project, (iv) equpping him with basic managerial understanding and (v) helping him to secure necessary financial, infrastructural and related assistance so that an industrial venture could materialise within the shortest possible time.

To facilitate and expedite implementation of projects, the Gujrat Industrial Development Corporation (GIDC) undertook a massive sheds-construction programme for industrial infrastructure and provid-ed ready factory buildings with essential facilities on liberal terms at multiple points in the state.

The three innovative schemes simultaneously introduced and operated by the conglomerate of Industrial Corporations fed and strengthened each other. Careful selection and training of entrepreneurs under EDPs, needs-based financing with ready infrastructure and sheds for expeditious implementation of the projects proved to be highly effective ways of promoting small enterprises. According to the World Bank Sponsored Research Study 'Innovations in Banking: The Gujrat Experiments', of the 1238 new entrepreneurs trained by March 1977, 74% in the category of 'experienced persons' 95% of 'jobless engineers', and 55% of the 'educated unemployed' eventually set up their industrial ventures.[5] It was, in fact, the Gujrat EDP that gave momentum to the entrepreneurship development movement in

5 Ibid., p.12.

the country and served as a model for adopting similar programmes in other States as also some other developing countries of South East Asia. It paved the way for the developmental and financial institutions in India to realise the need for identifying and implementing the ways of promoting entrepreneurship and undertake EDPs as an integral part of their promotional activities to widen the entrepreneurial base and create opportunities for self-employment.Several financial, promotional and educational institutions in the country are now engaged in the sphere of entrepreneurship development. The EDP conducting agencies include Technical Consultancy Organisations (TCOs) sponsored by all-India financial institutions, the Entrepreneurship Development Institute of India (EDII), an apex-level organisation set up and sponsored by all-India Financial Institutions, the State-level Institutes of Entrepreneurship Development (IEDs), Xavier Institute (REDI) Ranchi, Management Development Institute (MDI) sponsored by IFCI, the Regional Engineering Colleges and various other Technology Institutes throughout the country.

IFCI's Support for Entrepreneurship Development:

As a national level financial institution, IFCI's contribution in the field of entrepreneurship development has been by:

a) according in project financing cases, a preferential treatment to the projects promoted by new/technician entrepreneurs[6] and relaxing financing norms in respect of such projects,

b) assisting the TCOs and other specified agencies in different states by filling in the gap in the funding arrangements of the cost of EDPs conducted by them and

c) providing support to the Entrepreneurship Development Institute of India, and helping in the establishment of state or regional-level Institutes of Entrepreneurship Development in collaboration with other financial institutions and promotional agencies in the country, as also support to the Science and Technology Entrepreneurs' Parks (STEPs).

---

6 IFCI, Promotional Activities, 1984, p.26.

In its project financing operations, IFCI provides financial assistance for setting up new industrial projects as also for the expansion, diversification or modernisation of the existing ones. **Table 9.1** gives an extract of IFCI's project financing operations for the years 1983-84 to 1986-87 in order to highlight IFCI's sanctions to the projects promoted by new and technician entrepreneurs. From the figures of Table 9.1, following observations are noted:

i) In aggregate, IFCI's cumulative sanctions upto 30th June, 1987 amount to Rs. 4042.58 crores to 2541 projects. Out of this, Rs. 2683.03 crores were sanctioned to new projects of which Rs. 230.95 crores were claimed by 291 projects promoted by new/technician entre-preneurs. The sanctions to projects promoted by such entrepreneurs amounts to 8.6% of the sanctions to new projects and only 5.7% of the total sanctions. Though the number of projects promoted by technician entrepreneurs is about 11.4% of the total (291 out of 2541), the assistance sanctioned in respect of these is 5.7% of the total sanctions. Therefore, it is only to the extent of 5.7% of IFCI's total sanctions that has gone in favour of projects promoted by first generation entrepreneurs.

ii) During the past four years, i.e. 1983-84 to 1986-87, 76 projects promoted by new technician entrepreneurs were sanctioned Rs. 99.21 crores of assistance by IFCI. This implies that out of IFCI's cumulative sanctions to projects promoted by such entrepreneurs, as much as 43% (Rs. 99.21 crores out of Rs. 230.95 crores) has been given out to over 26% of the number of projects (76 out of 291) only during these four years. This apparently indicates that the trend to encourage new technician entrepreneurs to set up their industrial ventures in the industrial horizon of the country is quite recent in origin. The reason for this can be attributed to the fact that entrepreneurship development movement in India itself has gained momentum only during the last decade.

iii) To support the development of entrepreneurship, it is said, that in project financing cases, IFCI accords a preferential treatment to the projects promoted by new/technician entreprenuers. The analysis of the relevant data from **Table 9.1**

Table 9.1

IFCI's Sanctions to Projects Promoted by New/Technician Entrepreneurs

Year	Total Projects		New Projects out of the total		Projects promoted by new/technician entrepreneurs out of new projects		% of sanctions to projects promoted by technician entrepreneurs to sanctions to new projects	% of sanctions to projects by technician entreneaurs to total sanctions
	No. of Projects	Sanc. (Rs. Crores)	No. of new Projects	Sanc. (Rs. Crores)	No.	Sanc. (Rs. Crores)		
(1)	(2)	(3)	(4)	(5)	(6)	(7)	(7/5x100)	(7/3x100)
1983-84	337	353.62	147	252.25	20	18.33	7.3%	5.2%
1984-85	418	450.64	141	244.54	18	17.56	7.2%	3.9%
1985-86	365	579.45	127	361.59	12	20.36	5.6%	3.5%
1986-87	556	853.02	203	514.51	26	42.96	8.3%	5%
Cumulatively upto 30th June, 1987		4042.58 (2541 Projects)		2683.03		230.95 (291 projects)	8.6%	5.7%

Source: The figures have been drawn from the Annual Reports and Operational Statistics of IFCI of the year 1983-84, 1984-85, 1985-86, 1986-87.

for the years 1983-84 to 1986-87, however, questions the validity of this claim. In 1983-84, IFCI sanctioned assistance to 337 projects of which 20 were those promoted by new entrepreneurs involving Rs. 18.33 crores from IFCI's sanctions, which was 5.2% of the total sanctions by IFCI. In 1984-85, out of 418 projects, 18 were those promoted by new entrepreneurs with Rs. 17.56 crores assistance, which was 3.9% of IFCI's total assistance sanctioned. In 1985-86, out of 365 projects, only 12 projects promoted by new entrepreneurs were sanctioned Rs. 20.36 crores, which was 3.5% of IFCI's total sanctions. There was a slight improvement in 1986-87 when out of 556 projects, 26 projects promoted by new entrepreneurs were sanctioned Rs. 42.96 crores, i.e 5% of IFCI's total sanctions.

Therefore, barring 1986-87, not only the number of projects promoted by new technician entrepreneurs, assisted by IFCI, has declined in absolute terms, but also the sanctions in respect of such projects as a percentage of IFCI's total sanctions has gone down during the said period. With this, it seems, that the efforts of IFCI in encouraging first generation technician entrepreneurs by giving them preference in project financing cases are rather illusionary.

It may be due to lesser number of applications received for assistance from new entrepreneurs in general, or due to the meagre number of available trained technician entrepreneurs themselves who might be eligible for availing assistance from IFCI. In either case, it calls for more committed efforts on the part of development finance institutions like IFCI in encouraging first generation entrepreneurs and inducing them to take up industrial activity so as to broad-base entrepreneurship and create opportunities for self-employment.

Another aspects of IFCI's contribution for entrepreneurship development is to indirectly assist the TCOs, and other specified agencies like the National and the State-level Entrepreneurship Development Institutes, Management and Technology Development Institutes, Regio-nal Engineering Colleges etc. by sharing the cost of Entrepreneurship Development Programmes (EDPs) conducted by them throughout the country. It also includes the

Science and Technology EDPs organised under the auspices of National Science and Technology Entrepreneurship Development Board (NSTEDB) and conducted through these accredited institutions so as to harness the scientific and technical manpower talents in the country and make them available employment opportunities suited to their needs.

If the movement of entrepreneurship development has been able to gain momentum over the last few years, it is to a large extent, due to the patronage and liberalised support being provided by the all-India financial Institutions including IFCI. Cumulatively upto the 30th June, 1987, IFCI alongwith IDBI and ICICI had shared the cost of 747 EDPs conducted by various institutions, benefitting 17,920 potential entrepreneurs. The funds support provided by IFCI towards sharing of EDPs costs up to the 30th June, 1987, aggregated to Rs. 27.01 lakhs out of the Benevolent Reserve Fund and the Interest Differential Funds.

In addition to this, as a national-level development bank, IFCI has been assisting in the establishment of EDP centres at the national and state-level in collaboration with other financial institutions and promotional agencies and providing resources support to them.

Entrepreneurship Development Institute of India (EDII):

An important step in the direction of creating a network of institutions committed to spread the entrepreneurship movement throughout the country was the establishment of Entreneurship Development Institute of India (EDII) at Ahmedabad in 1983, with the joint efforts of the all-India financial institutions including IFCI, the state-level institutions and banks. IDBI contributed Rs. 56 lakhs towards the cost of setting up the centre, IFCI and ICICI contributed Rs. 28 lakhs each and a sum of Rs. 102 lakhs was jointly contributed by the Government of Gujrat, the state-level institutions and banks.

The prime objective of EDII is to serve as an apex level institution to initiate, support and accelerate entrepreneurship training, development and research efforts in all parts of the country. To accomplish this task, EDII organises model EDPs in different states, conducts seminars, workshops and research projects and provides faculty and professional support as a resource of experience and expertise for the benefit of various EDP conducting agencies like TCOs, State-level Entrepreneurship Development Institutes, Management and Technology Development Institutes etc. engaged in the field of entrepreneurship development. The aim is not only to support the accredited EDP conducting institutions in their on-going activities but also to create and build up a cadre of skilled, dedicated trainers and motivators for the country, i.e., the people who can make the EDPs a success all over the country. Since the inception of EDII in 1983, IFCI has provided resources support to it to the order of Rs. 72.50 lakhs out of the Benevolent Reserve Fund as upto 30th June, 1987.

State-level Institutes for Entrepreneurship Development (IEDs):

Sequential to the establishment of EDII as the national focal point for the development of entrepreneurship, many State Governments also initiated institutionalising the entrepreneurship development activities by setting up state-level centres/Institutes of Entrepreneurship Development. In Gujrat, a Centre for Entrepreneurship Development (CED) has already been in existence, and the all-India financial institutions including IFCI, have supported/agreed to support the setting-up of such institutions in Uttar Pradesh, Bihar, Orissa, Madhya Pradesh and North-Eastern Region.

The first in the battery of State-level Institutes of Entrepreneurship Development (IEDs) was the IED, U.P. established in February, 1986 at Lucknow. This Institute made a good start by conducting 14 training programmes covering 350 participants representing various target groups during the first year of its operation. Four Entrepreneurship Awareness Camps and an EDP exclusively for women entre-preneurs were successfully conducted at Lucknow. IFCI provided resource support of Rs. 7.50 lakhs to IED, Lucknow out of the Benevolent Reserve Fund during 1986-87.

In 1986-87, two more Institutes of Entrepreneurship Development came into existence, one in Bihar and the other in Orissa.

The IED, Bihar was established at Patna and had its formal inauguration in March, 1987. IFCI's contribution to IED, Patna, upto 30th June, 1987 was Rs. 1.00 lakh out of the Benevolent Reserve Fund. IED, Orissa was set up at Bhubaneshwar and has become operational only from May, 1987.

Support to Science & Technology Entrepreneurs' Parks (STEPs):

IFCI has provided/agreed to provide funds support on a sharing basis, alongwith other all-India financial institutions, Department of Science and Technology, Government of India and other sponsoring bodies, for the setting up and development of Science & Technology Entrepreneurs' Parks (STEPs) in India on the lines of 'Science Parks' in U.S.A. and U.K. The STEPs are nursery industrial estates attached to selected Universities and Institutes of Technology envisaging creation of suitable conditions and providing necessary facilities to the technocrates coming out of these institutions to make them fledgling entrepreneurs and enable them to translate their project ideas into viable industrial projects at a pilot level. The first STEP was set up at the Ranchi, Bihar, sponsored by Birla Institute of Technology (BIT). The BIT-STEP provides facilities to accommodate technocrats particularly in the field of electro- mechanical industries, electronics, pharmaceuticals and lubrications. Another STEP at Tarapur, Maha-rashtra, sponsored by the C.C. Shroff Research Institute has been set up essentially as a National Entreprenurs Chemical Park for the upcomig chemical engineers. During 1986-87, IFCI has agreed to assist two more STEPs being set up by the Regional Engineering College, Tiruchirapally, and Harcourt Butler Technological Institute, Kanpur. The REC-Trichi STEP will specialise in providing facilities to mechanical, electrical and electronic engineering units and the HBTI-STEP at Kanpur will specialise mainly in the field of chemical engineering, non-edible oils and food technology. It is stipulated that within a short period, the aforesaid STEPs would be able to transform potential entrepreneurs with scientific and technical know-how into confident entrepreneurs by matching their `talents' with `tasks' and `facilities' with `experience' so as to nurture applied research and translate it into productive development of the industry.

IFCI's contribution to the cause of entrepreneurship development by way of providing funds support to the Entrepreneurship Development Programmes and Organisations/Institutes set up for carrying out entrepreneurship development activities has been Rs. 108.01 lakhs, cumulatively upto the 30th June, 1987. As most of these activities are of very recent origin, it is premature to evaluate their impact on evolving a suitable entrepreneurial climate for the industrial pro-gress of the country. They are at best like the first steps in a long journey, where the goal is clear but the path is thoroughly uneven and uncertain.

Here, the aspect of entrepreneurship development in relation to the lesser developed areas[7] of a developing country like India needs to be emphasised. If industrial and entrepreneurial development is to assume the form of a movement or some kind of continuity, it is not only enough that few individuals establish industrial units and bear the risk, but it is also necessary that the initiation of entrepreneurship is followed by the required proliferation in the hitherto industrially less-developed areas of the country. The task of developing entrepreneurship in backward areas, in turn, requires entrepreneurship of a somewhat unusual nature from the financial and developmental agencies. While contemplating on the issue of carrying EDP movement to the backward areas, they are often confronted with some basic problems, such as, what kind of industrial unit, industrial activity, technology etc. could be fostered in such areas. In the context of backward areas, more often, the solutions are likely to be found in the development of entrepreneurship through self-employment by encouraging tiny and small scale ventures in the rural and cottage industries or engaged in simple manufacturing activities with relatively simple or less complex technology. This requires innovativeness on the part of institutions working for entrepreneurship development in:

i) designing EDPs suited to different target groups in consonance with the type of industrial activity to be undertaken

---

7 Sh. H.N. Pathak's Paper on The Entrepreneur & Manager in Backward Districts Profile and requirements, IDBI Seminar on EDPs, 1980.

and the kind of entrepreneurs to be developed from backward areas;

ii) the right kind of training institutions needed to be set up at the block and district level, and not just in few metropolitan cities and

iii) linking of such technical institutions to industrial estates for the in-plant training.

Further, conducting EDPs successfully alone may not be effective in inducing industrial activity in backward areas unless the efforts of the EDP organising agencies are linked and coordinated with the district and state level development finance institutions entrusted with the responsibility of providing financial assistance and infrastructure facilities to such areas under the overall guidance and promotional support of all-India financial and developmental institutions. To increase the effectiveness of entrepreneurship development efforts, they have to be conceived as a part of comprehensive workable programme so as to institutionalise and regulate the entrepreneurship development activities in a better way; and the success of such programmes will depend upon the extent to which they shift the educated or skilled unemployed youths gifted with entrepreneurial traits from the position of 'job-seekers' to 'job-givers', thus helping in the growth of the overall industrialisation process in the country.

10

Rural Development

Beginning with the Second-Five-Year Plan, India launched an ambitious programme of industrial development with the twin objectives of accelerating the pace of industrial growth and diversifying the pattern of development. The last three decades have no doubt witnessed growth and diversification in the industrial structure of the economy, yet this has not been able to fulfil certain expectations which were derived from its assumed role as a catalytic agent for generating growth in employment and in related activities and also in bringing about reduction in the inter-regional disparities in the levels of development. The trends in industrialisation point to clustering of large, medium and small-scale industries in urban areas or areas having most of urban facilities, rather than dispersal of small industries to rural areas.

Therefore, in the post 1970 period, when the backward areas had already been identified, increasing emphasis has been placed on devising special measures for the development of employment oriented industries in relatively backward regions and rural areas especially for weaker groups of population. In a country like India, where major part of the backward regions consists of rural areas and where more than three-fourth of the population lives in villages and remote areas, rural development assumes a special significance. Rural development does not simply consist of doing some nice things in a few selected villages but calls for evolving a strategy capable of implementation within a credible time span. It requires motivation of the villagers and their leaders, involvement of the local people in the planning and implementation of rural development plans, in village training in the skills required to implement these plans, and integrating these local efforts with the resources made available by the Central/State Government, financial institutions and other voluntary organisations.

Several programmes for rural development initiated by the Central/ State Governments have been in operation for quite a few years, but what is more relevant in this context is the role of financial institutions, especially that of Industrial Finance Corporation of India, for the development of rural areas. A large part of the initial programmes for rural development relates to the agriculture and other traditional activities, and it is quite natural that these sectors attract major attention in the programmes for development of rural and backward areas where agriculture is the mainstay of population. Of late, however, efforts have been made towards diversification of industrial activity into such areas. The rationale for emphasis on rural industrialisation in the development policy in India lies primarily in the following reasons:

a) Agricultural growth, even if rapid, is unlikely to be able to provide productive employment to all the labour force in the rural areas, with the result, underemployment would continue to be a feature of rural employment;

b) Organised industrial sector mainly concentrated in urban areas finds it difficult to absorb the growing labour force in the cities, not to mention the rural workers migrating to seek work in the urban industrial sector. As a result, a large part of the rural labour force either remains unemployed or earns very low incomes for most part of the year;

c) Industrial development provides a lasting and more effective stimulus to development since it brings about greater spread effects and linkages than the primary activities.

Therefore, development of industrial activity in the rural areas becomes imperative for diversification of rural economy, and rural industrialisation becomes as much an essential ingredient of rural development strategy as industrialisation as such is of the development strategy for the country.

The financial institutions can help achieve the objective of diversifying industrial activity in rural areas by assisting industrial units in such areas. They can also help in the geographical distribution of industries and consequent creation of future income in these regions. Depending upon the kind of entrepreneurs that these institutions assist, they can help determine the emerging composition of ownership of means of production in the economy. To the extent they assist small entrepreneurs in rural and backward areas, they can help in the upliftment of rural economy.

The role of financial institutions with regard to rural industrialisation can take different dimensions of which the following may be undertaken more prominently:

i) Diversification of industries into smaller towns, villages and backward areas;

ii) Protecting and developing cottage industries and traditional crafts and other rural industries;

iii) Assistance by way of subsidies and concessions to industries coming up in rural areas and

iv) Development of rural entrepreneurship.

The question of diversification of industries into rural and backward areas needs to be examined in the context of certain necessary conditions conducive to make these places attractive for industrial location. Required infrastructure, service facilities, availability of skilled labour and economies of concentration are some of the factors important for the establishment of certain industries. In areas where these are available, the financial institutions should spare no opportunity to divert liberal financial assistance for setting up of industries. But constraints arise where such pre-requisites are not adequately available. Then the problem relates to the selection of those types of industries which have locational flexibilities and can be advantage-ously located in small towns and villages so that they can serve as the nucleus of industrial activities to generate employment and income effects in these areas. In this regard, Industrial Cooperatives can be an effective instrument for rural development and the role of IFCI is worth mentioning in the development of rural economy through assistance to industrial cooperatives.

IFCI's Assistance to Industrial Cooperatives:

Table 10.1 gives IFCI's assistance to Industrial Cooperatives cumulatively upto June, 1987. The total number of projects assisted in the Cooperative Sector is 301 to which Rs. 379.43 crores had been sanctioned and out of this Rs. 341.28 crores had

Table - 10.1

IFCI's Assistance to Industrial Cooperatives (1948-87) Upto June, 1987.

Rs. Crores

Nature of Industry	No. of Projects	Amount Sanctioned	Amount Disbursed
Sugar	200	224.25	217.73
Textiles	86	84.90	71.23
Jute	1	.79	.79
Paper	4	4.45	4.34
Fertilizers	4	47.75	42.60
Synthetic Fibres	2	13.00	2.50
Vegetable Oil	1	.22	.22
Cocca Processing	1	1.87	1.87
Chemicals	1	.20	--
Industrial Estate	1	2.00	--
	301	379.43	341.28

Source: IFCI, Annual Report, 1987, Table 8, p. 53

INDUSTRIAL COOPERATIVES ASSISTED BY IFCI

(TABLE 10.1)

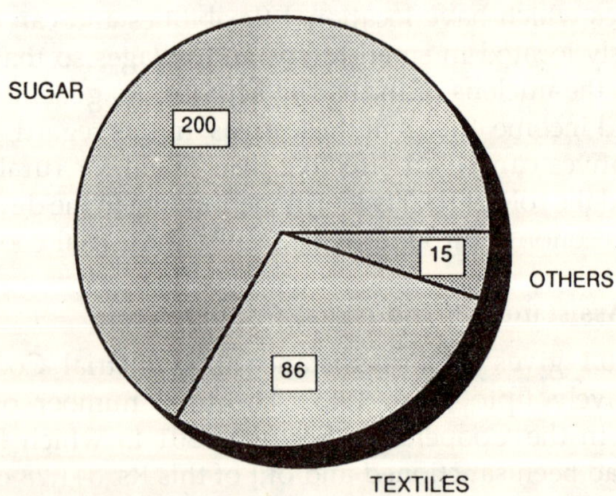

Table 10.2

State-wise Distribution of Industrial Cooperatives assisted by IFCI (upto June, 1987)

State	No. of Cooperatives Assisted by IFCI
Maharashtra	108
Uttar Pradesh	39
Karnataka	27
Andhra Pradesh	24
Gujarat	23
Tamil Nadu	19
Punjab	15
Orissa	10
Haryana	8
Assam	5
Bihar	5
Madhya Pradesh	5
Kerala	4
Rajasthan	4
W. Bengal	2
Pondicherry	2
Goa	1
Other states & UTs	Nil
Total	301

Source: Annual Report of IFCI, 1986-87, p. 67, Para 2.73.

COOPERATIVES ASSISTED IN DEVELOPED AND BACKWARD STATES

(TABLE 10.2)

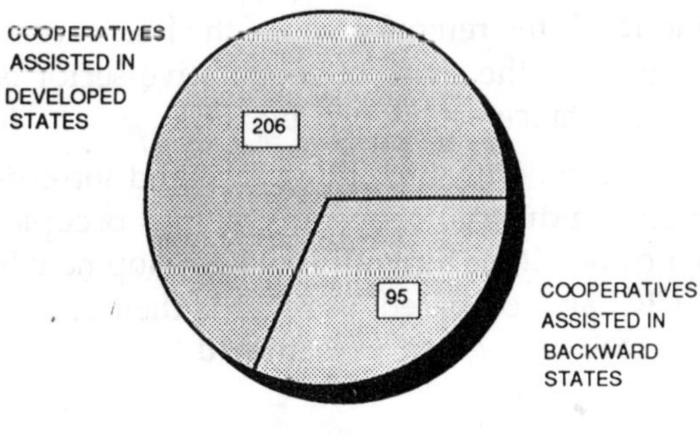

already been disbursed. Sugar and textile industries have been the major bene-ficiaries of IFCI's assistance. Since almost all the Cooperatives in the industrial sector are either agro-based or provide inputs to agriculture, IFCI has been able to develop, by providing impetus to the cooperative movement in the industry, a good nexus between agriculture and industry, thereby inducing economic growth of rural areas. Sugar cooperatives have been instrumental in promoting a number of ancillary and associate industries like distilleries for the manufacture of industrial alcohol, confectionary units, bagasse-based paper plants and production of mixed and granulated fertilizers. Textile spinning cooperatives have also provided opportunities for the development of the handloom sector in the rural and semi-urban areas. The spread of the cooperative movement in many other industries like jute, fertilizers, synthetic fibres, vegetable oil, cocca processing, paper and development of industrial estates indicate to the strength and success achieved by the industrial cooperatives all over the country.

Table 10.2 gives a state-wise distribution of the industrial cooperatives assisted by IFCI during the last four decades. The distribution indicates that 200 cooperatives (two-thirds of the total) assisted by IFCI are in the six developed states, namely, Maharashtra, Karnataka, Gujarat, Tamilnadu, Punjab and Haryana. Maharashtra has been the fore-runner in the cooperative movement in the industrial sector and alone accounts for over 35% of the industrial cooperatives assisted by IFCI. Only 95 cooperatives out of 301 (31.5%) assisted by IFCI are spread over all the backward states together. Despite the nature of industrial activity undertaken in the cooperative sector, which is so closely related to the rural economy, the cooperative movement has not been able to reach the remote areas of the less developed states. Also, in aggregate, the share of cooperative sector is just 9.4% in the total assistance sanctioned by IFCI.

However, even with this little share and lop-sided pattern of assistance to industrial cooperatives, IFCI occupies the most significant position if the three all-India development banks IDBI, IFCI and ICICI are compared, as regards their assistance to the cooperative sector; as given in **Table 10.3.**

Table 10.3

Institution wise Assistance to Cooperative Sector (Cumulative upto March, 1987)

Institution	% share of Cooperative Sector in the cumulative sanctions up to March, 1987	Disbursements as a % of Cumulative sanctions in the Cooperative Sector
IDBI	2.5%	80.5%
IFCI	9.4%	91.5%
ICICI	4.1%	83.1%

Source: Compiled from Report on Development Banking in India, IDBI, 1986-87.

The percentage share of cooperative sector in the cumulative sanctions upto March, 1987 is only 2.5% in case of IDBI and 4.1% in case of ICICI. IDBI disbursed 80.5% and ICICI 83.1% out of the cumulative sanctions, whereas IFCI's disbursements are 91.5% of the sanctions to the cooperative sector. Thus, the role of IFCI in assisting industrial cooperatives has been more prominent than that of IDBI and ICICI, yet this is not enough. To the extent the financial institutions are expected to help diversify industries into rural and backward areas, the cooperative sector definitely deserves a much better deal in their assistance portfolio, since the nature of industries in the cooperative sector is generally such as it helps in channelising the savings of agricultural sector for productive purposes, e.g. sugar, textile, jute, paper industries etc.

These industries are usually labour-intensive and create substantial direct and indirect employment. The industrial cooperatives set up in rural areas have a tremendous impact on the economic and social life of the community in their area of operations, since their establishment is accompanied by improvements in roads, irrigation facilities, education and health services etc. They strengthen the villagers' faith in the cooperative movement and in themsleves by creating a new class of entrepreneurs in the country, as has been in the case of milk cooperatives in Gujarat. Therefore, a more liberal approach on the part of the financial institutions is called for in assisting industrial cooperatives as an instrument for rural development.

Rural Industrialisation Efforts: Encouragement to Industries in VSI sector and Development of Rural Entrepreneurs:

The other dimension of the role of financial institutions in rural industrialisation for uplifting rural economy relates to the development of village and small industries and traditional handicrafts, provision of subsidies and concessions to such and other industries coming up in rural areas and development of rural entrepreneurship. These aspects are closely interconnected as far as the all-India Financial Institutions, like IFCI, are concerned, in the sense that their role can be indirect and promotional rather than direct and financial in nature with respect to such developmental efforts. The reason is that it is the local bodies, district and state level institutions that are directly related to the remote rural and backward areas than the national level institutions. The local efforts in turn can be strengthened and supported by institutions like IFCI for the implementation of rural development programmes.

The rural and backward areas are characterised by low levels of infrastructure development and lack of industrial culture as reflected in deficiencies in human capital, skilled labour and entrepreneurship, all acting in a vicious circle. As a consequence, entrepreneurship does not develop from local population and outside entrepreneurs do not get attracted to these areas on economic criterion. Even when some manufacturing units get located in these areas which may be using the local materials, they are confronted with the problems of financial constraints, unorganised activity and lack of marketing faci-lities. Thus, these units either face the problem of survival, or are at best, not in a position to bring about the desired benefits of linkages to these areas. Therefore, special treatment of units located in rural and backward areas becomes essential if these areas have to be developed industrially.

Financial institutions like IFCI can take certain measures in this regard and devise such integrated programmes for rural development which combat all the three major problem fronts of rural economy, viz., entrepreneurship, finance and infrastructure facilities. These programmes should be comprehensive in nature and need to be carefully monitored right from the concept to the fruition stage. To achieve this, they should encompass and integrate the following distinct aspects to promote industrial activity in rural areas:

i) Development of rural entrepreneurship through identification and training of potential entrepreneurs;

ii) Organisation of viable industrial activities of various kinds suited to rural background and provision of finance, concessions and subsidies to encourage such activity in rural areas and

iii) Provision of necessary infrastructure facilities and extension services essential for successful implementation of such projects.

The programmes for rural industrialisation can be effective only when all these factors are taken into consideration in their developmental efforts so as to push the rural and backward areas out of the vicious circles of industrial backwardness.

The process of industrial developmental of rural areas requires, as a first step, the motivation and development of villagers and involvement of the local people in the planning and implementation of rural development plans. They should be encouraged to take up industrial activity and their initial inhibitions can be overcome by imparting in-village training in the skills required to undertake such activities. Financial institutions like IFCI have contributed to the development of rural entrepreneurship in several ways:

i) IFCI has agreed to contribute Rs. 5 lakhs to the Xavier Institute of Social Service, Ranchi, for setting up a Rural Entrepreneurship Development Institute (REDI) to cater to the tribal population in the state of Bihar. The objective of the Institute is to motivate and nurture through training and follow-up the village and tribal youths to become successful entrepreneurs and generators of self-employment. The Village Entrepreneurship Development Programme is in the form of adult education covering the aspects of upgrading the skills of people for revitalising the village economy. IFCI has also sponsored a Rural Entrepreneurship Development Programme for unemployed boys and girls at the Institute and funded its entire cost. More such programmes are proposed to be sponsored in other areas to be conducted by the local Technical Consultancy Organisations there.

ii) IFCI also agreed in 1983-84 to provide support both for capital and recurring expenditure for a period of three years to Gram Vikas Trust for setting up of a Rural Management and Entrepreneurship Development Centre (RMEDC) in Karjat Taluka, Raigarh District of Maharashtra. The objective of RMEDC is to provide training and management inputs which are necessary to rural development so as to bring about sustained growth and meaningful development in rural and semi-urban areas. In order to make the training more effective and practical, RMEDC proposes to provide demonstration units in the field of dairy and rural industries, for example, soap-making, match-making, oil extraction, carpentry, poultry-farming etc. It is expected that in due course the activities of RMEDC would help in generating self employment, better management of the existing rural industries and setting up of new industries suited to the rural scenario. The IFCI's share in the programme is of Rs. 2.3 lakhs.

iii) Apart from this IFCI also participated in an International Exposition of Rural Development (IERD) organised by the Institute of Cultural Affairs, India in 1984 and made a contribution of Rs. 1 lakh out of the Benevolent Reserve Fund.

This role of IFCI with regard to rural development is too indirect and inadequate. To quote William Diamond, "*Financial Institutions need not be passive instruments of economic activity. With dynamic management and an adequately permissive environment of available opportunities and of favourable policies, they can be active engines of economic development. Among financial institutions, one particular type the development bank has an explicit special task, aside from the conventional function of providing finance. It has been created to do something which needs to be done to foster development and which is not being done by others. The development bank can not avoid the responsibility to behave accordingly.*"[1] In India, where development

1 Diamond William, Second IFCI Silver Jubilee Memorial Lecture, The Interplay between Financial Institutions and Economic Development, IFCI, Compendium of IFCI Silver Jubilee Memorial Lectures, p.55-56.

will have little meaning unless the three-fourth rural and backward areas of the country are developed, the development banks like IFCI should actively participate in bringing about rural industrialisation by formulating comprehensive programmes for rural development and carrying them through, from conception to realisation, rather than being content with merely providing passive support for the development of rural entrepreneurship. With the guidance and support of national and state-level financial Institutions, many more Institutes for development of rural entrepreneurship, like REDI and RMEDC, need to be set up so as to cover all the rural blocks and districts of the country in a phased manner. These centres should give training to the rural entrepreneurs and encourage them to exploit available industrial opportunities. In a rural set up, they can be broadly of two types. On one hand, attention should be paid for the promotion and development of village and small industries which can be organised in tiny and small scale sector based on local resources, local market and local skills and entrepreneurship. Such activities can include processing of agro-based products, poultry-farming, manufacture of soaps, matches, chalks, wood and cane furniture, other items in carpentry, extraction of oils, textile production etc. based on the local resource endowment. The Industrial Policy Statements have also reserved a number of products exclusively to be produced in the tiny and small scale sector. Entrepreneurs can be trained to produce a wide spectrum of other products from automobile ancillaries, beverages, food products etc. to even sophisticated electronic instruments and equipment in the small scale sector both for indigenous markets and exports. However, only training the entrepre-neurs would not be sufficient for the implementation of identified projects especially in rural areas. Among the services to be provided to rural industrial units, finance and infrastructure facilities are equally important. Financial institutions like IFCI can play a significant role by making available liberal financial assistance on concessional terms for industrial units in these areas.

The district and the state level institutions can endeavour to provide infrastructure facilities like power, sheds, equipment and machinery, without which even the trained entrepreneurs would find it hard to commission and organise industrial projects and the cost of these can in turn be subsidised by the national level institutions through their various subsidy schemes for rural development.

The other category of industries, on which a developmental and protective emphasis is laid, for bringing about rural industrialisation is that of traditional crafts and cottage industries. This is based on a number of economic and social considerations. Using available traditional skills and requiring little capital, they provide suitable self-employment to rural households, artisans, and craftsmen without involving dislocation and migration costs. They use more labour per unit of capital and output as compared to modern industries and their operations can be adjusted to suit the fluctuations in labour requirements of agricultural sector. Such activities include handloom weaving, handicrafts, coir and silk products and other village industries like pottery, ceramics, leather, etc.

Both types of industrial activity, viz. tiny and small scale industrial sector as also the handicrafts and village industries, have yet another utmost important common problem, that of marketing. Whether they are electronic instruments and ancillaries produced in the small sector or products of the cottage, village, handicrafts and peasant industries, all require effective marketing channels for procurement of raw materials and marketing of the finished products. It is here that the national-level institutions like IFCI can help bridge the gap between the rural production centres and urban consumption centres. The local bodies and district-level institutions should be entrusted with the responsibility of providing transport facilities, credit facilities for the purchase of raw materials etc. and making arrangements so that finished goods reach the centres of demand. The block level efforts should be linked with the State-level Organisations for the necessary support and marketing assistance as also for availing of the concessions and subsidies offered by these institutions. At the national level, these organisations should work in close cooperation and coordination with all-India Institutions so that every possible policy, promotional and marketing support can be extended to them.

Thus, the problem of rural development is a challenging multi- dimensional task, requiring financial, organisational, technical, man-agerial and marketing support at every stage. The role of national-level development banks like IFCI has to be indirect and promotional in nature, yet it can be devised in a much more active and effective way within the framework of three-tier institutional infrastructure i.e. at the district level, state level and at the national level; providing guidance and support at various stages.

The national level institutions, through their state and district-level branches, or through small industry organisations like National and State Small Industries Development Corporations and through other institutions like Commercial Banks, Khadi and Village Industries Commission etc. can help establish small-scale, low-capital production and processing units in rural areas so as to generate extra incomes in such areas and strengthen inter-sectoral linkages between agriculture and industry.

There should be a determined and conscientious effort on the part of the national level institutions to search out for the methods by which they can participate effectively in the task of rural mobilisation for national progress.

11

Promotional Schemes

In addition to the hitherto discussed promotional activities which have been undertaken by IFCI either individually or in collaboration with other financial institutions, IFCI has been operating, on its own, several promotional schemes. The objective of IFCI in launching these promotional schemes as a part of its promotional activities is to:

i) Fill in gaps in the promotion and growth of industries specially in the rural, tiny, small scale and ancillary sectors so as to help and encourage self-employment, entrepreneurship and enterprise setting thereby creating opportunities for inducing industrial activity in relatively less-developed areas,

ii) Provide the much-needed guidance in identification, formulation, implementation and operation of industrial projects in the rural, tiny, small or medium scale sectors, as also provide assistance in marketing and market research, modernisation, pollution control etc.,

iii) Catalyse the promotion of technological research and development in the industry and

iv) Improve the productivity of material and human resources, at the same time, ensuring a better deal to the women and weaker sections of the society, in consonance with the national policies.

The philosophy that permeates in IFCI's promotional schemes is to provide industrial projects set up in rural, tiny and small scale sectors such supportive measures as can lead them to 'growth with stability.' With this aim, as at the end of June, 1987, IFCI's promotional schemes included seven Consultancy Fee Subsidy Schemes, four Interest Subsidy Schemes and one Assistance Scheme, as under: (The brackets give the dates from which the schemes have become operational).

Consultancy Fee Subsidy Schemes:

— Schedul of subsidy to small entrepreneurs in the rural, cottage, tiny and small scale sectors for meeting cost of feasibility studies etc. (1.7.1978).

— Scheme of subsidy for promotion of ancillary and small scale industries (1.9.1978).

— Scheme of subsidy to new entrepreneurs for meeting cost of market research/surveys (30.11.1977).

— Scheme of subsidy for providing marketing assistance to small scale units (1.8.1985).

— Scheme of subsidy for revival of sick units in the tiny and small scale sectors (28.6.1982).

— Scheme of subsidy for implementing the modernisation programmes of tiny, small-scale and ancillary units (1.1.1986).

— Scheme of subsidy for control of pollution in the small and medium scale industrial units (1.1.1986).

Interest Subsidy Schemes:

— Scheme of interest subsidy for self-development and self employment of unemployed young persons (26.6.1982).

— Scheme of interest subsidy for women entrepreneurs (1.1.1986).

— Scheme of interest subsidy for encouraging the adoption of indigenous technology (30.11.1977).

— Scheme of interest subsidy for encouraging quality control measures in small scale sector (1986-87).

Assistance Scheme:

— Scheme of assistance for development of technology through in-house R&D efforts (1.7.1984).

The Consultancy Fee Subsidy Schemes are aimed at providing subs-dised consultancy services to industrial units in tiny, small scale and ancillary sectors for specified purposes through Technical Consultancy Organisations (TCOs). The Interest Subsidy Schemes are intended to provide encouragement to unemployed youths and women entrepreneurs, and for adoption of quality control measures, harnessing the indigenously available technology, etc., and are being operated through the State Financial Corporations (SFCs), IFCI bearing the burden of interest on SFCs' loan assistance to such entrepreneurs during the first year upto specified limits. The Assistance Scheme for development of technology through in-house R & D efforts is being operated by IFCI directly. Following is a brief introduction of the aforesaid promotional schemes stating their objectives, eligibility criteria, limits of subsidy/assistance offered and other terms and conditions in nutshell and an analysis of the extent to which these schemes have been utilised by the TCOs and other specified agencies through which they are operated by IFCI.

Consultancy Fee Subsidy Schemes:

1. Scheme of subsidy to small entrepreneurs for meeting cost of feasibility studies etc.:

The objective of the scheme is to encourage the smallest among small entrepreneurs to avail themselves of the facilities of consultancy services offered by the TCOs through the various phases of the project cycle, i.e. project identification, formulation, implementation and operation. The scheme is applicable to small entrepreneurs who propose to set up new or expand/diversify their existing industrial unit in rural, cottage, tiny or small scale sector with total project cost not exceeding Rs. 10 lakhs. An entrepreneur is eligible for subsidy in respect of consultancy assignment only once during the project's life cycle, and for one project only, however, subsidy to two new projects promoted by the same entrepreneur but at different locations may be considered on merits. IFCI subsidises assignments taken up by the TCOs upto Rs. 2 lakhs per annum per TCO, an additional 0.50 lakhs p.a. per TCO may be considered on merit. The fees for the assignment taken up by the TCO is subsidised to the extent of 90% or Rs. 2700/- whichever is lower, and the balance 10% is normally expected to be borne by the entrepreneur. The TCO may be subsidised to the extent of 100% of the fee for the assignment or Rs. 3000/- whichever is lower where the assignment is from a SC/ST or physically handicapped entrepreneur, or relates to the use of bio-gas and/or renewable/alternative sources of energy, or where the project is proposed to be set up in notified industrially backward district or where the entrepreneurs are covered under the Integrated Rural Development Programme of the Government of India.

2. **Scheme for development of ancillary and small scale industries:**

The scheme is in consonance with the national objective of rapid industrialisation on a decentralised and dispersed basis through encouragement of small-scale and ancillary industries. The scheme covers entrepreneurs of ancillary and small scale industries who manufacture intermediate goods and products according to the designs and specifications given to them by other industrial units persuant to a minimum take-off arrangement, as also the downstream ancillary and small scale units of medium and large industries from whom they obtain their major raw materials under a supply arrangement for further processing. The subsidy is given for identification of products suitable for ancillarisation, preparation of feasibility/project reports for setting up ancillary units and for providing guidance in technical, financial and marketing areas to such units. IFCI subsidises the fees for assignments taken up and completed by the TCOs upto Rs. 1 lakh per annum per TCO (an additional 0.50 lakh p.a. per TCO may be considered on merit). 50% of the subsidy or Rs. 7500/-, whichever is lower, is reimbursed by IFCI upon completion of the assignment by the TCO and the balance when the ancillary unit has been sanctioned financial assistance and the minimum supply/take-off arrangements have been formalised with the parent unit.

3. **Scheme for subsidy to new entrepreneurs for meeting cost of market surveys/research:**

One of the aspects in project formulation, which is often overlooked by enthusiastic first-timer entrepreneurs in the small and medium scale industrial sector, is the assessment of the Market Potential for the product which they intend to manufacture. With a view to helping as also motivating the entrepreneurs to make a careful assessment of the market before deciding upon the scale of operations, the product-mix and the market strategy, this promotional scheme of IFCI envisages grant of subsidy to new entrepreneurs setting up industrial projects with a capital cost not exceeding Rs. 3 crores for the first time in the country, for their going in for a market survey/study for their project through a TCO. Such entrepre-neurs can avail themselves of the facility of IFCI subsidy for the fee for market survey payable to TCO to the extent of 75% or Rs. 7,500/-, or, 75% or Rs. 15,000/-, whichever is less, in case of industrial projects in small or medium scale sectors respectively. IFCI subsidises assignments completed by a TCO upto Rs. 1.50 lakhs per annum per TCO.

4. Scheme of subsidy for providing marketing assistance to small-scale units:

Problems relating to marketing have often been responsible for the tardy growth of small scale industrial units leading to sickness. The objective of this scheme is to provide marketing assistance to units in rural, cottage, tiny and small scale sectors at subsidised cost through the marketing assistance facilities offered by the TCOs. The nature of assistance may cover investigating client's marketing prob-lems, evolving a marketing strategy on distribution system, pricing, discount and credit policies etc., designing a marketing organisation for the unit or a tie-up with some other agency, and counselling on product improvement, technology upgradation and other matters so as to improve the overall marketing competitiveness of the products. Under the scheme, the TCO undertakes the assignment for a minimum period of one year and charges its fees from the beneficiary unit, 20% while accepting the assignment, 20% when it prepares the blueprint of the scheme, 20% when the scheme is implemented and the final 40% when the beneficiary unit certifies that the implementation of the scheme has resulted in perceptible improvement in its sales turnover. IFCI subsidises the last 40% of the fee or Rs. 7500/-, whichever is lower, and the aggregate subsidy available from IFCI is upto Rs. 2.00 lakhs per annum per TCO.

5. Scheme of subsidy for revival of sick units:

Sickness in industry implies hardship and unemployment to the labour, waste of already invested resources in such units and disincentive to new entrepreneurs coming up in those fields of industry where their predecessors have not been successful. The objective of this IFCI's scheme is to help revive the inherently viable sick industrial units in the tiny and small scale sectors so that existing investment becomes productive. Under the scheme, the fee chargeable by a TCO for carrying out a diagnostic study, implementing a rehabilitation programme or for nursing a unit is subsidised by IFCI to the extent of 80% or Rs. 7500/- whichever is lower. (100% subsidy is available where the assignment is routed through the State Corporation for SC/ST or backward classes). IFCI subsidises assignments completed by TCOs upto Rs. 1.00 lakh per annum per TCO.

6. Scheme of subsidy for modernisation programme of small-scale units:

The objective of the scheme goes with the emphasis of the Seventh Plan on modernisation and technology upgradation of Indian industry with a view to improving quality of products and productivity and reduce cost of production. Quite similar to IDBI's scheme of Refinance for modernisation of small and medium industries subsidising cost of modernisation studies to the extent of 50% or Rs. 5,000/- whichever is lower, IFCI's scheme aims to help entrepreneurs in implementing unit specific modernisation proposals through TCOs. The scheme applies to all small and ancillary units including those in rural, cottage and tiny sectors, which have been in operation for atleast 5 years, and where implementation of modernisation programme is considered to be necessary to keep pace with the changing technology or consumer needs or for productivity improvement, export orientation, import substitution, energy saving, recycling of wastes and by-products, improved capacity utilisation and enhancing operating efficiencies. If the TCO is involved not only with the formulation of the modernisation scheme but also in its implementation, the extent of subsidy in the fee chargeable by the TCO is 90% or Rs. 9000/- whichever is lower. IFCI subsidises assignments of modernisation programmes taken up by the TCOs upto Rs. 2.00 lakhs per annum per TCO.

7. Scheme of subsidy for pollution control:

Alongside the objective of promoting industrial development in the country, increasing importance is being placed on environmental protection measures to control industrial effluents and abate pollution of air water and soil. The objective of the scheme is to meet the growing need for formulating appropriate proposals for prevention of pollution in industrial units, specially for the small and medium scale entrepreneurs who often face problems due to inadequacy of such measures in conformation with the requirements of the concerned authority and/or Pollution Control Board.

The scheme applies to all tiny, small, ancillary and medium scale industrial units with capital cost upto Rs. 3 crores, which come under the category of pollutive industries as determined by the Central Government or State Pollution Control Boards. Under the scheme, IFCI subsidies the fees for the consultancy assignment payable to a TCO for preparing, and if required implementing a need-based scheme of pollution control in specific industrial units or for improving the existing effluent treatment and disposal system with a view to make gainful utilisation of wastes and by-products, energy conservation, and improve the overall working efficiency of the unit. Where the assignment involves only formulation of the scheme, IFCI subsidises 50% of the fees or Rs. 5000/- or 50% of the fees or Rs. 10,000/-, whichever is lower, in case of tiny, small scale and ancillary units, and medium scale industrial units respectively. Where TCO is involved also with the implementation of the scheme to the satisfaction of the concerned authorities, the subsidy available is 75% or Rs. 7500/- or 75% or Rs. 15,000/- in case of small and medium scale units respectively. IFCI subsidies assignments taken up by TCOs upto Rs. 3.00 lakhs per annum per TCO.

Interest Subsidy Schemes:

Under Interest Subsidy Schemes, IFCI bears the burden of interest during the first year upto specified limits on SFC's loan assistance given to certain categories of entrepreneurs.

1. Interest subsidy scheme for unemployed young persons:

The objective of the scheme is to introduce unemployed young persons to industrial vocations and settle them through the process of self-development and self-employment. The scheme applies to literate unemployed young persons who have successfully undergone a full course of EDP conducted by a TCO or specified agency, and persuant to that, decided to set up a new project which may be a shop, trade, repair service, production unit etc. for which they have got prepared a complete project report and financial assistance has been sanctioned and disbursed by any SFC. The assistance under the scheme is in the form of one-time subsidy, determinable on a case to case basis, equivalent to the amount of interest payable to the SFC for the loan assistance sanctioned for the project for a period of one year subject to a ceiling of Rs. 5,000/- and Rs. 10,000/- for tiny sector and small-scale sector projects respectively. (The ceiling is Rs.7,500/- and Rs. 12,500/- for SC/ST or physically handicapped young persons). The amount of subsidy is released by IFCI directly to the SFC to be adjusted against the interest liability of the entrepre-neurs thus passing the benefit of subsidy to the project set up by an unemployed young person.

2. Interest subsidy scheme for women entrepreneurs:

In consonance with the socio-economic objectives particularly the thrust given under the 20 Point Programme of Government of India to give a better deal to the women, weaker and underprivileged sections of the society, the objective of the scheme is to provide incentives to the women having business acumen and entrepreneurial traits to contribute their mite in the industrial development of the country. The scheme applies to all industrial projects set up by women entrepreneurs in rural, cottage, tiny, small (including ancillary) and medium scale sectors with capital cost upto Rs. 3 crores. To be eligible, the woman entrepreneur must have undergone a full course of EDP and must have been sanctioned and disbursed financial assistance by any SFC as in the case of earlier scheme. The assistance under the scheme is in the form of one time subsidy, determinable on a case to case basis, equivalent to the amount of interest payable by the woman entrepreneur on the SFC loan assistance sanctioned for the project for a period of one year subject to a ceiling of Rs. 25,000/- or Rs. 50,000/- in case of small and medium sector projects respectively, which is released by IFCI to the concerned SFC to be adjusted against the interest liability in favour of the woman entrepreneur.

3. Interest subsidy scheme for encouraging adoption of indigenous technology:

In line with the national objective of promoting scientific and technological self-reliance, the scheme offers subsidy to projects which play a pioneering role in the commercial exploitation of indigenously developed technology. The scheme covers all projects in tiny, small and medium scale sectors with capital cost upto Rs. 5 crores, and is operated in case of small scale projects through SFCs and in respect of other projects directly by IFCI. The assistance under the scheme is in the form of one-time subsidy, determinable on a case to case basis, subject to 80% of the cost of acquisition of indigenous know- how with a ceiling of Rs. 20,000/- or 10% of the cost of project, whichever is lower, in case of tiny and small scale project, and, same as above with ceiling of Rs. 5 lakhs or 10% of the cost of project, whichever is lower, in case of medium sector units. For being eligible the project must be based on indigenous technology developed in Government laboratories, Universities, National Research Development Corporation etc. which has not already been exploited on a commercial scale in the country, and the project must have been sanctioned financial assistance either by any SFC or by IFCI/ IDBI/ICICI. The amount of subsidy is released by IFCI in favour of the concerned financial institution providing financial assistance for the project to meet the interest liability.

4. Interest subsidy scheme for encouraging quality control measures in small scale sector:

The objective of the scheme is to help the small scale sector industrial units to equip themselves with proper' testing and quality control equipments so as to improve the quality of their products and increase their domestic and international competitiveness. The scheme applies to all small scale units (including rural, cottage, and tiny sector) existent in production who have been sanctioned and disbursed financial assistance by any SFC or state level financial institution for procuring testing and quality control equipment. IFCI's assistance under the scheme is in the form of one time subsidy, determinable on a case to case basis, equivalent to the amount of interest payable by the industrial unit for one year to the concerned SFC or financial institution on the loan assistance availed by the project for acquiring quality control equipment, subject to a ceiling of interest subsidy of Rs. 25,000/-

Assistance scheme for development of technology through in-house R&D efforts:

The objective of the scheme is to help the development of technology indigenously through in-house Research and Development efforts undertaken by concerns in the corporate and cooperative sectors (excluding MRTP/FERA companies). To be eligible, the applicant concern should be actively engaged in developing a technology, through in-house R&D efforts, which is basic to the manufacture of a product and is not already available indigenously. The cost of R&D efforts for developing technology from laboratory to commercial scale should be above Rs. 5 lakhs but not exceed Rs. 50 lakhs. Further, the concern should be an assisted unit of either any SFC or IDBI/ IFCI/ICICI. Under the scheme, IFCI provides directly loan assistance on soft terms at 11% interest p.a. The loan amount is limited to 50% of the cost of in-house R&D efforts for developing technology indigenously and secured by a first charge on the fixed assets of the borrower concern.

The repayment of the loan begins after the developed technology has been succefully harnessed and operated on commercial scale, or after a period of three years from the date of the first disbursement, whichever is earlier.

The foregoing paragraphs give an account of the various promotional schemes of IFCI as in June 1987. The discussion that follows endeavours to probe the extent to which these have been utilised by the TCOs, SFCs or directly by IFCI and identify the lags thereof.

Subsidies/Assistance disbursed under Promotional Schemes:

Table 11.1 gives a scheme-wise distribution of the subsidies/ assistance given under IFCI's Promotional Schemes. Following observations are made from the data given in the table:

Table - 11.1

Scheme-wise subsidies/assistance given under IFCI's Promotional Schemes.

Sl. No.	Name of the Scheme	(Year - July-June) 1983-84	1984-85	1985-86	1986-87	(Rs. lakhs). 1978-87 cum upto 30th June 1987
I.	**Consultancy Fee Subsidy Schemes:**					
1.	Scheme of subsidy to small entrepreneurs in the rural cottage, tiny and small scale sectors for meeting cost of feasibility studies etc.	20.36	37.29	31.45	21.91	158.28
2.	Scheme of subsidy for promotion of Ancillary and small scale industries	2.00	.83	2.48	2.84	152
3.	Scheme of subsidy to new entrepreneurs for meeting cost of market research/surveys	.72	.15	2.04	2.27	5.18
4.	Scheme of subsidy for providing marketing assistance to small-scale units				.14	.14
5.	Scheme of subsidy for revival of sick units in the tiny and small-scale sectors	.43	2.05	1.31	2.65	6.44
6.	Scheme of subsidy for implementing the modernisation programmes of tiny, small-scale and ancillary units					
	Sub Total (1)	**23.51**	**40.32**	**37.28**	**30.05**	**186.10**
II.	**Interest Subsidy Schemes:**					
1.	Scheme of interest subsidy for women entrepreneurs				.03	.03
2.	Scheme of subsidy for encouraging the adoption of indigenous technology	16.94	18.58	--	--	42.95
	Sub Total (2)	**16.94**	**18.58**		**.03**	**42.98**
III.	**Assistance Scheme:**					
1.	Scheme of assistance for development of technology through in-house R&D efforts **Sub Total (3)**	--	--	23.50	--	--
	Total (1) + (2) + (3)	**40.45**	**58.90**	**60.78**	**30.08**	**252.58**

Source: Compiled from IFCI, Operational Statistics; 1986-87, 1985-86, 1984-85, 1983-84.

1. Cumulatively upto 30th June, 1987, IFCI had disbursed subsidy and loans under its various promotional schemes aggregating Rs. 252.58 lakhs, benefitting 5180 industrial units, largely in the small-scale and ancillary industries sector.[1]
2. IFCI operates Consultancy Fee Subsidy Schemes through TCOs and Interest Subsidy Schemes through SFCs or other state-level institutions like SIDCs/SIICs. However, the Interest Subsidy Scheme for Encouraging Adoption of Indigenous Technology is operated directly by IFCI except in respect of tiny and small- scale projects. This scheme was started in 1977 and since then only three units have been the beneficiaries under the Scheme. IFCI subsidised a sum of Rs. 7.43 lakhs to an industrial unit in Kerala which had obtained the technology for the manufacture of electrolytic manganese-dioxide from the National Metallurgical Laboratory, Jamshedpur. Another unit granted subsidy of Rs. 16.94 lakhs under the scheme by IFCI is in Rajasthan, which had obtained the technology developed by the Regional Research Laboratory, Hyd-erabad, for the manufacture of glyoxal 40% solution. The third unit granted a subsidy of Rs. 18.58 lakhs is in Gujarat for the manufacture of Ethylene diamines and Polyamines which had obtained the process know-how invented and developed by the National Chemical Laboratory, Pune, a constituent unit of the Council of Scientific and Industrial Research. The total subsidy granted under the scheme by IFCI is Rs. 42.95 lakhs to the aforesaid three units.[2]
3. The Assistance Scheme for Development of Technology through in-house R&D efforts, started in July, 1984, is also operated directly by IFCI. Since then, the list of beneficiaries under the scheme consists of just one company engaged in the manufacture of bulk drugs, fine chemicals and formulations, to which a loan assistance of Rs. 23.50 lakhs was sanctioned by IFCI during 1984-85, the same being disbursed in 1985-86, for financing a part of its R&D project aimed at developing and scaling up the technology from laboratory to commercial scale in the areas of research in drugs, natural

1 IFCI, Annual Report, 1986-87, p.91.

2 IFCI, Promotional Activities, p.35 and IFCI, Annual Report, 1983-84, p.67.

products, steriods and pharmaceutical formulations.[3]

4. Of all the other promotional schemes which are operated by IFCI through the specified agencies like TCOs and SFCs, the consultancy fee subsidy scheme to small entrepreneurs in the rural, cottage, tiny and small scale sector for meeting cost of feasibility studies etc. has been exploited the most. This scheme became operational from 1st July, 1978, and since then, cumulatively upto 30th June, 1987, a sum of Rs. 158.28 lakhs has been subsidised by IFCI under this scheme to various TCOs for meeting the cost of feasibility/project reports etc. prepared by them for the prospective entrepreneurs. This amounts to over 85% of the assistance granted by IFCI under its promotional schemes by way of subsidies. All other subsidy schemes together accout for only about 15% of the total amount subsidised by IFCI to various TCOs under the promotional schemes.
5. Three of the IFCI's promotional schemes are yet to make a headway. The subsidy scheme for control of pollution in the small and medium scale industrial units, which was started from 1st January, 1986, and the interest subsidy scheme for encouraging quality control measures in the small-scale sector, which was introduced in 1986-87, have not been utilised at all. A matter of greater concern is that the scheme of interest subsidy for self-development and self-employment of unemployed young persons, which became operational from 28th June, 1982, even after five years of its introduction still awaits a beneficiary.
6. IFCI granted subsidy for the first time during 1986-87 under three of its promotional schemes. A sum of Rs. 0.14 lakhs was subsidised by IFCI under the scheme of subsidy for providing marketing assistance to small scale units, which had become operational since August, 1985. Under the subsidy scheme for implementing modernisation programmes of tiny, small scale and ancillary units, which was started from 1st January, 1986, a sum of Rs. 0.24 lakhs was subsidised by IFCI, and under the interest subsidy scheme for women

---

3 IFCI, Annual Report, 1984-85, p.111.

entrepreneurs, which was also started from 1st January, 1986, a sum of Rs. 0.03 lakhs was subsidised by IFCI in favour of a women entrepreneur in Maharashtra[4] for the first time during 1986-87.

The facts above reveal that though there are twelve promotional schemes offered by IFCI as till June, 1987, but if the two schemes operated by IFCI directly i.e. the schemes for encouraging adoption of indigenous technology and for promoting technology development through in-house R&D efforts, (in which the subsidy/assistance given is determinable on case-to-case basis, and only four industrial units have been benefited so far under the said two schemes), and, the subsidy scheme for meeting cost of feasibility studies are put aside, the utilisation of all other schemes has been negligibly small. There is too wide a gap between the limits of subsidies offered by IFCI that could be availed of and what has been availed by the TCOs/SFCs through which the promotional schemes of IFCI are being operated. This places an inevitable question mark,

i) on the efficacy of TCOs/SFCs in implementation of these schemes, in relation to their basic objective of filling in vital gaps in the promotion and growth of industries specially in the rural, cottage, tiny, small and ancillary sectors thus creating industrial opportunities for developing industrially backward areas, as also,

ii) on the adequacy of TCOs/SFCs as channels through which IFCI's promotional schemes are operated.
In this context, **Table 11.2** gives a TCO-wise distribution of the subsidies disbursed to TCOs under IFCI's promotional schemes. Based on this data, following observations are made:

1. Cumulatively upto 30th June, 1987, a sum of Rs.186.10 lakhs has been subsidised to various TCOs under IFCI's promotional schemes. This is in respect of 5175 projects, of which more than 85% relate to feasibility studies and project reports[5] prepared by the TCOs.

---

4 IFCI, Annual Report, 1986-87, p.90.

5 As per the information in the Balance Sheets of various TCOs.

Table 11.2

Subsidies disbursed to TCOs under IFCI's Promotion Schemes

Amt. in Rs. Lakhs

Name of	1978-83 (5 Yrs.)		1983-84		1984-85		1985-86		1986-87		1978-87	
TCO	No. of Proj.	Amt. Sub.	No. of Proj.	Amt. Sub.	No. of Proj.	Amt. Sub.	No. of Proj.	Amt. Sub.	No. of Proj.	Amt. Sub.	No. of Proj.	Amt. Sub.
APITCO	99	5.76	19	1.71	23	1.58	29	4.09	11	1.51	181	14.65
BITCO	53	2.54	16	.70	27	1.24	29	1.06	9	.28	134	5.82
GITCO	167	7.44	73	3.17	151	7.67	63	3.67	28	1.13	482	23.08
HARICON	-	-	-	-	-	-	2	.08	37	1.47	39	1.55
HIMCON	319	9.90	83	3.18	121	5.46	76	3.48	70	2.04	669	24.06
ITCOT	48	2.28	27	1.25	2	.10	38	1.62	110	5.16	225	10.41
J&KITCO	47	2.06	18	1.29	12	.74	9	.60	1	.26	87	4.95
KITCO	105	4.29	57	2.04	68	3.59	51	2.79	28	1.83	309	14.53
MPCON	278	5.62	158	2.73	245	6.18	182	3.87	88	1.44	951	19.84
MITCON	-	-	4	.19	33	1.91	31	2.13	25	1.54	93	5.77
NEITCO	23	1.13	10	.50	12	.64	6	.43	1	.03	52	2.73
NITCON	-	-	-	-	32	1.41	34	.96	415	3.08	481	5.45
ORITCO	12	.62	23	1.09	12	.81	6	.42	14	.88	67	3.83
RAJCON	176	6.11	57	2.02	43	1.74	162	3.10	84	2.00	522	14.97
TECSOK	34	1.56	37	1.12	76	2.34	91	3.35	98	3.47	336	11.84
UPICO	172	5.12	32	1.22	33	1.58	37	2.11	77	2.63	351	12.66
WEBCON	11	.51	23	1.30	62	3.33	65	3.52	35	1.30	196	9.96
Total	1544	54.94	637	23.51	952	40.32	911	37.28	1131	30.05	5175	186.10

Source: IFCI, Operational Statistics, 1986-87, p. 72.

2. The five TCOs directly under IFCI's lead, viz, HARICON, HIMCON, MPCON, NITCON and RAJCON, together account for 35.4% of the total subsidies disbursed under various schemes (Rs. 65.87 lakhs out of Rs. 186.10 lakhs). A similar share of 35.3% (Rs. 65.63 lakhs out of Rs. 186.10 lakhs) has been subsidised to five TCOs GITCO, ITCOT, KITCO, TECSOK and MITCON all of relatively developed states of Gujarat, Tamil Nadu, Kerala, Karnataka and Maharashtra respectively, the rest of the amount of subsidies being disbursed to all other TCOs mostly in the less-developed states. It appears from the former fact that the TCOs directly under IFCI's lead have an easier accessibility on the subsidies offered under IFCI's promotional schemes, which is reflected in the greater amounts of subsidies availed by HIMCON as compared to J&KITCO and NEITCO (all TCOs are of hill-states), and, by RAJCON and MPCON as compared to ORITCO and BITCO (all are identified less-developed states). Alternately, the underlying reasons for this may be in a higher degree of commitment of IFCI in the TCOs directly under its lead as also in the length of the period for which the concerned TCOs have been in operation. The latter observation is indicative of fewer opportunities available of inducing industrial activity in the less-developed regions due to the deep-seated vicious circles of industrial backwardness as reflected in inadequate infrastructure facilities, deficiencies in human capital, lack of entrepreneurship and other supportive activities for which most of these schemes grant subsidies.

3. The aggregate amount of subsidies disbursed to TCOs under IFCI's promotional schemes has declined after 1984-85. IFCI subsidised Rs. 23.51 lakhs in respect of 637 projects to various TCOs in 1983-84, which rose to Rs. 40.32 lakhs for 952 projects in 1984- 85. However, in 1985-86, all the TCOs together were given a subsidy of Rs. 37.28 lakhs in respect of 911 projects, the amount of subsidy and the number of projects both registering a decline. In 1986-87, the amount subsidised to various TCOs under IFCI's promotional schemes further declined to Rs. 30.05 lakhs, though the number of projects handled by TCOs increased to 1131. It has been already

pointed out that over 85% of the consultancy assignments handled by the TCOs relate to the preparation of feasibility/project reports, as a consequence of which, the consultancy fee subsidy scheme of IFCI for meeting cost of feasibility studies etc. is the singlemost scheme utilised by the TCOs the most, the subsidies availed under other schemes being very small. The conspicuous decline in the amount subsidised to the TCOs under IFCI's promotional schemes in the past two years may be attributed to the fact that maximumm limit for subsidy under the aforesaid IFCI's scheme for meeting cost of feasibility reports was reduced from Rs. 7500/- to Rs. 2700/- per assignment with effect from 1st August, 1985.

4. Out of 5180 industrial units benefited under IFCI's promotional schemes upto 30th June, 1987, 5175 units are those which have been given subsidies through TCOs. The remaining five units include four projects which were directy subsidised by IFCI under the schemes for encouraging adoption of indigenous technology and for developing technology through in-house R&D efforts,[6] and the one project of a woman entrepreneur in Maharashtra, to which an interest subsidy was given through the Bank of Maharashtra[7] in 1986-87. This implies that the role of State Financial Corporations (SFCs) and other state-level institutions like SIDCs/SIICs entrusted with the responsibility of serving as channels to operate the interest subsidy schemes of IFCI has been nil. The foregoing analysis conspicuously brings out the following revelation:

1. Though the promotional schemes of IFCI envisage grant of subsidies/assistance for undertaking a wide range of supportive measures for the promotion and growth of industries especially in the rural, tiny, small and ancillary sectors, yet, the institutions TCOs/SFCs through which they are operated at the state-level appear to be inadequate. The SFCs and other state- level institutions like SIDCs/SIICs in particular have

---

6 as has been discussed earlier in the chapter.

7 as per Operational Statistics, IFCI, 1987-88, p.75. (The conditions in the scheme for women entrepreneurs may be relaxed in special circumstances).

proved to be a wrong choice for operating some of the schemes.

2. All the promotional schemes of IFCI except one have been highly underutilised. It is worth noting that the scheme of subsidy for meeting cost of feasibility studies etc. under which over 85% of the aggregate amount subsidised by IFCI under its several promotional schemes has been availed by the TCOs, is general in nature, as the preparation of feasibility studies/ project reports is a pre-requisite in the process of identification, formulation and implementation of the industrial projects, whatever be their kind, to be undertaken by the prospective entrepreneurs. The other promotional schemes with more speci-fic objectives practically get defeated in their very purpose for which they have been formulated, if they remain bold only in concept and are availed only to an insignificant level, to the extent, that some of the schemes are yet to see an actual start.

   It is true, that for some of the schemes, it is premature to evaluate them or comment upon their efficacy, however, this excuse does not apply to all the schemes, for example, the scheme of interest subsidy for the unemployed young persons, which even after five years of its commissioning has failed to attract a single beneficiary. The channelisation of this scheme through the SFCs and other state-level agencies SIDCs and SIICs seems to be one of the reasons for such a stagnant situation. To be eligible to avail interest subsidy under this scheme, the unemployed young person must have been sanctioned and disbursed financial assistance by one of these institutions for meeting capital cost of the project. It is relevant to point out here that these institutions have their offices situated in few big cities of India which may not have an easy access to the unemployed youth from the rural and backward areas who wish to set up small projects of their own, may be a shop, trade or small scale industrial unit, for their self-employment. The institutional network of commercial and cooperative banks including the Regional Rural Banks can prove to be a better channel for implementation of this scheme. Usually it is these banking organisations to which the small entrepreneurs aspiring to create opportunities for self-employment approach to for their requirements of financial assistance.

Another requirement to become eligible for availing subsidy under this scheme is that the unemployed young person must have undergone a full course of EDP conducted by a TCO/ Specified Agency, and persuant to which the prospective entrepreneur must have got prepared a complete project report in consultation with the TCO/ Specified Agency. This eligibility criteria should be relaxed specially for those unemployed persons who already have knowledge and/or experience in the type of project they wish to set up, or whose prospective projects are not technical in nature like a shop, trade or service unit, if this scheme is to become more attractive.

Similar eligibility requirements of financial assistance been sanctioned and disbursed by SFCs or SIDCs/SIICs and successful completion of EDP course hold true in case of scheme of interest subsidy for women entrepreneurs also. It has already been discussed that SFCs etc. have proved to be inappropriate channels for operating these schemes. The requirement of accomplishing through the EDP course also needs careful consideration in relation to the women entrepreneurs in India. If the objective is to create avenues of self-development and self-employment for few elite women of metropolis in India, there is nothing to object to. But if the task seeks to involve the near-half the total population of the country of women, belonging to the over 70% of the backward areas of the country, such scheme is nothing more than a jumble of words. In accordance with one of the objectives of IFCI's Promotional Schemes, which seeks to ensure a better deal to the women and weaker sections of the society in consonance with the national policies[8] if any promotional scheme exclusively for women is formulated so as to provide them incentive to exploit their entrepreneurial traits, it should be conceived as a part of an integrated programme for creating employment opportunities for women, and not just as an isolated scheme. In-village training programmes to create

8 As has been spelt out in the objectives of IFCI's Promotional Schemes, p.3 of Promotional Schemes, IFCI, 1986.,

development consciousness and arouse interest in women for self-development and self-employment should be organised as the first step. The educated women interested in taking up small industrial projects may be imparted formal training through EDPs conducted by TCOs and other institutions, which may also be organised exclusively for women.[9] Rural and cottage industries, traditional handicrafts and village industries linked to agricultural products are other industrial activities which should be collectively organised for the women from rural and backward areas. Suitable incentives in the form of subsidies/assistance/supportive measures etc. will then have to be offered by the financial and developmental institutions to encourage women to take up such activities.

Several other subsidy schemes of IFCI, for example, Schemes for revival and rehabilitation of sick units, for providing marketing assistance, for implementing modernisation programmes etc. in the tiny, small-scale and ancillary sectors have remained highly underutilised, and the reason for this could be partly due to the fact that there has been duplication of similar schemes offered by IDBI.[10] In May, 1986, IDBI set up Small Industries Development Fund (SIDF) exclusively for the development, expansion, modernisation, diversification and rehabilitation of the small-scale, tiny, village and cottage sectors to serve as the apex focal point to coordinate the availability of both financial and non-financial inputs required for the orderly and healthy growth of this sector in the country.[11] In fulfilment of these objectives, IDBI liberalised the existing schemes and introduced several new schemes[12] as measures to increase the

9 In recent years, many TCOs like RAJCON, HARICON, MPCON, APITCO, KITCO etc. have organised EDPs exclusively for women entrepreneurs.

10 IDBI's Refinance Scheme offers assistance for rehabilitation of sick units, marketing support schemes and for modernisation of small-scale industrial units.

11 IDBI, Annual Reports, 1985-86, p.59, 1986-87, p.51.

12 New Schemes include:
  i) Package of assistance exclusively to women entrepreneurs.
  ii) Concessional assistance to existing and new SSI units going in for in-house quality testing facilities and
  iii) Scheme of resource support to SSIDCs to enable them to finance the marketing operations of SSI units and other activities like raw material distribution and extension services. IDBI, Annual Report, 1986-87 pp.54-55.

quantum of assistance to this sector.

Consequent to these developments on one hand, and the unsatisfactory level of operations of the existing package of IFCI's promotional schemes on the other, IFCI has recently made extensive reviews of its promotional schemes.[13] The existing promotional schemes have been liberalised for the benefit of entrepreneurs in North-Eastern Region and in Sikkim. Ex-servicemen and repatriates from Sri Lanka have been considered as preferred categories for similar benefits as available under various schemes to SC/ST and physically handicapped entrepreneurs. In an effort to reduce duplication of schemes, it has been decided to dispense with three schemes, viz., Subsidy Schemes for revival of sick units and for implementing modernisation programmes of tiny, small scale and ancillary units, which have been taken up by IDBI on a much wider scale, and, Assistance Scheme for development of technology through in house R&D efforts, as a similar scheme of Technology Finance has been introduced by the Risk Capital and Technology Finance Corporation Ltd. (RCTC). In addition to this, three new consultancy fee subsidy schemes[14] have been introduced which relate to:

i) activities like animal husbandry, dairy farming, poultry farming and fishing;
ii) industries based on or related to agriculture, horticulture, sericulture and pisciculture and
iii) use of non-conventional source of energy and energy conservation measures.

Also, the eligibility criteria of some of the existing schemes have been revised, for example, the requirement of completion of EDP course in case of only women entrepreneurs[15] has been relaxed, and for operating interest subsidy schemes for unemployed young persons and for women entrepreneurs, a major relaxation has been given by way of incorporating banks as one

---

13 The schemes have been reviewed in December 1987, and the revised promotional schemes of IFCI have become operative from 1st July, 1988.

14 IFCI, Promotional Schemes, July, 1988.

15 For unemployed men, completion of EDP course is still essential to be eligible for availing subsidy under the scheme.

of the specified institutions alongwith SFCs/SIICs whose loans would qualify for the interest subsidy to be passed on to the entrepreneurs.[16]

It is expected that the recent liberalising of the eligibility requirements of some of the existing schemes would make them more attractive so as to benefit a wider cross-section of the prospective entrepreneurs especially those who want to set up industrial ventures in the rural tiny and small scale sectors. The impact of new schemes for providing consultancy services devised for industries related to animal breeding, dairy and poultry farming, fishing, agriculture and horticulture etc. is awaited. These are the activities which are closely related to each other as well as to the agricultural set-up of the rural and backward areas, and therefore can provide positive encouragement to the entre-preneurs from these areas to take up such ventures more conveniently. What is needed to support this is a more committed and concerted effort to carry out implementation of these schemes by the financial and promotional institutions at the state and district level.

16 This relaxation is not applicable to the other two interest subsidy schemes for encouraging adoption of indigenous technology and quality control measures. It is desirable to remove such inconsistencies and extend similar provisions to other schemes as well, if their benefits are to reach those entrepreneurs for whom they are meant.

12

Promotion of Research and Development

Probably every gift of modern age, whether material, financial, social or educational etc., owes its existence to an unending zeal for research and development in its own area. In the field of search and research in disciplines relating to development banking, financial and industrial management and other allied areas, IFCI's contribution has been in more than one ways as a part of its promotional role.

Reasearch Studies:

IFCI has provided funds support to a number of research projects connected with the promotion of industrialisation in various areas undertaken by the consultancy organisations, national and state level developmental agencies or financial institutions. Some of the prominent Research Studies funded by IFCI are mentioned here below:

— Study of oilseeds processing industry: Undertaken during 1975-78, in response to a suggestion from the World Bank, the study provided useful material concerned with the oilseeds production and processing industry in India regarding not only the major oilseeds like groundnut, rapeseed, mustard, sesamum, linseed and castor but also non-traditional source of vegetable oil, as cotton seeds, rice-bran, sunflower and soyabean.

— Study of standardised 1,250 tonnes capacity per day of sugar plants: Commissioned by IFCI, the study of standardised 1250 tonnes capacity per day of sugar plants capable of expansion to 2000 tonnes capacity per day, suggested improvements in the design of plant and equipment to optimise energy use and conserve baggasse for other applications. The study, completed by National Productivity Council in 1983-84, provided useful data on sugar plant specifications to improve energy productivity, technical practices and economic viability of standard sugar plants, which had been passed on to the Technical Committee of Government of India for consideration.

— Study on management of turn around of sick industrial projects: The study, sponsored and funded by all-India financial institutions, including IFCI, and undertaken by IIM, Ahmedabad, provides useful clues to managements of sick enterprises as also to the financial institutions which have a big stake in such units as to how to revive them and formulate policies for their take-over and management.

— Study on manpower plan for industries and strategy for local people participation: The study, sponsored and funded by all-India financial institutions including IFCI, and undertaken by Gujarat TCO (GITCO) provides an insight into the manpower needs and problems of industries in developing areas, particularly the three category B, backward districts of Bharuch, Panchmahals and Surendra Nagar in Gujarat, which have over 2000 small scale sector industrial units. Based on the study, the manpower plans provide ways to ensure effective fulfilment of industry needs and enlarge local people involvement in employment generation.

These are the examples of a few Research Studies, related to industrial development in respective fields, that have been funded by IFCI. Apart from providing funds support to such studies, IFCI has also instituted four IFCI Research Fellowships for carrying out research work in the field of development banking, industrial economics, financial and industrial management and regional economics.

IFCI Chairs:

The Benevolent Reserve Fund, created in 1972, made it possible for IFCI to utilise the same for certain specified purposes, one of which was creation of Chairs in Universities, academic institutions and research foundations with the objective of promotion of research in the field of management and development banking. Over the years IFCI has built up good nexus with the Universities and Management Institutes by creating six Chairs for promoting research in specified areas.

The first Chair was set up in 1974 in the Indian Institute of Management, Ahmedabad, in the field of 'Industrial and Financial Management & Development Banking' and thereafter five more Chairs were set up at the Universities of Delhi, Bombay, Calcutta, Guwahati and Madras.

The Chairs created by IFCI envisage that IFCI Professors, in addition to their normal functions, would guide and conduct the research in their field of specialisation and deliver an Annual Public Lecture related to their subject of specialisation and research. Over the years, some very useful research work has been done, and is being done, under the auspices of IFCI Chairs,[1] based on which the IFCI Professors have delivered lectures on topics of considerable interest to the academicians, economists, administrators, bankers and public at large. Some of these have been published by IFCI in the form of a compendium for the reference and benefit of research scholars, econo-mists and development bankers.

The progress of research work under IFCI's Chair at the Calcutta University has been rather slow on account of disturbed political conditions. At the Madras University also, the IFCI Chair, though established in April 1982, remained unoccupied till April 1986. Most of the research projects under IFCI Chair, Madras University (mentioned in Appendix I) are under way. It is expected that under the able guidance of Chair Professors, research activities under all six IFCI Chairs would gain momentum in the years to come.

IFCI Silver Jubilee Memorial Lectures:

IFCI completed 25 years of its service to Indian industry in 1973. To commemorate the Silver Jubilee of IFCI, it was decided to institute IFCI Silver Jubilee Memorial Lectures to be delivered every year by a distinguished development banker. The objective was to build up expertise and professional literature in the field of development banking, provide an opportunity to focus attention on the complex problems confronting the development banks and augment the fund of experience of the development

1 This is given in Annexure 12.1 at the end of ths chapter.

bankers operating in different countries.[2]

The various development finance institutions all over differ in structure and experiences. They are conditioned to different political, economic and social setting under which they have been set up. The problems of development also differ significantly from country to country. However, in spite of these inherent difference, their goal is the same, namely, to eradicate poverty and provide better and higher standards of living. It is this common interest which brings the various development financing institutions the world over together and it is natural, therefore, that they explore avenues to share their experience and professional expertise. The institution of IFCI Silver Jubilee Memorial Lectures has provided a forum for the development bankers to share their thought and experiences with their counterparts in this country.

Since 1973, ten lectures have been delivered in this series till 1987 by eminent development bankers.[3] On the completion of a decade of IFCI's Silver Jubilee, a compendium of the professional literature provided by these lectures was published by IFCI in 1984 for the benefit of the development bankers, academicians, research scholars and authorities connected with the formulation of developmental and promotional policies.

Cumulatively upto to June, 1987, IFCI has utilised Rs. 44.91 lakhs out of its Benevolent Reserve Fund for the promotion of research studies, IFCI Chairs, which also includes the contributions made to the VIII World Economic Congress, Indian Economic Journal and Conference on Research and Information Systems for the non-aligned and other developing countries.

The activities of IFCI mentioned hitherto are mostly of academic interest and research oriented in nature. The success of such work from the nations' point of the view depends largely to the extent to which it provides a useful content for the policy makers to devise more effective strategies for tackling the practical problems of development and enhancing skill and

---

2 Quoted from the 'Foreword' by Sh. D.N. Davar, from Search Light on Development Banking, IFCI Publication, 1984.

3 Refer to Annexure 12.2 at the end of this chapter.

efficiency in industry. Most of the research work and innovations in the field of development banking and industry would practically remain as the epitomes of pure academics unless they are suitably exploited by the decision-makers for industrial advancement of the country.

Funding of Special Assignments:

IFCI has also been sharing from time to time, on case to case basis, the consultancy cost of special assignments relating to the feasibility studies, project reports, market surveys, techno-economic surveys, project profiles, industrial potential surveys, research studies etc. sponsored and/or undertaken by the Consultancy Organisations, and various other national and state-level developmental and financial institutions engaged in the promotion of industrialisation in their respective areas, in participation with other institutions, where these can not be subsidised under the existing promotional schemes of IFCI.

Some of the research studies funded by IFCI, alongwith other financial institutions, have already been mentioned. Of the other special assignments which IFCI has funded in an agreed proportion with other institutions, mention may be made of the following:[4]

1) Industrial potential surveys and project profiles in respect of six districts of Bihar, i.e. Bhagalpur, Darbhanga, Samastipur, Begusarai, Madhubani and Purnea, undertaken by the Bihar Industrial & Technical Consultancy Organisation Ltd. (BITCO).
2) Hundred project profiles in the small and medium scale sector as downstream to Haldia Petro-Chemical Complex prepared by West Bengal Consultancy Organisation Ltd. (WEBCON).
3) Assignment relating to the establishment of a Functional Ceramics Industrial Complex in the Bankura Distt. West Bengal by WEBCON.
4) Techno-economic survey of Purulia district in West Bengal by Jadavpur University.

---

4 IFCI, Promotional Activities, 1984, p. 36.

5) Assignment relating to the establishment of two functional industrial complexes, viz. Agro Products Complex and Leather Complex in Chindwara and Dewas districts respectively, undertaken by Madhya Pradesh Consultancy Organisation Ltd. (MPCON).

6) Studies relating to electronics industry and mineral resources in Himachal Pradesh, carried out by Himachal Consultancy Organisation Ltd. (HIMCON).

7) Economic survey of Tamil Nadu by Tata Economic Consultancy Services.

8) Industrial potential surveys for ancillary development in automobiles and chemical group of industries, and preparation of 50 project profiles for the benefit of the prospective entrepreneurs in Tamilnadu, undertaken by Industrial and Technical Consultancy Organisation of Tamilnadu Ltd. (ITCOT).

9) Sectoral study for the purpose of industrialisation of Kota-Chittorgarh broad gauge rail line area, undertaken by Rajasthan Consultancy Organisation Ltd. (RAJCON).

10) Industrial potential surveys of 4 districts in Haryana viz. Mohindergarh, Hissar, Bhiwani and Jind, undertaken by National Industrial Development Corporation (NIDC).

Thus, in addition to providing funds support under various promotional schemes, IFCI has also been sharing the consultancy cost of such special assignments as mostly relating to carrying out of techno-economic surveys of backward districts or preparing project profiles for the industrial projects that could be profitably undertaken in the less-developed areas of the country. This is a modest effort on the part of IFCI to bridge the gap in the funds needed by TCOs and other developmental and financial institutions for carrying out promotional work for the industrial development of backward areas.

Annexure 12.1

Topics of Research Work done under IFCI Chairs:

In IIM Ahmedabad:

— Structural and control problems in Credit Administration.

— Determinants of Effective Working Capital Management.

— Problems in Promotion and Financing of New Projects.

— Success and Sickness of New Projects.

— Financial Behaviour of Growth Companies.

— The Sugar Economy: A cobweb of Policies.

— Predicting Corporate Sickness The case of Indian Textile Industry.

— Valuation of Securities and influence of value on Financial Decisions of a firm.

— Economic Performance of the Ancillary Industry in India; Managerial and Policy Implications.

— Human Resource Development and Organisation Development in a large organisation.

— Some Aspects of Financing and Pricing of Sugar Industry in India.

— Some Issues of Project Appraisal and Bank Lending in India.

— Some Aspects of Credit Planning in India.

— Flow of Bank Funds and Balanced Regional Development in India.

— Investment Behaviour in Automobile Industry.

— Financial Implications of Capitalisation of Interest on long term borrowings, and some Accounting Practices.

— Managing Productivity of Corporate Capital: A New Approach to its Measurement.

In Bombay University:

— Market for Government Securities in India.

— Some Issues of Industrial Policy and Finance in India.

— Off-shore Banking in India.

— A study of New Capital Issues in India and abroad.

— Merchant Banking in India.

— Financial Institutions and the Problem of Regional Imbalances in India.

— Development Banking and Economic Development of Backward Areas: Some case studies and evaluation.

— Socio-Economic Impact of Development Finance Institutions' Assistance to Cooperatives in Maharashtra with special reference to Sugar Industry.

— Lease Finance in India.

— Some aspects of Banking Policy in India.

In Delhi University:

— Design and Development of Information Systems for Development Banks A Systems Approach.

— Lead Industry Strategy for Developing Backward Areas.

— Information Systems for Investment Decisions in Backward Areas.

— Human Resource Development: Role of Technology.

— Management of Productivity in Jute and Mini-Steel Industry.

In Calcutta University:

— Behaviour of Capital Output Ratios and its Causative Influence on Sickness in Light Engineering Industry in West Bengal.

In Guwahati University:

— The role of Development Banking in North-East India.

— Role of Small-Scale Industries in Economic Development of North-East India.

— Rural Development Programmes and Role of Commercial Banks: A study on North-Eastern India.

In Madras University:

— Role of Development Banks in the Indian Capital Markets.

— Project Risk Analysis by Development Banks.

— Promotional Role of Tamilnadu Small Industries Development Corporation Ltd. (SIDCO).

— Evaluation of Chit Fund Schemes.

— Funds Management in Development Banks.

Source: IFCI, Promotional Activities, 1984, p. 38-39 and Annual Reports of IFCI, 1983-84 to 1987-88.

Annexure 12.2

Series of IFCI's Silver Jubilee Memorial Lectures

1. New Aspects of Development Banking by Mr. Hans Erich Bachem, Member, Board of Management, KFW, Federal Republic of Germany, (1973).
2. The Interplay between Financial Institutions and Economic Development by Mr. William Diamond, the then Director, South Asia Department, International Bank for Reconstruction and Development, Washington (1974).
3. The Development Bank in a Fast Developing Economy by Mr. A.G. Kheradjou, Managing Director, Industrial and Mining Development Bank of Iran (1975).
4. Development Banking in Latin America: The Role and Experience of IDB by Mr. Antonio Ortiz Mena, President, Inter-American Development Bank (IDB), Washington (1976).
5. Development Banks: A Growing Role by Mr. C.S. Krishnamoorthi, Vice President, Asian Development Bank, Manila (1977).
6. The International Capital and Credit Markets and the Developing Countries by Rt. Hon. Lord Roll of Ipsden (Retd. Chancellor of University of Southampton) (1979).
7. Rising Oil Prices Their Impact on Developing Countries by Mr. H. D. Krukenberg, Head: Main Department for Asia/ Oceania of KFW, Federal Republic of Germany (1981).
8. Industrialisation under Capital Constraints by Mr. Masao Fujioka, President, Asian Development Bank (1983).
9. Relationship between the Government and Private Sector the Japanese Experience by Mr. Isamu Miyazaki, Chairman, Daiwa Securities Research Institute, Tokyo, Japan (1984).
10. Financial Policy for Economic Development by Mr. Sung Sang Park, Governor, Bank of Korea (1987).

Note: The eleventh lecture in this series was recently held on 5th December, 1988, on Central Banking in an era of change by Shri Tan Sri Dato' Jaffar Hussein, Governor, Bank Negara, (Central Bank of Malaysia).

13

Merchant Banking Services: An emerging catalytic role of IFCI

With the background of experience for more than three and a half decades in the field of industrial finance and development banking, it was in 1982 that IFCI was authorised to undertake merchant banking operations. In 1986, with an amendment made to IFC Act, 1948, the scope of the merchant banking services of IFCI was further elaborated by including consultancy services and allowing its merchant banking operations to be carried out both in and outside India.

In its role as a catalyst for industrial growth, IFCI entered the merchant banking business with effect from 1st July, 1986, by setting up a Merchant Banking Division at New Delhi and subsequently, a Merchant Banking Bureau at Bombay. To serve the industrial community, the endeavour of IFCI is to act not just as an ordinary merchant banker, but as an institution, which understands the needs and requirements of the promoters and entrepreneurs on one hand, and the financial institutions, banks, stock exchanges and money markets on the other.

The accent of merchant banking operations of IFCI, besides rendering issue management services, is on providing a package of facilities, particularly to medium, medium-large and large-scale enterprises in the corporate sector, which need special assistance or guidance in the formulation and implementation of new projects of modernisation/diversification of their existing activities, as also in mobilising requisite financial resources for their block and working capital requirements.

The wide variety of merchant banking and advisory services offered by IFCI can be broadly categorised as follows:

1. Management of public issues and securities:

The services for managing issues of shares and debentures, whether by way of public issue, rights issue or private placement include:

— advice on designing a sound capital structure acceptable to the banks and financial institutions,
— assistance in obtaining consents from Controller of Capital Issues, appointment of bankers, brokers and underwriters, and their coordination with stock exchanges,
— preparation of budget for total expenses of the issues,
— drafting of prospectus, assisting in advertising campaigns, holding the press, brokers, investors conferences and preparing of complete action plan for grooming the issue etc.

2. Project Counselling:

The Merchant Banking Division of IFCI also offers guidance in relation to project viability, techno-economic soundness and organisational, managerial and marketing aspects of the project. It also advises on capital structuring and financial engineering, i.e., selecting the right mix of financing pattern, as also in selecting consultants for preparation of project reports and market surveys. The promoters are also assisted in complying with various procedural steps, e.g. obtaining clearances and Government approvals in relation to the project.

3. Credit Syndication:

Such services cover monitoring the pre and post sanction negotiations/liaison with financial institutions and banks for financial assistance in rupee and/or foreign currencies as term loans or for working capital requirements and assisting in the completion of legal documentation.

4. Consultancy to ailing/sick industrial units:

The Merchant Banking Division of IFCI also offers corporate counselling for the financial reconstruction and technical rehabilitation of old and sick industrial units on a tailor-made basis. The Division assists such units in locating areas/activities of growth and diversification, appraise and assess their requirements for restructuring technology and capital base, evolve rehabilitation programmes and explore possibilities for mergers or amalgamations wherever called for. The units are also assisted in obtaining approvals from the concerned authorities and in the implementation of the approved schemes of rehabilitation, mergers and/or amalgamations so as to push them out of industrial sickness.

15. Other allied services:

The allied services offered by the merchant banking division may cover services to the non-resident Indians for suitable investment opportunities in India, assistance in the negotiations of foreign collaborations and advice on leasing, equipment finance, technology finance and venture capital.

During the first year of its operation, IFCI's Merchant Banking Division successfully managed 12 public issues and had with it as on the 30th June, 1987, mandates from 32 companies for managing their public issues in the near future.

Merchant banking is a specialised financial function, a function of expertise in managing public issues of securities. To this, IFCI has added a promotional touch by offering consultancy and advisory services in relation to project counselling, credit management and assistance to sick industrial units. Such supportive avtivities though are not directly related to the objective of industrial advancement of backward areas in the country in particular, but certainly endeavour to fulfil some rapidly growing needs and requirements of the industry as a whole.

14

Summary & Suggestions

Industrial Finance Corporation of India (IFCI) has been the pioneer national development bank of the country, set up in 1948, with the objective of providing medium and long term capital funds to eligible industrial enterprises. The present operations of IFCI can be broadly grouped under two heads, namely, project financing operations and promotional activities.

The accent of this study has been on the 'promotional role of IFCI in the development of backward areas'. Therefore, in the background of the exercise of identification of backward areas in the country, the study has assessed (i) the qualitative aspect of IFCI's project financing operations reflected in the assistance given to projects set up in backward regions, and (ii) the various promotional activities undertaken by IFCI as supportive measures to improve the productivity of human and material resources and accelerate the process of industrialisation in its multi-faceted form.

The important findings and conclusions of the study are summarised herebelow:

IFCI's Assistance to Backward Areas:

Successive Five Year Plans have placed increasing emphasis on the development of backward areas and reducing regional imbalances, yet there had been no methodic approach towards this problem, and as such, the share of backward areas in the total financial assistance sanctioned by all-India development banks, including IFCI, was merely about 25% in pre - 1970 period. The first systematic endeavour to identify backward areas and introduce several fiscal and financial incentives for their industrial development was made only in 1969 as a result of the recommendations of Pande and Wanchoo Working Groups. These efforts have given an impetus to the flow of industrial finance to projects in backward areas, as their share in total sanctions by all-India development banks has gone up from 25-

30% in pre - 1970 period to 40-45% during 1983-87. IFCI's financial assistance to projects in backward areas which was a meagre 26% of its total sanctions in pre - 1970 period more than doubled to 54.4% in post- 1970 period.

Despite this, out of 412 districts in the country of which 301 are declared backward, IFCI's cumulative assistance of Rs. 2109.87 crores (52.2% of the total sanctions) has been spread over 1184 projects (46.6% of total projects assisted) in 196 backward districts (BDs), leaving out 105 BDs yet to be covered under IFCI's assistance portfolio. The share of eight developed states is 46.2% and the least developed of the backward states like Assam, Himachal Pradesh, J&K, Orissa and Bihar together account for mere 8.7% of IFCI's assistance to backward areas. Only six states together have drawn 59% of IFCI's assistance to 666 projects in 93 BDs, the rest 41% to be shared by 518 projects in 103 BDs spread over remaining 19 states and 5 Union Territories.

Therefore, not only more than half of the projects assisted by IFCI claiming nearly half of its sanctions are located in areas not identified as backward, but also the distribution of IFCI's assistance to backward areas is highly uneven amongst different states, with unduly high proportions of assistance converging to projects in relatively developed states.

IFCI's Promotional Role:

While fiscal and financial incentives have their own role in activising efforts for industrialisation of backward areas, non-financial inputs like project-counselling and extension services, resourceful entrepreneurship, technical and managerial competence etc. become increasingly important to facilitate establishment of new projects in these areas. The "Promotional Activities" undertaken by IFCI since 1970s on its own or in collaboration with other development banks are an endeavour to identify industrial potential and project opportunities in such areas and create `entrepreneurial interests' for their implementation. These include the following:

1. Industrial Potential Surveys:

The first step of the promotional strategy of IFCI in collaboration with other financial institutions was to have "Industrial Potential Surveys" of backward states and Union Territoriries, which were completed by 1976-77. As a follow-up, the detailed surveys of backward areas, adpoting district as a unit, to identify industrial opportunities and the extent of infrastructural requirements have been initiated under the "Institutional Intensive Developmental Efforts Programme for NIDs". Out of 134 No-Industry Districts (NIDs)/Special Region Districts, surveys have been completed by 1987 only in respect of 45 NIDs.

2. Technical Consultancy Support:

Setting up a chain of Technical Consultancy Organisations (TCOs) in the country, jointly with other financial institutions, has been an important aspect of IFCI's promotional role towards fortifying institutional infrastructure for accelerated development of backward areas. The TCOs provide a total package of consultancy services to small and medium scale entrepreneurs from 'concept' to 'commissioning' of the projects. Over 23,000 consultancy assignments completed, of which more than 80% relate to projects in village and small industries (VSI) and ancillary sectors, coupled with 591 Entrepreneurship Development Programmes (EDPs) conducted which trained over 16,500 persons till June, 1987 do bear testimony to the thrust being built by the TCOs in developing a consultancy culture in the country. However, the assessment of the impact of such developmental efforts in terms of the proportion of project plans that have been translated into action reveals that on an average not more than one-third of the assignments involving investment, for which TCOs provided consultancy services, have actually been implemented into viable projects.[1] This underlines the need to find out ways for improvement and extension in the TCOs' services.

3. Risk Capital Assistance:

To encourage technologists and professionals and develop them into first generation entrepreneurs, IFCI sponsored Risk Capital

1 Refer to Chap. 6.

Foundation (RCF) in 1975 to provide them Risk Capital Assistance. Upto December, 1987, RCF assisted 234 promoters for setting up 137 projects with total project cost of Rs. 611.31 crores and employment potential for about 33,000 persons. About 80% of the projects whose promoters have received RCF's assistance are located in the declared backward areas. With the recent thrust on technology upgradation and development, RCF now known as RCTC (Risk Capital and Technology Finance Corporation Ltd.), has introduced the "Scheme of Technology Finance" and also revised the existing scheme of risk capital assistance under which, henceforth, assistance would normally be granted to high-tech ventures or projects manufacturing new products for new usages and markets. In its new role, RCTC is expected to strengthen technological entrepreneurial base in the country, but may latently disappoint many deserving entrepreneurs contemplating projects in the conventional manufacturing industries.

4. Upgradation of Managerial Skills:

For the cause of enriching human capital and upgrading managerial skills, IFCI set up Management Development Institute (MDI) in 1973 and its wing Development Banking Centre (DBC) in 1977. MDI and DBC have conducted 794 management development programmes upto June, 1987, relating to finance, marketing, technical, personnel and other functions for the entrepreneurs and executives of industry and development finance institutions. MDI has come a long way since 1973, yet no systematic series of training programmes have been devised for the small entrepreneurs of relatively less-developed areas, who as much need technical and managerial expertise as their urban counterparts. The programmes like "Identification, Promotion and Implementation of Industrial Projects (IPIIP)" and "Training the Trainers"[2] need to be taken up by institutions like MDI in a big way to decentralise the pool of technical and managerial skills for the benefit of entrepreneurs from industrially backward areas.

---

2 Refer to Chap. 8.

5. Development of Entrepreneurship:

IFCI's support for entrepreneurship development has been by

(i) giving preference to financing the projects promoted by new and technician entrepreneurs,

(ii) providing funds support to the TCOs and other specified agencies for conducting EDPs and

(iii) assisting in the establishment of EDP Centres at the national and regional level, like Entrepreneurship Development Institute of India (EDII), Ahmedabad, Institutes of Entrepreneurship Development (IEDs) at Lucknow, Patna, and Bhubaneshwar, and Science and Technology Entrepreneurs' Parks (STEPs) at Ranchi, Bombay, Tiruchirapalli and Kanpur.

Most of the entrepreneurial development activities, however, are in nascent stage, and the success of these efforts depends upon the extent to which the young technocrats explore and exploit opportunities to become fledgling entrepreneurs in the industrial horizon of the country on one hand, and the educated/skilled unemployed youth of relatively less-developed areas find avenues for small-scale self-employment ventures on the other, which could elevate their position from "job-seekers" to "job-givers".

6. Rural Development:

IFCI's assistance to industrial cooperatives has helped in developing rural scenario by inducing promotion of a number of ancillary and associate industries, creating opportunities for direct and indirect employment and uplifting the rural economy. Upto June 1987, IFCI assisted 301 industrial cooperatives (of which 200 are located in six developed states, with 108 units in Maharashtra alone) with Rs. 379.43 crores, which is 9.4% of its cumulative sanctions. As industrial cooperatives are mostly agro-based and provide good nexus between agriculture and industry, they deserve a better deal in the assistance portfolio of development banks, ensuring at the same time, a wider dispersal of the benefits to the less-developed areas. To give impetus to rural industrialisation efforts with focus on the development of

VSI sector, it is necessary that the national development banks like IFCI, extend their financial and promotional support for establishing EDP Centres in rural areas and reinforcing the efforts of state and regional level institutions in providing finance, infrastructure and other facilities to small-scale units in these areas.

7. Promotional Schemes:

IFCI operates several promotional schemes to help the entrepreneurs in the VSI and ancillary sectors. The analysis of the subsidies/ assistance disbursed under these schemes reveals that:

i) Except for Scheme of Consultancy Fee Subsidy for meeting cost of Feasibility Studies etc., all other schemes have remained highly under-utilised,

(ii) Subsidies have been granted under three schemes only for the first time in 1986-87 and three schemes are yet to make a headway and

(iii) State Financial Corporations (SFCs) and State Industrial Development/Investment Corporations (SIDCs/SIICs) have been inappropriate channels to operate the Interest Subsidy Schemes.[3]

Though it is premature to comment on the efficacy of several schemes which have been started only recently, it is imperative to relax eligibility criteria in some cases to make them more attractive to entrepreneurs in VSI sector for whom they are meant.

8. Other Activities:

Some other promotional activities of IFCI include:

(i) Sharing the cost of research studies, market and techno-economic surveys etc. undertaken by consultancy organisations, financial and developmental agencies,

(ii) Publication of "Directory of Industrial Consultants" jointly with IDBI and ICICI for the benefit of entrepreneurs,

---

3 Refer to Chap. 11.

(iii) Creation of IFCI Chairs in six Universities for promoting research in the field of management and development banking,

(iv) Organising IFCI Silver Jubilee Memorial Lectures providing a forum for the development bankers from different countries to share their experience, thought and professional expertise and

(v) Merchant Banking Services to medium and large scale corporate enterprises.

Undoubtedly, these activities are not particularly addressed to the industrial advancement of backward areas, but do fulfil some rapidly growing needs of industry in the competitive national and international environment.

In essence it can be said that,

i) Only about half of IFCI's cumulative financial assistance, as a part of its project financing operations, has gone to projects in backward areas; its distribution has been disproportionate, the important beneficiaries being the developed states.

ii) IFCI's promotional activities introduced during the last decade and a half can best be regarded as a modest beginning in initiating to create "development consciousness" in the less-developed areas; and need manifold proliferation at the regional level to accelerate the process of industrialisation in the country.

This disproportionate allocation of resources for development and the slow pace in creating development consciousness may be attributed to the following:

Anomaly of Criterion for backwardness:

The fact that the benefits of concessional finance and other incentives for backward area development have converged over the years to few backward districts favouring the relatively developed states owes one of the reasons in the built-in bias in favour of BDs of developed states right from the stage when backward areas were identified in 1969. The adoption of "State Averages" as the criterion for declaring a district backward led to the anomalous classification of backward areas in as much as certain districts of developed states classified as "backward" were far more developed than the "developed" districts of backward states. In other words, some of the districts of backward states which were in fact much more backward than the so-called "backward" districts of developed states were excluded from the list of BDs.

The result was that some of the backward states like Bihar, Orissa, Rajasthan were able to get lesser percentage of their districts declared backward as compared to some of the developed states like West Bengal, Tamil Nadu and Gujarat, the top three states according to Pande Index. Inevitably, the backward districts of relatively developed states have been able to corner most of the finance meant for backward areas as a whole.

Constraints of Industrial and Social Infrastructure:

The tendency for larger capital inflow to backward areas of developed states was further accentuated by the difference in the level of general amenities as between the developed and backward states. The developed states could comparatively offer better industrial infrastructure facilities in terms of roads, transport, communications, power, industrial sheds etc., and therefore, the entrepreneurs preferred to set up their industrial projects in the less-developed areas of relatively developed states rather than in those of backward states. Another plausible explanation for this trend lies in the fact that an industrialist seeking a site for his project will not only evaluate the area in terms of purely economic factors and availability of industrial infrastructure, but also from the point of view of its endowment of such amenities as good housing, education, shopping and entertainment facilities, i.e. the social infrastructure. Since entrepreneurs, managerial staff and key workers of modern industries are those who are highly skilled and highly paid personnel who can afford to have strong preferences for a pleasant environment, it would be difficult to attract them to an area unless it can offer good social amenities. An area with a retarded level of industrial and social infrastructure is unattractive for setting up industrial ventures, whatever the financial incentives offered, and the resultant gravitation of industrial activity to developed areas aggravates regional disparities.

Nascent Entrepreneurial Culture:

Besides inadequate infrastructure, there are several other constraints in the location and development of industry in backward areas. High incidence of poverty, illiteracy and unemployment are some of the root level problems of such areas. Further, lack of an industrial culture as reflected in dearth of technical and managerial skills, a near-absence of entrepreneurial climate and narrow linkage with supporting activities like marketing etc. acting in a vicious circle have perpetuated for so long and so deep in the backward areas that no amount of fiscal and financial incentives alone can bring success in industrialisation efforts unless coupled with multifarious catalytic and promotional activities; and even such developmental efforts, howsoever well conceived, are not likely to yield tangible results in a short time span. The only immediate satisfaction that could be derived is from creating an awareness of the development prospects which could urge the people to make endeavour to correct the prevailing pattern of industrial imbalances and backwardness.

Regional Disparities of Resource Endowment:

A basic limitation with the whole approach to industrial development of backward areas so far appears to be the underlying concept of treating this problem more from a techno-economic angle, without giving due regard to the inter and intra regional variations in resource-endowment, available infrastructure facilities and development potential. All regions may not be equally endowed, equally prepared and equally respond to the emerging challenges of the process of industrialisation. Hence, a general set of incentives, concessions and subsidies, conceived from a macro angle, can not be extended to be operative throughout the country evenly without creating distortions. It would be difficult to narrow down regional disparities of development unless the resources to be provided and the programmes to be taken up in each area are determined on the basis of local assessment of problems, resources and productive potential.

To expedite the pace of industrial development of backward areas as also to enhance the efficacy and effectiveness of IFCI's on-going promotional efforts, following measures may be considered:

1. The high correlation between availability of physical and social infrastructure and industrialisation necessitates adoption of "growth centre approach" for promoting industrial development of backward areas. While it is necessary to persuade setting up of new industries away from the existing centres to ensure industrial dispersal, it is equally important that the new centres to be developed must be of sufficient size so as to reap the economies of agglomeration. Given the limited economic resources, the strategy of developing growth centres with adequate infrastructure facilities to act as seats of "decentralised concentration" of medium and large industries which could generate sufficient linkages to promote and sustain industrial development of backward areas, has been aptly advocated for a long time. In 1981, National Committee on Development of Backward Areas (NCDBA) recommended 100 such centres to be selected for development in the Sixth Plan. A much delayed decision has been recently taken by the Government[4] for developing 100 growth centres, to begin with throughout the country over the next about 5 years. It is sincerely hoped that this is implemented as a time-bound programme.
2. The impact of close link between urbanisation and industrialisation is that big cities which are already crowded and congested continue to attract large and medium industries. It is, as such, suggested that a system of disincentives be introduced as a device to dissuade establishment of industries near the urban centres.
3. Licensing Policy may also help in achieving the desired objective by restricting issue of industrial licenses for estab-

4 Through press-note dated 3.6.1988, details of which are given in Appendix II at the end.

lishment of industrial units near urban centres and exempting from the obligation of obtaining licenses those projects which could serve as nucleus plants for promoting ancillary units in backward areas.[5]

4. The all-India Financial Institutions should decide as a policy matter that one out of two medium and large projects assisted by them, if not more, should be located in backward areas. Institutions like RCTC which provide risk capital assistance up to 50% of the promoters contribution to the equity of the project may raise this limit for entrepreneurs setting up their projects in backward areas. Such concessions should be available to industries coming up in the growth centres as well.

5. While due to infrastructural requirements, it is prudent to promote large and medium industries at growth centres, and the number of such growth centres to be developed will necessarily have to be limited within a specific plan period to achieve concrete results, there need be no such restriction on a wide spread growth of small-scale industries to promote industrialisation in the entire backward areas. It is more in the context of small-scale industries (SSI) sector that the promotional efforts of financial institutions like IFCI assume significance to bring out latent entrepreneurial talents and provide them the requisite guidance, assistance, training and other services. For convenience in discussion, the small industries may be broadly grouped as traditional and non-traditional industries.

6. The traditional handicrafts and village and cottage industries like handloom, coir and silk products, ceramics, making of soaps, matches, chalks etc. which use local resources, more of traditional skills and little capital can provide suitable self-employment to rural households, artisans and craftsmen, relieving at the same time, dysfunctional pressure on urban areas due to migration of rural work force to seek work in urban industrial sector. The village entrepreneur, however,

5 Through press-note dated 3.6.1988, Industrial Licensing System has also been liberalised to certain extent, details of which are given in Appendix II at the end.

is a highly dispersed production unit, producing so infinitely small quantity that an individual can not think of getting any technical, financial or marketing assistance on his own. The need is, therefore, to organise and integrate these units at the village or block level and extend them the much-needed support with regard to supply of raw materials, credit, marketing facilities and training in the concerned activity.

As it is impossible for a single organisation to take care of these diverse needs, the efforts for promoting rural industries have to be framed within a three-tier institutional structure. The responsibility for motivation of village entrepreneurs, in-village training and integration of local efforts with the resources essentially rests with the local organisations whose activities have to be closely linked to the regional and state-level financial and promotional agencies so that the rural produce could be made available where the consumer demand exists. The national/apex level institutions are expected to reinforce these developmental efforts with their financial and promotional support.

7. It is the development of ancillaries and small industries of non-traditional type in which the entrepreneurs can be trained to produce a wide spectrum of products[6] from automobile ancillaries, beverages, food products etc. to even sophisticated electronic instruments and equipment, both for indigenous markets and exports, that has the real potential of dispersing industrial activity to backward areas. As these areas suffer from a basic lack of entrepreneurial culture, any policy package for promoting small industries must incorporate three different but equally important ingredients:

   i) Entrepreneurship development,

   ii) Service infrastructure, providing facilities for factory sheds, repair and maintenance, raw material supply, marketing etc. and

   iii) Needs-based financing.

---

6 The number of items reserved for exclusive manufacture in the small-scale sector stood 835 at the end of January 1989. *Economic Survey*, 1988-89, Para 4.41.

8. Careful selection and training of small entrepreneurs under Entre-preneurship Development Programmes to equip them with basic technical, managerial and entrepreneurial skills is of paramount importance so that the projects set up by them are well-conceived technically, financially and economically and not such as would eventually tend to become sick/weak units.[7] Carrying EDP movement to the backward areas is a challenging task and requires innovativeness on the part of institutions working for entrepreneurship development in:

   i) Designing EDPs suited to different target groups in consonance with the type of industrial activity to be undertaken,

   ii) Setting up a network of training institutions with their branches at the district level and

   iii) Linking of such training centres to industrial estates for practical in-plant/on-the-job training.

9. The entrepreneurial development activities at the regional level would gain considerable momentum if the apex institutions like Management Development Institute and Entrepreneurship Development Institute of India undertake such programmes as 'Training the EDP trainers' on a wide scale. The TCOs, state level financial and promotional institutions and other accredited agencies for conducting EDPs should get a core group of personnel trained, who in turn can conduct EDPs for small entrepreneurs at the local level thus assuming the role of 'trainers'. The trainers should establish a good rapport with the organisations working at the village and block level which would act as 'linkage agencies' for pre-training motivation and identification of prospective entre-preneurs of the particular area and follow-up and feed back. This would help spread the EDP movement countrywide at a much faster rate and encourage entrepreneurs to not only get self-employed but also generate employment for few more persons.

---

7 The number of sick units in the portfolio of scheduled commercial banks as at the end of June 1987 stood at 1,59,938, of which an overwhelming number of 1,58,226 units belong to SSI sector. *Economic Survey*, 1988-89, Para 4.46.

10. The Technical Consultancy Organisations, jointly set up by all-India financial institutions as a part of their promotional activities, are a vital territorial link entrusted with heavy responsibilities of providing developmental consultancy to projects in small and medium sector including carrying out EDPs. There is a wide scope for improvement and extension in their services for effective implementation of the identified projects. It is suggested that branch offices of the TCOs/Consultancy Cells be opened in as many districts as possible, so that there could be close follow-up and monitoring of the projects to which TCOs have provided consultancy services. This is all the more needed in case of projects promoted by new and small entrepreneurs who lack adequate experience and require assistance and guidance at every stage of project execution. Further, Field Officers should be empanelled who should work in close association with the local organisations to conduct spot surveys and identify the needs and difficulties of the entrepreneurs. This kind of information can serve as a useful feedback to the TCOs to identify thrust areas for their services as well as to devise EDPs suited to the needs of the local entrepreneurs. Such an excercise would build a better nexus between training and placement in the EDPs conducted by the TCOs and likely to result in a higher percentage of trained entrepreneurs being able to set up viable industrial projects. Considering their immense promotional value, the TCOs deserve to be strengthened with larger financial resources and greater promotional assistance from their sponsoring institutions.
11. The Promotional Schemes of IFCI specially addressed to encourage entrepreneurs in VSI and ancillary sectors require certain relaxations in their eligibility criteria to make them more attractive. In case of Interest Subsidy Schemes, loans raised by the entrepreneurs from commercial and regional rural banks, apart from SFCs and SIDCs/SIICs, should also qualify for the interest subsidy to be passed on to them. The requirement of successful completion of EDP course by an unemployed person to be eligible to avail interest subsidy may be relaxed at least for those persons who already have knowledge and/or experience in the type of project they wish

to set up or whose prospective projects are not technical in nature like a shop or a trade. The women entrepreneurs may be entirely exempted from this requirement, as in the Indian context, it is few elite women having business acumen and entrepreneurial traits who opt for self-employment industrial ventures. Successful completion of EDP course may only be treated as an additional and not a necessary qualification for them.

12. The financial institutions should bring out informative pamphlets giving full details of their various development schemes and widely circulate them to the regional and local level organisations so as to fill the information gap which many times prevents the small entrepreneurs from backward areas from getting the full benefits of such schemes.
13. The initial survey work of NIDs and other backward areas for identification of projects as also of infrastructural requirements is of prime importance as it forms the basis of subsequent developmental efforts, and must be completed expeditiously.
14. Promotional efforts are essentially complementary to the availability of needs-based finance and supportive extension services for pro-moting industrial development of backward areas. Various agencies like Central and State Governments, financial and promotional institutions at the national, state and regional level and consultancy organisations have specific roles to play in supplying one or more of the essential ingredients of industrial development. Therefore, the way to speedy implementation of project plans lies in the committed, concerted and coordinated efforts of all the institutions concerned with the development of backward areas. To ensure undivided attention to the result-oriented pursuit of policies and programmes for backward area development and their effective coordination and monitoring, the setting up of a Central Authority for backward area development, suggested by Nayak Committee[8] deserves a close look.

---

8 Appointed by the Government of India under the Chairmanship of Shri P.C. Nayak, 1976, to evolve a strategy for development programme for small scale industries in backward areas.,

15. The rapidly changing economic environment, scientific and technological innovations and growing complexities of development financing are continuously throwing newer challenges for developing nations in the realm of financing of industries. Human resource development, technology upgradation, environmental protection and pollution control, energy management and development of non-conventional energy sources and enhancing the productivity of industry alongwith the quality of industrial products, are some of the thrust areas on the industrial scene to which greater attention will have to be paid in the years to come; and industrial development especially of backward areas will have to be brought about with stability, updated technology and competitive strength.

To conclude, careful selection of backward areas having potential for industrial development, identification of projects with the desired linkage effects and suited to the material and human resource endowment of the specific area, proper project planning and availability of finance, infrastructure facilities and human capital enriched with technical, managerial and entrepreneurial skills, are all important aspects of industrialisation process, which require greater attention than hitherto if industrial investment in backward areas is to pay richer dividends than in the past.

Appendix - I

LIST OF NO-INDUSTRY DISTRICTS/NOTIFIED LESS DEVELOPED DISTRICTS ELIGIBLE FOR CONCESSIONAL FINANCE FROM ALL INDIA FINANCIAL INSTITUTIONS UNDER BACKWARD AREAS DEVELOPMENT SCHEME.

INCENTIVES FOR SETTING UP OF INDUSTRIES IN NO-INDUSTRY DISTRICTS/ BACKWARD AREAS:

1. One of the important objectives of Government's policy is to correct regional imbalances and to secure the industrialisation of backward areas of the country. Towards this end, Government has provided several incentives to enable entrepreneurs to establish industrial undertakings in backward areas. These include concessional finnce extended by the all-India term-lending institutions, outright subsidy on fixed capital investment, preferential treatment in the grant of industrial licences, etc. The revised scheme of incentives announced by the Central Government on the 27th April, 1983 together with the modifications made in the Scheme from time to time are as under:

Categorisation of Backward Areas

2. The backward areas in the country have been divided into the following three categories:

Category 'A'	Comprise no-industry districts plus special regions (134 districts).
Category 'B'	Comprise the districts currently eligible for Central Subsidy minus districts included in Category 'A' (54 districts).
Category 'C'	Comprise existing 246 concessional finance districts minus those included in Catagories

'A' and 'B' (113 districts including Amritsar District of Punjab).

Eligibility to Central Investment Subsidy:

3. The Central Investment Subsidy for the three categories as mentioned above is as under:

Category 'A'	25% of the fixed capital investment subject to a maximum of Rs. 25 lakhs.
Category 'B'	15% of the fixed capital investment subject to a maximum of Rs. 15 lakhs.
Category 'C'	10% of the fixed capital investment subject to a maximum of Rs. 10 lakhs. (In case of Electronics Industries set up in Hill districts, in category 'A' the maximum ceiling on subsidy has been raised from Rs. 25 lakhs to Rs. 50 lakhs with effect from 1st April, 1985).

4. Under the revised Scheme, the blocks/taluks/urban agglomerations/extension of townships, in categories 'B' and 'C' districts where investments have exceeded Rs. 30 crores as on the 31st March, 1983, are not eligible for further investment subsidy or concessional finance.
5. The Central Government have notified 71 Blocks in 'B' & 'C' category districts, where the investment had exceeded Rs. 30 crores as on the 31st March, 1983 in which projects would not be eligible for concessional finance and central subsidy. So also MRTP/FERA houses are not eligible for Central Investment Subsidy for projects in category 'C' districts.

EXPLANATIONS:

i) Investments maturing on or after the 1st April, 1983 are eligible for subsidy in the specified districts.

ii) In those areas where investments on ground as reflected in the creation of physical assets, have exceeded Rs. 30 crores as on the 31st March, 1983, further investments are not to qualify for subsidy.

iii) For working out the ceiling of Rs. 30 crores, only investment in industrial enterprises i.e. private sector, public sector or departmental, would to taken into account and investments, if any, made in infrastructure like industrial estates/areas, power sub-stations, water works, common utilities and services, etc. would be excluded.

iv) Investment in projects, where approval in terms of letters of Intent/C.G. Clearance/Foreign Collaboration Approvals, etc. had been obtained on or before the 1st April, 1983, would continue to be eligible for Central Investment Subsidy irrespective of the ceiling of Rs. 30 crores as on the 31st March, 1983 applicable to category 'B' and 'C' districts.

Special Concessions to MRTP/FERA Companies located in Industrially Backward Areas:

6. According to the existing policy, MRTP/FERA companies can participate in Industries included in Appendix-I to the Press Note of the 2nd February, 1973 as amended from time to time. Their entry into the non-Appendix-I items is subject to export obligation of 75%, if the item is reserved for small scale and 60% if the item is not reserved for small scale. Keeping in view the need for developing backward areas and the role that can be played by MRTP/FERA companies, it has now been decided to permit entry of MRTP/FERA companies into non-Appendix-I industries which are not reserved for small scale sector with an export obligation of 25% for setting up industries in category 'B' & 'C' districts without any export obligation in respect of category 'A' districts.

Scheme of Concessional Finance for Projects set up in Notified No-Industry Districts/Less Developed Areas:

7. In order to accelerate the pace of industrialisation in specified backward areas, specially in No Industry Districts', all-India Financial Institutions have also formulated a comprehensive scheme of concessional assistance and other incentives for the setting up of units in such areas. Under the new scheme, the policy thrust is on providing graded scale of incentives to attract investment in 'No-Industry-Districts' and other relatively more backward regions. The salient features of the

new scheme, introduced with effect from Ist April, 1983 are given as follows:

i) New projects in all the three category districts are eligible for concessional rupee finance on aggregate basis from the Financial Institutions as under:

(Rs. Crores)

Districts/Areas	Loan Assistance/ Payment Guarantee	Underwriting Assistance
Category 'A' (NIDs)	5.00	2.50
Category 'B'	3.00	1.50
Category 'C'	2.00	1.00

However, projects set up in 'Notified Blocks' in 'B' and 'C' category districts where the investment had exceeded Rs. 30 crores as on the 31st March, 1983, are not eligible for concessional .finance.

ii) The concessional portion of the loan assistance carries inteest @ 12.5% p.a. as against the normal lending rate of 14% p.a. So also, the rate of underwriting commission on shares, debenturs, etc. is reduced on the concessional portion of under- writing assistance by 50% and the rate of guarantee commission on deferred payment guarantee is reduced by 25% on the concessional portion of assistance as indicated above.

iii) In Category 'A' Districts (NIDs), as also in Category 'B' Districts, the norm of promoters' contribution has been reduced to 15% of the total cost of the project. In Category 'C' districts, the norm of minimum promoters' contribution is 17.5% of the total cost of the project.

iv) No commitment charge is levied on the undrawn portion of rupee loans sanctioned to projects in Category 'A' districts (NIDs) (costing up to Rs. 50 crores). In respect of projects in 'B' and C' Category district, as also for projects costing more than Rs. 50 crores set up in Category 'A' districts, commitmment charge is levied on the undrawn portion of the rupee loan amount bearing concessional rate of interest, at half the normal rate; the normal rate of commitment charge being nil up to 180 days from the date of letter of intent or upto the date of signing of the loan agreement, whichever is earlier, 1% p.a. for a period of 365 days thereafter, and after that $^1/_2$% p.a.

Project-Specific Infrastructure Development Loan:

8. In Category 'A' districts (NIDs), new projects costing up to Rs. 50 crores are entitled to an interest-free loan for the development of 'project-specific infrastructure' during their construction period. After the project has gone into production, the 'project-specific infrastructcure loan' which is limited to 20% of the project cost or Rs. 5 crores, whichever is lower, carries concessional rate of interest of 12% p.a. No promoters' contribution is expected in respect of expenditure on 'project- specific infrastructure'. Further, 'project-specific infrastructue loan' is over and above the project-finance loan; in other words, a new project being set up in Category 'A' district (NID) can avail itself of concessional finance up to maximum of Rs. 10 crores, Rs. 5 crores for 'project-finace' and another Rs. 5 crores for 'project-specific infrastructure development'. Infrastructure for this purpose includes approach roads, railway siding, minimum housing facilities laying of power lines and water pipes, captive power plant (not in the nature of stand-by arrangement) and other items of developmental expenditure for infrastructue as may be considered necessary for the projects.

Preferential Treatment for New Industries in Punjab:

9. In respect of all new projects in Punjab, rupee loan assistance up to Rs. 3 crores carries, with effect from the Ist July, 1985, concessional rate of interest of 12.5% and underwriting assistance upto Rs. 1.5 crores in respect of such projects, carries concessional rate of underwriting commission. These concessions were valid up to 31st March, 1987. As regards promoters contribution and debt-equity ratio of projects proposed to be set up in the State of Punjab, Institutions adopt a flexible and liberal approach and special efforts are

made to dispose of expeditiously all applications for assistance for projects coming up in the State of Punjab.

Assistance for Infrastructural Development in Identified Growth Centres:

10. Under the scheme, the Central Government assists the State Government to take up infrastructural development in one or more of the identified growth centres in each no-industry district.

    The assistance from the Central Government is limited to $^1/_3$rd of the total cost of the infrastructural development subject to a maximum of Rs. 2 crores per district. The cost of infrastructure development is not normally to exceed Rs. 6 crores which is shared to the extent of Rs. 2 crores each by Central Government, State Government and IDBI. In case more than one 'Growth Centre' is envisaged in a 'No-industry District', establishment of two growth centres per NID can be allowed but within the total expenditure limit of Rs. 6 crores. The assistance from IDBI is provided by way of loans through the State Industrial Development Corporations (SIDCs) or any other designated Corporation. In the case of District in the North Eastern Region, the State Government's share upto Rs. 2 crores can be met either by the Stage Government concerned from its own budget or obtaining a loan from IDBI.

Setting up of Nucleus Plants and Ancillaries:

11. As rapid industrialisation of backward areas would be facilitated by providing an impetus for the setting up of such industries as can promote the development of ancillary units in the area, Government have recognised certain industrial units of this type as Nucleus plants. An industrial unit will qualify as Nucleus Plant if it fulfills the following criteria:

    i) The nucleus plant will have to be located in any one of the identified central subsidy districts/areas.

    ii) The obligations and concessions in respect of nucleus plant would be available to it if it is conferred with the status of a nucleus plant through a procedure of certification by the Ministry of Industry. On being so certified, the nucleus plant would be entitled, subject to performance of obligations, to all the Central, and State-level incentives.

iii) To be certified as a nucleus plant, the project report should indicate that 50 per cent of production in the plant would be through off-loading specified assemblies/sub-assemblies components to ancillaries. The nucleus plant itself would not be permitted to set up manufacturing facilities in respect of such identified items to be off-loaded. The condition regarding such off-loading would be monitored by the State Government, DC (SSI) and DGTD.

iv) The nucleus plant would be expected to promote new ancillaries in the local areas as part of its programme of 50 per cent ancillarisation. The project report should contain specified plan about the products and items; the number of units and the technology promoting greater employment that would be involved in setting up such ancillaries. In respect of such ancillaries, the nucleus plant would be under an obligation to supply technology, design and documentation, training and, wherever possible new raw materials.

v) In order to promote widespread employment through this programme, the ancillarisation plan of the nucleus plant should provide for at least three times direct employment in the ancillaries.

12. In order to obtain certification as Nucleus Plant, an entrepreneur will have to apply in the prescribed Proforma while applying for Industrial Licence/Registration Certificate approvals to the competent authority.

13. The rate of Central Investment Subsidy for Nucleus Plant is as follows:

Districts in Category 'A'	25% up to a ceiling of Rs. 25 lakhs.
Districts in Category 'B'	20% up to a ceiling of Rs. 20 lakhs.
Districts in Category 'C'	15% up to a ceiling of Rs. 15 lakhs.

14. MRTP/FERA companies are not, however, entitled to Central Investment Subsidy in respect of nucleus plants in Category 'C' areas. Nevertheless, the following additional concessions and incentives are available to all nucleus plants including the MRTP/FERA companies.

i) Inter-corporate-investments will be allowed on case to case basis upto a ceiling of 30% instead of the present ceiling of 10% under section 372 (1) of the Companies Act. This would be adopted as a guideline by the Department of Company Affairs which would consider applications on case to case basis.

ii) Convertibility clause imposed by the term-lending Institutions will not apply to nucleus plants located in Category A, B & C districts for a period of 7 years from the date of sanction or 5 years from the date of disbursement, whichever is later.

iii) State Governments will extend to nucleus plants composite package of assistance similar to the Pioneer Unit Scheme in force in Maharashtra like exemption from Sales Tax liability, interest free sales tax loan, capital investment subsidy from State funds, etc.

15. This Scheme, has now been extended up to the 30th September, 1988.

LIST OF NOTIFIED BACKWARD AREAS/ DISTRICTS CLASSIFIED UNDER 'A' 'B' AND 'C' CATEGOREIS

CATEGORY 'A' (134 Districts)

Sl. States/UTs	Districts	
No-Industry Districts:		
1. Bihar:	Aurangabad, Bhojpur, Khagaria, Nalanda, Purnea, Saharsa (including Madhepura).	6
2. Gujarat:	Dangs.	1
3. Karnataka:	Bidar	1
4. Kerala:	Idukki, Wynad.	2
5. Madhya-Pradesh:	Balaghat, Bhind, Chhatarpur, Chhindwara, Damoh, Datia, Dhar, Guna, Jhabua, Mandla, Narsinghpur, Panna, Rajgarh, Seoni, Shivpuri, Sidhi, Surguja, Tikamgarh.	18
6. Maharashtra:	Gadchiroli.	1
7. Orissa:	Balasore, Bolangir, Boudh Khondmal (Phulbani).	3
8. Rajasthan:	Jaisalmer, Sirohi, Barmer, Churu.	4
9. Uttar Pradesh:	Banda, Fatehpur, Hamirpur, Jalaun, Jaunpur, Sultanpur, Kanpur Dehat.	7
10. West Bengal:	Bankura, Cooch Behar, Jalpaiguri, Malda.	4
	Sub total	47
Special Region Districts:		
1. Assam:	Cachar, Goalpara, Kamrup, Karbi Anglong, Nowgong, North Cachar Hills*, Lakhimpur*, Darang, Dibrugarh, Sivsagar.	10

2. Himachal-Pradesh:	Chamba*, Kangra*, Kulu*, Kinnaur*, Lahaul & Spiti*, Solan, Sirmur, Bilaspur, Hamirpur, Mandi, Shimla, Una.	12
3. Jammu &-Kashmir:	Anantnag, Baramula, Doda*, Jammu, Kathua, Ladakh*, Poonch*, Rajori*, Srinagar, Udhampur*, Badgam, Kargil, Kupwara*, Pulwama*,	14
4. Meghalaya:	East Garo Hills*, West Garo Hills*, Jayantia Hills*, East Khasi Hills, West Khasi Hills*.	5
5. Manipur:	Manipur Central*, Manipur East*, Manipur North* Manipur South*, Manipur West*, Tangoupal*.	6
6. Nagaland:	Kohima, Mekokchung, Tuensang*, Phek, Mon, Wokha, Zunheboto.	7
7. Sikkim:	Gangtok*, Gyalshing*, Mangan*, Namchi*	4
8. Tripura:	Tripura North*, Tripura South*, Tripura West*.	3
9. Uttar Pradesh:	Almora, Chamoli*, Pauri Garhwal*, Tehri Garhwal*, Uttar Kashi*, Pithoragarh, Dehradun, Nannital.	8
10. Andaman & Nicobar Islands:	Andaman Islands, Nicobar Islands.*	2
11. Arunachal-Pradesh:	Tirap*, East Kameng*, West Kameng*, East Siang*, West Siang*, Lower Subansiri*, Upper Subansiri*, Dubang Valley, Lohit.	9
12. Dadra & Nagar Haveli:	Dadra & Nagar Haveli*.	1

13. Lakshadweep:	Lakshadweep*.	1
14. Mizoram:	Aizawal*, Lunglex*.	2
15. Goa, Daman & Diu:	Goa, Daman & Diu.	1
16. Pondicherry:	Pondicherry.	1
17. West Bengal:	Darjeeling*.	1
	sub-total	87

Total No. of districts: 134.

*No-Industry Districts within the Special Region Category.

CATEGORY 'B' (54 Districts)

1. Andhra-Pradesh : (equivalent to 6 districts).

Srikakulam district and 5 'areas'. Two areas from Rayalseema region comprising 22 blocks.

Area - 1: Comprising 13 blocks, viz., Chittoor, Bangarupalem. Pulicheria, Puttur, Chandragiri and Kalahasthi (from Chittoor District) and Kodur, Rajampet, Sidhout, Cuddapah, Kamalapuram, Proddutur and Pulivendla (from Cuddapah District).

Area - II: Comprising 9 blocks viz. Tadapatri, Singanamala, Gooty, Kudai (from Anantaput district) and Dhone, Kurnool, Banganapalli, Nandyal and Giddalur (from Kurnool district).

Three areas from Telengana region comprising 43 blocks:

Area - I: Comprising 14 blocks viz. Mahbubnagar, Jadcherla, Shadnagar, Kalwakurthy and Amangal (from Mahbubnagar district) and Nalgonda, Mungadi, Makrakal, Suryapet, Kodad, Huzurnagar, Miryalguda, Peddavora and Devarakonda (from Nalgonda district).

Area - II: Comprising 14 blocks, viz., Khammam, Thirumalaipalem, Kallur, Yellandu, Kothagudem, Aswaraopeta, Burgampad and Bhadrachalam (from Khammam district) and Mahabubabad, Narasampet, Hanmakonda, Ghanapur, Jangaon and Mulug (from Warangel district).

Area - III: Comprising 15 blocks. viz., Zaheerabad, Patancheruvu, Narsapur, Medak and Siddipet (from Medak district) Yedappalli, Nizamabad, Kamareddy and Domakonda, (from Nizamabad district) and Sircilla, Karimnagar Sultanabad, Peddapalli, Monthani and Huzurabad (from Karimnagar district).

2. Bihar Bhagalpur, Darbhanga, Champaran, Palamau and Santhal Parganas. (5)

3. Gujarat Panchmahals, Broach and Surendranagar. (3)

4. Haryana - (equivalent to 3 districts).

Reorganised Mohindergarh district (comprising Mohindergarh) and Rewari sub divisions). Bhiwani district comprising Bhiwani and Dadri sub divisions and one 'area' comprising S blocks, viz., Hissar block No: 1 and Barwana Block (of Hissar Tehsil), Hansi Block No: 1 (from Hansi Tehsil), Bahuna Block (from Fatehabad Tehsil), Tohana block/tehsil (from Tohana Tehsil) from district of Hissar, Jind Block and Julana Block (from Jind Tehsil), Uchana Block (Narwana Tehsil) from the district of Jind.

5. Karnataka Raichur, Mysore and Dharwar. (3)

6. Kerala Alleppey, Cannanore and Malapuram. (3)

7. *Madhya Pradesh: (equivalent to 4 districts) 'Six Areas'

Area - 1: (From Eastern Region) comprising blocks, viz. Korba, Baloda, Champa, Kota, Masturi and Bilha (Bilaspur) blocks (from Bilaspur district), Bhatapara, Simga, Tilda, Dharsiwa (Rajpur), Abhanpur and Rajim blocks (from Raipur district).

Area - II: (From Western Region) comprising blocks, viz. Dewas and Tonk Khurad Block (from Dewas district). Gulana, Shujalpur and Shajapur blocks (from Shajapur district).

Area - III: (From Northern Region) comprising blocks Morena and Jeura (from Morena district).

Area - IV: (From Central Region) comprising blocks, viz., Bhind-Itawa, Khuri - Banda (Binaika), Rahatagarh, Sagar, Sehgarh (Amarmau) (from Sagar district), Vidisha and Gyaraspur (from Vidisha district).

Area - V: (From Western Region-II) comprising blocks viz., Maheswar and Barwana (from Khargona district), Ratlam and Jaura (from Ratlam district). Mandsaur, Malhargarh and Neemuch (from Mandsaur district).

Area - VI: (From North-Eastern Region) Comprising Blocks, viz. Rewa and Raipur (Garh) (from Rewa district).

*N.B.: As far as Madhya Pradesh is concerned, out of the 65 blocks equivalent to six districts, 29 blocks are in the Districts included in No-Industry Districts.

8. Maharashtra Ratnagiri, Aurangabad and Chandrapur. (3)

9. Orissa Kalahandi, Mayurbhanj, Dhenkanal, Keonjhar and Koraput. (5)

10. Punjab Hoshiarpur, Sangrur and Bhatinda. (3)

11. Rajasthan Alwar, Jodhpur, Bhilwara, Nagaur and Udaipur. (5)

12. Tamil Nadu : (equivalent to 3 districts)

Three Areas/Tracts comprising 33 taluks:

Area - I: Comprising 12 Taluks (including Sub-Taluks) viz. Ramanathapuram, Mudukulathur, Sivaganga, Parmakudi, Thiruvadani, Karaikudi and Thirupathur Taluks (from Ramanathapuram district), Melur Taluk (from Madurai district), Pudukkottai, Thirumayam, Alamgudi and Kulathur Taluks (from Puddukkottai district).

Area - II: Comprising 11 Taluks viz. Dharmapuri, Palacode, Hosur, Denkanikottah, Krishnagiri, Uthangarai, Harur (from Dharmapuri district). Tirupattur. Vaniyambadi, Vallore, Walajapet (from North Acrot district).

Area - III: Comprising 10 Taluks, viz., Aruppukkotai, Sattur, Virudhunagar, Srivilliputtur, Rajapalayam (from West Ramanathapuram of Ramanathapuram district) Thirumangalam, Usilampatti, Nilakottai, Dindigul and Vedasandur (from Madurai district).

13. Uttar Pradesh — Ballia, Basti, Faizabad, Jhansi and Rae-Bareli. (5)

14. West Benga Purulia, Midnapur and Nadia. (3)

Total No. of Distt. 54.

CATEGORY 'C' (113 Districts)

1. Andhra Pradesh — Anantpur (excluding Tadpatri, Singanamala, Gooty and Kudai blocks), Chittoor (excluding Chittoor, Bangarupalem, Pulicherla, Puttur, Chandragiri and Kalahasthi blocks), Cuddapah (excluding Kodur, Rajampet, Sidhout, Cuddapah, Kamalapuram, Proddutur and Pulivendla blocks), Karimnagar (excluding Sircilla, Karimnagar, Sultanabad, Peddapalli, Manthani and Huzurabad blocks), Khammam (excluding Khammam, Tirumalaipalem, Kullur, Yelllandu, Kothaguden, Aswaraopeta Puragampad and Bhadrachalem blocks), Kurnool (excluding Dhone, Kurnool, Banganapalli, Nandyal and Giddalur blocks), Mahabubnagar (excluding Mahabubnagar, Jedcherla, Shadnagar, Kalwakurthy and Amangal blocks), Medak (excluding Zaheerabad, Patancheruvu, Narsapur, Medak and Siddipet blocks), Nalgonda (excluding Nalgonda, Mungaid,

	Nakrakal, Suryapet, Kodad, Hazurnagar, Miryalguda, Peddavora and Devarakonda blocks), Nellore, Nizamabad (excluding Yedapalli, Nizamabad, Kamareddy and Demakunda blocks), Ongole, Warangel (excluding Mahbubabad, Narsampet, Hanmakonda, Ghanapur, Jangaon and Mulug blocks).	(13)
2. Bihar	Muzaffarpur, Saran, Nawadah, Gaya, Begusarai and Monghyr.	(6)
3. Gujarat	Amreli, Banaskantha, Bhavnagar, Junagadh, Kutch, Mehsana, Sabarkantha.	(7)
4. Haryana	Bhiwani (excluding Bhiwani and Dadri Sub divisions, Hissar (excluding Hissar, block No. 1 and Barwana blocks of Hissar Tehsil, Hansi block No. 1 from Hansi Tehsil, Bahuna block from Fatehabad Tehsil, Tohana block/tehsil from Tohana Tehsil), Jind (excluding Jind block and Julana block from Jind Tehsil and Uchana block from Narwana Tehsil), Mohindergarh (excluding Mohindergarh and Rewari sub-divisons).	(4)
5. Kerala	Trichur and Trivandrum.	(2)
6. Karnataka	Belgaum, Bijapur, Gulbarga, Hassan, North Kanara, South Kanara and Tumkur.	(7)
7. Madhya-Pradesh	Bastar, Betul, Bilaspur (excluding Korba, Baloda, Champa, Kota, Masturi and Bilha (Bilaspur blocks), Dewas (excluding Dewas and Tonk Khured blocks), Hoshangabad, Khergone (excluding Maheshwar and Barwana blocks). Mandsaur (excluding Mandsaur, Malhargarh and Neemuch blocks), Morena (excluding Morena and Jeura blocks), Panna, Raigarh, Raipur (excluding Bhatapara, Simga, Tilda, Dharsiwa (Raipur), Abhanpur and Rajim blocks), Rajnandgaon, Raisen,	

	Shajapur (excluding Gulana, Shujalpur and Shajapur blocks), Ratlam (excluding Ratlam and Jaura blocks), Rewa (excluding Rewa and Raipur (Garh) blocks, Sagar (excluding Bina-Itawa, Khuri-Banda (Banaika), Rahatgarh, Sagar, Sahgarh (Amarmau) blocks, Vidisha (excluding Vidisha and Gyaraspur blocks). New Sehore.	(19)
8. Maharashtra	Bhandara, Bhir, Buldhana, Colaba, Dhulia, Jalgaon, Nanded, Osmanabad, Parbhani and Yeotmal.	(10)
9. Orissa		(Nil)
10. Punjab	Amritsar, Ferozpur, Gurdaspur.	(3)
11. Rajasthan	Banswara, Dungarpur, Jalore, Jhunjunu, Jhalawar, Sikar and Tonk.	(7).
12. Tamil Nadu	Dharmapuri (excluding Dharmapuri, Pala-code, Hosur, Denkanikottah, Krishnnagiri, Uthangarai and Harur Taluks), Kanyakumari, Madurai (excluding Melur, Thirumangalam, Usilampattai, Nilakottai, Dindigul and Vedasandur Taluks), North Arcot (excluding Tirupattur, Vaniyambadi, Vellore, Walajapet Taluks), Ramanathapuram (excluding Ramapathapuram, Madukulathur, Sivaganga, Paramakudi, Thiruvadani, Karaikudi, Thirupa-thur, Aruppukkottai, Sattur, Virudhunagar, Srivilliputtur, Rajapalayam Taluks), South Arcot, Thanjavur, Tiruchirapalli, Pudukottai (excluding Pudukottai, Thirumayam, Alangudi and Kulathur Taluks).	(9)
13. Uttar Pradesh	Azamgarh, Badaun, Bahraich, Barabanki, Bulandshahar, Deoria, Etah, Etawah, Farrukhabad, Ghazipur, Gonda, Hardoi, Mainpuri, Mathura, Muradabad, Pilibhit, Pratapgarh, Rampur, Shahjahanpur, Sitapur and Unnao.	(21)

14. West Bengal	Birbhum, Burdwan, Hooghly, Murshidabad and West Dinajpur.	(5)

The total No. of Distt:	113
Category - A	134
Category - B	54
Category - C	113
Grand Total :	301

List of Blocks/Taluks/Urban Agglomeration/ Extension of Townships in Category 'B' and 'C' Districts (where the level of investments have exceeded Rs. 30 crores as on 31.3.1983) which are not eligible for further Investment Subsidy or Concessional Finance.

Sl. State	Name of blocks/taluks/urban agglommeration/extension of township	District
1. Andhra-Pradesh	1. Kamalapulam Block	Cuddapah
	2. Patancheru Block	Medak
	3. Kurnool Block	Kurnool
	4. Pedapalli Block	Karimnagar
	5. Eturnagaram Block	Warangal
	6. Kothagudem Block	Khammam
	7. Borgampadu Block	Khammam
	8. Miryalaguda Block	Nalgonda
2. Bihar	1. Barauni Block	Begusarai
3. Gujarat	1. Bhavnagar (Urban Agglomeration)	Bhavnagar
	2. Jafrabad (Taluks)	Amreli
	3. Ranavav (Taluka)	Junagadh
	4. Anjar (Taluka) (excluding Kandla Free Trade Zone).	Kutch
	5. Kalol (Taluka)	Mehsana
	6. Bharuch (Taluka)	Bharuch
	7. Ankleshwar (Taluka)	Bharuch.
4. Haryana	1. Rewari Block	Mohindergarh
5. Karnataka	1. Mysore (Urban Agglomeration Area)	Mysore
	2. Hosahalli Industrial Area.	Raichur
	3. Kumarapatnam Industrial Township	Dharwad

	4. Kangrali Industrial Area.	Belgaum
	5. Wadi-Shahabad Industrial Area.	Gulburga
	6. Benaga Industrial Area	North Kanara (Uttar Kannada).
	7. Ammasandra Industrial Township.	Tamkur
	8. New Mangalore Port Area & Baikampady Industrial Area.	South Kanara
	9. Devarayapatna Industrial Township	Tumkur.
6. Kerala	1. Chalakkudy Block	Trichur
7. Maharashtra	1. Panvel (Taluka)	Raigad (Kulaba)
	2. Alibag (Taluka)	Raigad (Kulaba)
	3. Khalapur (Taluka)	Raigad (Kulaba)
	4. Roha (Taluka)	Raigad (Kulaba)
	5. Aurangabad (Taluka)	Aurangabad
	6. Chandrapur (Taluka)	Chandrapur
	7. Rajura (Taluka)	Chandrapur
	8. Uran (Taluka)	Raigad (Kulaba)
	9. Bhandra (Taluka)	Bhandra
8. Madhya-Pradesh	1. Akaltara Block	Bilaspur
	2. Korba Block	Bilaspur
	3. Dewas Block	Dewas
9. Orissa	1. Talcher Block	Dhenkanal
10. Punjab	1. Hoshiarpur-II Block	Hoshiarpur
	2. Balachaur Block	Hoshiarpur
	3. Ahmedgarh Block	Sangrur
	4. Bhatinda Urban Agglomeration/extension of township	Bhatinda
11. Rajasthan	1. Ramgarh Block	Alwar
	2. Girwa Block	Udaipur

	3. Rajasamand Block	Udaipur
	4. Jodhpur Urban Agglomeration.	Jodhpur
	5. Khetri Block	Jhunjhunu
12. Tamil Nadu	1. Hosur Block	Dharmapuri
	2. Katpadi Block	North Arcot
	3. Madhanur Block	North Arcot
	4. Wallajah Block	North Arcot
	5. Cuddalore Block	South Arcot
	6. Karur Block	Tiruchirappalli.
	7. Ariyalur Block	Tiruchirappalli.
	8. Thiruvenambur Block	Tiruchirappalli.
13. Uttar-Pradesh	1. Dibai Block	Bulandshahr
	2. Bulandshahr Block	Bulandshahr
	3. Sikandrabad Block	Bulandshahr
	4. Farah Block	Mathura
	5. Rahi Block	Rae-Bareli
	6. Bisrakh Block	Ghaziabad (erstwhile Bulandshahr district)
14. West-Bengal	1. Serampore-Uttarpara Block	Hooghly
	2. Chinsurah-Mogra Block	Hooghly
	3. Chandannagar-Bhadreswar-Singur Block	Hooghly
	4. Chakda Block	Nadia
	5. Sutahata-I Block	Midnapur.
	6. Durgapur-Faridpur Block	Burdwan
	7. Hirapur Block	Burdwan
	8. Salanpur Block	Burdwan.

Total number of blocks/taluks/urban agglomerations/extension of townships is 71.

Note:

1. Small Scale units would, however, continue to be eligible for concessional finance facilities.
2. Industrial units in the above blocks will continue to be eligible to the various backward area incentives except Central Investment Subsidy and Concessional Finance.
3. Investments in projects where Government of India's approval in terms of letters of intent/CG Clearance/ Foreign Collaboration approval/DGTD Registration/ State Government's Approvals in terms of SSI Registration or allotment of land or any other infrastructural facilities has been received on or before 1.4.1983, will continue to be eligible for investment subsidy.

Appendix - II

Package of de-licensing of Industries and Incentives for Industrialisation in Backward Areas

Press Note 3.6.1988

In order to accelerate the industrial growth and give a strong imeptus to the industrialisation of backward areas of the country, Government have decided upon a major package of delicensing and incentives. The salient features of the decision of the Government are as follows:

A. Liberalisation of the Industrial Licensing System:

The Industrial Licensing System has been liberalised in a very substantial manner for non-MRTP/Non-FERA Companies. Henceforth, there will be no need for non-MRTP/Non-FERA companies to obtain Industrial Licences under the Industries (Development & Regulation) Act, except in the following cases:

1) Projects involving an investment in fixed assets of more than Rs. 50 crores if they are located in Centrally declared backwrd areas, or more than Rs. 15 crores, if they are located in non-backward areas, provided however, that the facility of delicensing will not be available in both cases if the project is located within --

   a) 50 kms. of the periphery (i.e, boundary of the urban area limits) of cities having a population of more than 25 lakhs.

   b) 30 Kms of the periphery of cities having a population of more than 15 lakhs but less than 25 lakhs.

   c) 15 kms. of the periphery of cities having a population of more than 7.5 lakhs but less than 15 lakhs.

   d) the standard urban areas/municipal limits of other cities and towns.

2. Projects falling in industries includes in a "special list" (the special list is attached). This list supercedes the existing Schedules IV & V of the notification under the IDR Act.
3. Projects which require foreign exchange for Imported raw material (other than steel and specified items) and components for more than 30% of the value of ex-factory production from the first year of commercial production. So far as the reservation for small scale or Public Sector is concerned, the existing policy would continue.

B Development of Growth Centres:

1. For promoting industrialisation of backward areas in an effective manner, the focus would henceforth be on the development of growth centres that would act as the magnet for attracting industries to backward areas. Such growth centres would be endowed with infrastructural facilities on par with the best available in the country, particularly in respect of power, water, telecommunications and banking.
2. To begin with at least 100 such growth centres, would be developed throughout the country over the next about 5 years. Each growth centre would be provided with funds of the order of Rs. 25-30 crores in order to create infrastructural facilities of a high order. In other words an investment of the order of Rs. 2500-3000 crores is envisaged over the next about 5 years for creating sound and efficient infrastructural facillities in selected growth centres in backward areas. The funds for this purpose will be found by the Centre, the States and the all India Financial Institutions acting together.
3. The growth centres will be located within a reasonable proximity of district headquarters or tehsil head-quarters in backward areas at such places that have a good potential for attracting industries. A committee of Secretaries and representatives of all India financial Institutions, headed by the Secretary, Planning Commission is being appointed to formulate the criteria and guidelines for the selection and location of the growth centres. The States will be asked to submit their proposals for location of growth centres in accordance with these criteria guidelines.

4. As stated above, atleast 100 growth centres would be selected to begin with and developed over the next about 5 years. Thereafter, the development of growth centres would be further expanded so that over the next 10 to 15 years, most of the backward areas of the country are covered by them. The ultimate objective is to develop one growth centre in each of the 430 odd districts in the country.

5. The development of the growth centres is in addition to the existing backward areas scheme and is not in substitution of it. However, the backward areas scheme would be reviewed periodically with the progress in the establishment of the growth centres and such modifications will be made in it as are necessary

C. Financial Incentives:

At present, any new industrial undertaking established in a Centrally declared backward district is eligible to Income Tax relief under Section 80HH of the Income Tax Act by way of deduction of 20% of the profits for a period of 10 years. Furthermore, under section 80 I of the Income Tax Act, all new industrial undertakings are entitled to an income tax relief by way of deduction of 25% of the profits for a period of 8 years. The benefits of both these Sections are available cumulatively to industrial undertakings established in notified backward districts. The investment allowance scheme has recently been reintroduced and industrial units will be eligible to claim its benefit also. All these benefits will be available both to the industrial units established in the growth centres as well as those located in other centrally declared backward areas.

D. Monetary Incentives:

In order to provide greater assistance, the norms for working capital funds required by industrial units established in backward areas would be reviewed and they will be accorded a more liberal treatment. The committee under Planning Secretary would also look into this matter and make its recommendations.

Government hope that these measures will give a boost to the investment climate and industrialisation of backward areas in the country.

List of Industries for which Industrial Licensing is Compulsory

1. Coal.
2. Textiles: units operated by power;
   a) All Weaving units.
   b) All Spinning units with investment in fixed assets of more than Rs. 15 crores.
3. Milk foods and Malted Foods.
4. Vegetable oil including solvent extracted oils & Vanaspati.
5. Leather.
6. Matches.
7. Distillation and Brewing of Alcoholic Drinks.
8. Hot Rolling of Semis, Bars, Wire Rods and Structural Sections of Steel.
9. Tractors & Self-propelled combine harvestors.
10. Motor Cars, Buses, Trucks, Jeeps, Vans, Scooters, Motor Cycles and all other types of automobiles.
11. Asbestos and Asbestos based products.
12. Slitting/Confectioning of photosensitized material form Jumbo rolls.
13. Plywood, Decorative veneers, particle board, medium density fibre board and block board.
14. Sugar
15. All types of steel manufactured through induction and electric arc furnaces.
16. Iron & Steel pipes and tubes, and Stainless Steel Tubes.
17. Wires of mild Steel, Special Steel and Alloy Steel Coated and uncoated.
18. Cold and Hot Rolled Strips, Sheets and Plates of all categories of Steel including box strappings.
19. Non-ferrous semis, Alloys, Flat products and Extrusions.
20. Cold Rolled Formed Sections.

21. Ferro Alloys.
22. a) Telecommunication Equipment.
    b) Subscriber (And user) Communication Terminals Equipment.
    c) Wireless equipment: All equipment.
23. Computer Peripherals excluding key boards and monitors.
24. Micro-processor based industrial control instrumentation system.
25. Electronic Aerospace and Defence Equipment: All types.
26. Industrial explosives, including detonatinng fuse, safety fuse, gun powder and nitrocellulose.
27. Chemicals (Other than Fertilizers):
    - i) Sodium/Potassium Chlorate.
    - ii) Calcium Carbonate.
    - iii) Calcium Carbide.
    - iv) Elemental phosphorous.
    - v) RHC Technical
    - vi) M - Aminophenol.
    - vii) O - Dinitro benzene.
    - viii) Nitro benzenes.
    - ix) Nitro Chloro benzenes.
    - x) Nitro Toluenes.
    - xi) Alcohol based chemicals, namely Acetaldehyde, Acetic acid,Acetic Anhydrides, Ethyl Acetate and Diethyl ether.
    - xii) Formaldehyde.
    - xiii) Nylon Chips/Nylon moulding powder
    - xiv) Polyester chips/polyester moulding powder.
    - xv) Industrial Alcohol.
    - xvi) Sodium/Potassium Cyanide.

xvii) Pesticides/Insecticides formulations based on technical material obtained from sources other than own manufacture.

xviii) Carbaryl.

xix) Quinalphos.

xx) Dimethoate.

xxi) Aluminium phosphide.

xxii) Isoproturon.

xxiii) Phorate.

xxiv) Monocrotophes.

xxv) Carbondazine.

xxvi) Fanitrophion

xxvii) 6-APA.

Population of Selected Cities and Towns According to the 1981 Census Data

Category I (Cities with a population of above 25 lakhs).

	Population in lakhs
1. Calcutta	91.9
2. Bombay	82.4
3. Delhi	57.3
4. Madras	42.9
5. Bangalore	29.2
6. Ahmedabad	25.5
7. Hyderabad	25.5

Category II (Cities having population of above 15 lakhs but less than 25 lakhs).

1. Pune	16.9
2. Kanpur	16.4

Category III (Cities and towns with a population of above 7.5 lakhs but less than 15 lakhs).

1.	Nagpur	15.0
2.	Jaipur	10.2
3.	Lucknow	10.1
4.	Coimbatore	9.2
5.	Patna	9.2
6.	Surat	9.1
7.	Madurai	9.1
8.	Indore	8.3
9.	Varanasi	8.0
10.	Jabalpur	7.6
11.	Agra	7.5
12.	Vadodra	7.5

BIBLIOGRAPHY

Books & Articles

1. Basu S.K., *Theory and Practice of Development Banking,* 1965.
2. Bhatt V.V., -Financial Institutions and Technical Consultancy Services", Article in the *Economic and Political Weekly,* Bombay, November 1981.
3. Bhattacharya S.N., *Rural Industrialisation in India - Its Nature and Problems,* 1980.
4. Bhattacharya S.N., *Industrial Potential Survey - Its Nature and Problems in Developing Economies,* 1981.
5. Bhattacharya S.N., *Development of Industrially Backward Areas - Indian Style,* 1981.
6. Boskey Shirley, *Problems and Practices of Development Banks,* 1959.
7. Development Banking Centre, *Selected Readings in Development Banking,* A compilation of DBC, edited by S.P.S. Deol, 1982.
8. Diamond William, *Development Banks,* 1957.
9. Gupta L.C., *Changing Structure of Industrial Finance in India,* 1969.
10. Gupta L.C., *Readings in Industrial Finance (Ed),* 1976.
11. Gupta L.C., *Growth Theory and Strategy: New Direction - A unified systems approach to regional and national growth,* 1983.
12. IDBI, *Handbook of Information on Industrial Development of Backward Regions,* 1974.
13. IDBI, *Industrial Development of Backward Areas,* Seminar Papers, 1980.
14. IDBI, *Entrepreneurship Development Programmes,* Seminar Papers, 1980.
15. IFCI, *Search and Research - A Compendium of Lectures delivered by IFCI Chair Professors,* 1984.
16. IFCI, *Searchlight on Development Banking - A Compendium of*

IFCI Silver Jubilee Memorial Lectures, 1984.

17. IFCI, *A Saga of 35 years of Service to Industry,* 1983.
18. *Industrial Finance Corporation Act, 1948,* (as amended upto date), 1987.
19. Jain P.K., *Industrial Finance Corporation of India - A Study in Financial Management,* 1988.
20. Khan M.Y., *Indian Financial System,* 1981.
21. Management Development Institute, *Backward Areas Development Strategies and Policies (Role of Financial and Promotional Institutions),* Seminar Papers, 1977.
22. Management Development Institute, *Management of Development Banks* Seminar Papers, 1975.
23. Mandal S.K., *Regional Disparities and Imbalances in India's Planned Economic Development,* 1987.
24. Menon K.S.V., *Development of Backward Areas through Incentives,* 1979.
25. Mukharjee Sakti and Mukharjee Indrani, *Role of Development Banks in Industrial Finance,* 1985.
26. Papola T.S., *Rural Industrialisation - Approaches and Potential,* 1982.
27. Patel V.G., *Innovations in Banking: The Gujrat Experiments,* published by IDBI, 1981.
28. Poonia M.S., *Development Banking in India,* 1987.
29. Ranade Sudhanshu, *Rural Banking Adrift - A study of Development Banking for underdeveloped rural areas in India as if the weaker sections really mattered,* 1984.
30. Rao V. Lakshmana, *Progress of Development Banking in India,* 1986.
31. Schumpeter J.A., *Theory of Economic Development,* 1959 Ed.
32. Shreekantaradhya B.S., *Regional Dispersal of Industries and Industrial Development,* 1985.
33. Simha S.L.N., *Development Banking in India,* Institute for Financial Management and Research, Madras, 1976.

34. Singh Prabhu N, *Role of Development Banks in a Planned Economy*, 1974.

35. Singh Vimal Shankar, *Development Banking in India*, 1985.

36. Verma J.C., "Role of Industrial Finance Corporation of India as a development bank", paper presented at the Faculty Development Programme, 1984-85, Department of Commerce, University of Delhi.

37. *Yojana*, Magazine, Vol. 31, No: 4, 6, 9.
Vol. 32, No: 4, 5, 6.

Reports And Other Publications

1. IDBI, Report on Development Banking in India for the years 1984-85, 1985-86, 1986-87.
2. IDBI, Annual Reports for the years 1980-81 to 1987-88.
3. IDBI, Industrial Potential Surveys of Backward States and Union Territories, 18 Survey Reports published by IDBI.
4. IFCI, Annual Reports for the years 1983-84 to 1987-88.
5. IFCI, Operational Statistics for the years 1983-84 to 1987- 88.
6. IFCI, Publications and brochures on:
   - Promotional Activities, 1984.
   - Promotional Schemes, 1986, 1988.
   - Backward Areas Development Scheme, 1986
   - Equipment Finance Scheme, 1986.
   - Modernisation Assistance Scheme, 1986.
   - Merchant Banking Services, 1987.
   - Suppliers' Credit Scheme, 1987.
   - Chairman's Statement, 1988
   - A Profile, 1987-88.
7. ICICI, Annual Reports for the years 1983-1987.
8. MDI, Management Journal, Vol. 1, No: 2, July, 1988.
9. RCTC, (Risk Capital and Technology Finance Corporation Ltd.),Annual Reports since inception in 1975 to 1987.

10. RCTC, Brochures on Risk Capital Assistance Scheme and Scheme of Technology Finance & Development.
11. TCOs, (Technical Consultancy Organisations), Annual Reports of past 3 years of RAJCON, HIMCON, NITCON.
12. Report of the Working Group on Identification of Backward Areas, 1969. (Pande Committee Report).
13. Report of the Working Group for suggesting fiscal and financial incentives for industrial development in backward areas, 1969 (Wanchoo Committee Report).
14. Report of the Committee to evolve a strategy for development programme for small-scale industries in backward areas, 1976, Ministry of Industry, Deptt. of Industrial Development, Government of India (Nayak Committee Report).
15. Report of the Indian Central Banking Enquiry Committee, 1931.
16. Report of the Estimates Committee, 69th Report, 1974-75, Lok Sabha Secretariat, New Delhi (Development of Backward Areas).
17. Planning Commission, Government of India, Five Year Plan Documents.
18. Planning Commission, Government of India, Reports of National Committee on Development of Backward Areas (NCDBA) on:
    - Organisation of Administrative and Financial Structures for Backward Area Development, 1980.
    - Industrial Dispersal, 1980.
    - Development of Backward Hill Areas, 1981.
    - Village and Cottage Industries, 1981.
    - Development of Tribal Areas, 1981.
    - Industrial Organisation, 1981.
    - Development of Drought Prone Areas and Desert Areas, 1981.
    - Development of Coastal Areas Affected by Salinity, 1981.

- Development of Chronically Flood Affected Areas, 1981.
- Development of North Eastern Region, 1981.
- General Issues relating to Backward Area Development, 1981.

19. Planning Commission, Programme Evaluation Organisation, Evaluation Report on Concessional Finance and other Incentives in Industrially Backward Areas, 1981.
20. Planning Commission, Government of India, Mid-term Appraisal of the Seventh Plan.
21. Economic Survey, 1987-88, 1988-89, Ministry of Finance, Economic Division.

INDEX